The Messenger, The Message, & The Community

Three Critical Issues for the Cross-Cultural Church Planter

Third Edition
2013

Roland Müller

Print history: The first editions of this book were published under three separate covers: Tools for Muslim Evangelism (2000), Honor and Shame, Unlocking the Door(2000) and Creating Christian Community (2005). The first edition of MMC combined these books under one cover and was printed in 2006. This book is the third edition of the combined books printed by Lightning Source.

First Edition: 2005, Second Edition: 2010, Third Edition 2013

ISBN: 978-1-927581-14-8

Other books by the same author:
    Understanding Islam
    The Man from Gadara
    Missionary Leadership by Motivation & Communication
    Missions: The Next Generation
    Honor and Shame, Unlocking the Door
    Tools for Muslim Evangelism

A Word of Explanation

The original intent of the first editions of this book was to produce a guide or manual for missionaries planting churches among Muslims. Yet it wasn't long before I began hearing back from missionaries working with other groups, such as Hindus, Buddhists, Animists, and post-modern young people. Requests for seminars came from many places outside of the Middle East such as Europe, East Asia, and North America (including First Nations people). It soon became apparent that many of the principles used for church planting among Muslims were actually principles applicable to most cross-cultural church planting situations. Many readers responded positively to the material on the effects of sin on human beings, and the worldviews that result. Many others expressed their appreciation for the materials that addressed the way God works and what God is doing as he moves across cultural barriers to bring people to himself.

Today we find ourselves living in a global community where it is important to understand many different cultural backgrounds and situations. Few missionaries work in a mono-cultural situation. The philosophies of Muslims, Buddhists, Hindus, post-moderns, agnostics, and many others influence those among whom we minister.

It is the aim of this book to explore a variety of very basic and simple principles that should be foundational to our ministry as cross-cultural church-planters. We start with examining ourselves as church-planters. In effect the church planter is a messenger who bears the Gospel message into a target community. If the Gospel is to be heard, then the church planter must gain a hearing. If the target community rejects the church planter as a valid messenger, then the ministry will go no farther.

Once the church planter is accepted as a valid messenger, he must move on and begin to share a message that is culturally appropriate and understandable to his audience. If his message is not understandable, the target community may reject the Gospel, because they fail to identify the message as being a valid message for their situation.

However, even if the messenger gains a hearing and shares a culturally appropriate message, the Gospel may still be rejected if the church being planted is not a viable community of faith for that situation. Thus we will explore three primary areas in this book: the messenger, the message, and the community.

As I mentioned, the original focus of this book was to act as a guide for those working in a Muslim context. Thus, many of the resources, examples, and case studies are taken from a Muslim setting. However this should not distract the reader from learning how God works with people across a variety of cultural backgrounds. Some of the pastors that reviewed this book in manuscript form shared with me that these materials have proven beneficial to them as they led established churches which were seeking to reach out to fast-changing multi-cultural communities. I trust that the principles shared in this book will also be useful to you and your ministry situation.

The questions at the end of each chapter are intended for personal reflection and team discussion. Many people find that working through questions helps them digest and absorb the material better. The questions are also intended to help you apply the material to your specific church planting ministry situation. ... Roland Müller

Acknowledgments

People are usually better resources than books. They are more current, personal, and can usually answer questions posed to them. In the CD version of this book and on the website is a bibliography of the related books that I have read. But this list pales in significance when I think of the many people with whom I have interacted and from whom I have learned as I researched the topics in this book.

So, in the beginning, I would like to acknowledge the many brothers and sisters laboring around the world who have shared with me their struggle to communicate the Gospel with those from a heritage other than their own. I would also like to thank all the missionaries, missiologists, and theologians who have given suggestions. So many things that they shared with me have become part of this book.

Special thanks, however, must go to a fellow church-planter: Kenneth Betts, a close friend, who spent many hours with me, talking through the issues that became fundamental to this book. Along with this he shared his own personal journey as a fellow cross-cultural church-planter. Without his insight and encouragement, this book might never have been written. Others, like Dr. George Kelsey, Dr. Mazen Hanna, Neil Krahn, Ken Guenther, Shane Cooke, Dr. Roger Sheehy and Ed Gruidier must also be thanked for the time they sacrificed and for all of the insights they shared from their own experience. Special mention must also go to Colin Bearup who faithfully labored through the manuscript, sharing from his years of experience, and challenging me to think more deeply and clearly on many issues.

Lastly, Daphne Spraggett, Bryan Wylie, Dorothy and Richard Wiman, John Lombard, Josiah Gibson, Keith Kline, and my wife Maria must be thanked for the time they put into checking manuscripts and correcting my grammar. Without their help, the manuscript would have been un-publishable.

Table of Contents

THE MESSENGER

Introduction to the Messenger

While I was researching and writing the original manuscript for this section, several people commented that I was trying to write a "how to" book on cross-cultural evangelism. They objected to the idea, as they felt I could not address the needs of everyone everywhere. Obviously, there are tremendous differences in religious understanding, cultural backgrounds, and personal situations. These people felt that a "how to" approach would be harmful in several ways. They believed that such a book would give the reader the false idea that having learned the contents, he could simply go out and "do it successfully." They argued that the "how to" approach does not minister to the personal needs and particular situation of any specific person. They also maintained that this approach could be so rigid that it would limit the work of the Holy Spirit.

I believe that all of these fears are well founded but I encourage the reader to understand from the beginning that I am not trying to set out a simple "how to" approach that will work in every case. Rather, this book contains bits of wisdom gleaned from a number of successful evangelists to Muslims, Hindus, Buddhists and others. I do, however, strongly believe that mission organizations today need to develop some kind of "how to" approach to help their new evangelists get started on the right foot.

When I first arrived in the Middle East in the late 1970s, I started asking, "How do I do it?" No one seemed to have any concrete answers. There was no one to point to and say, "They know how to do it!" Consequently, each new missionary developed his own approach by trial and error, often resulting in more error than success.

In 1992, I was asked to begin an apprenticeship program for a large group of new missionaries. This presented me with a real challenge. Who would be able to apprentice them all? I immediately began searching through the Middle East for those who were successful in their ministry and could apprentice or mentor these new missionaries.

In my search for successful evangelists I used a number of criteria. First, I looked for those who had numerical results. From this list I then looked for those who had experience in gathering new converts into fellowships, either through local church situations or into separate convert fellowships. Lastly

I looked for long-term results. My list was short, but I was encouraged as I discovered that there were some successful evangelists!

Once I had my list, I approached these evangelists to find those who would be willing to take on one or two apprentices. As the program progressed, I assessed each learning situation, seeking to find common denominators and, hopefully, the secrets of their success. I tried to look through the eyes of the evangelists, the apprentices, the community of local believers, fellow evangelists and missionaries, and sometimes, when possible, through the eyes of the converts themselves. In the end, the principles that I gleaned from these dedicated people have proved useful in many other cross-cultural situations.

This book is not about academic statistics, nor is it intended as an evaluation of those involved. Its aim is to record useful insights gained from those who are successful in ministry. The material was originally written from the perspective of Christians working with Muslims in the Middle East. However as I received positive feedback from missionaries and pastors working in other areas of the world, I expanded my perspective so that these would also be included. Regardless, individual missionaries will need to sift through the material and decide what is applicable for their situation, although the principles outlined here have since proven effective in many different countries and cultural settings.

I would like to add a short word about personal pronouns. When writing this material I became very conscious of wanting to enter he and/or she whenever dealing with evangelists and converts. I resorted to using the inevitable "he" but do not want to minimize the role that females have both as evangelists and as those who are evangelized.

May God bless you as he leads you through these pages.

Chapter One
Gaining an Acceptance

When a Christian worker or church-planter first arrives in a new culture he faces a credibility problem. He comes as a messenger of the Gospel, hopefully having prepared himself beforehand, and hopefully with some ministry experience in his own cultural setting. He should have a good knowledge of the Bible, an understanding of what the Gospel message is, and a tool-box which contains some useful tools for sharing that message. Usually these are tools that have proven useful in his own culture.

Once the Christian worker arrives on location, he usually discovers the credibility problem. Why should anyone listen to him? He doesn't speak the language, doesn't know the culture and isn't aware of the issues that people face among whom he is hoping to develop a ministry or plant a church. Thus, his first job is to overcome the hurdles that keep him from being accepted as a valid messenger, that is someone who can speak into the local situation with insight and understanding.

Language

The first task the Christian worker faces is that of learning language. This is not just learning to chat or use in the local lingo. It requires learning to express himself in terms which communicate deep truths. This is not a simple task. Language learning is a major effort that requires hours of time and great amounts of energy. No language can be mastered in a couple of months, even if someone spends their full time in concentrated study. If you find yourself in a cross-cultural situation where language learning is not required, you are in a very fortunate position. The rest of us, however, must spend the time and energy that is required. How much time and energy, will depend largely on four factors.

First, consider the mental abilities of the language learner. Every person has different mental skills and abilities. Some think globally, some more linearly. Some are quick with grammar, some better at pronunciation, and some with vocabulary. Others are more intuitive, and can pick up a great deal by simply observing situations. Whatever your ability, God has placed you in the situation you now find yourself, in order to use you. He is looking for a variety of different people that he can use in the ministry. Everyone who can speak can learn a foreign language. They have already learned one language and now they need to work on another language.

The second factor that comes into play is how many languages you already know. Our brains are made with what is known as neural networks. Connections between things can be formed and broken over time. Some people have had experience learning a second or third language and thus have already formed the neurological connections that are necessary to learn languages. Others, who are mono-lingual ceased learning languages as a child. Many of those connections no longer exist. The challenge now is not so much language learning, as teaching the brain how to learn another language. In fact some new workers spend the first six months on the field simply trying to convince themselves that the sounds they hear coming from other people's mouths have meaning. They have no network in which to place those sounds and sort them into meaningful expressions. Thus they must spend a great deal of time simply building the framework, so that they can actually start learning their target language. Usually they become very discouraged as others seem to rush ahead of them, absorbing the language with greater ease.

The third factor is the difficulty level of the language itself. Some languages are much more difficult than others. Now, this is not a case of simply creating a list of languages, ranging from simplest to the most difficult. It all depends from what language the learner is starting. If you are starting with a European language, then learning another European language is simpler than tackling a Semitic language or an Asian one. Likewise, languages are made up of many parts. Some languages contain sounds that are very difficult to pronounce if you are from Europe, but easier for those from some Asian countries. The reverse is also true. Along with this, grammatical structure varies widely from language group to language group. The writing system can also vary from simple to very complicated. Thus, the learner may find conversational Chinese to be relatively simple to speak, but reading and writing next to impossible. On the other hand, new workers in the Middle East may find that they can quickly read Arabic letters, but the complex grammatical structure of the language keeps them from being able to speak correctly despite months of language learning.

The fourth factor is the effort that the language learner applies. If you have a ministry, responsibility for children, or a personal crisis of some kind, it is hard to put concentrated effort and time into language learning. Sometimes our expectations also get in the way. Perhaps we think that we can learn the language in a couple of months, and when this doesn't happen we become discouraged. Some language learners put in many long hours of study and practice. Others don't try nearly as hard, or don't have the discipline to spend long periods of time concentrating on language learning. In some cases, language learners who experience difficulty with the first three hurdles, simply give up and only make a half-hearted effort at language learning. Everyone, however, can learn another language. For some it will be harder, and for some, a bit easier.

Culture

As with language, many new workers assume that cultural adaptation is a relatively simple thing comprised of learning a list of do's and don'ts. While this is true on a very superficial level, one will never grasp what is really happening in many situations if they do not have a feel for the culture, and the principles that are coming into play.

The primary tool that new workers must use in learning culture is that of language. Language affects culture, and culture affects language. Every language has various strengths and weaknesses. One of the strengths of the English language is nouns. The English language has names for everything. In fact, most things have two names, a scientific name and a common name. Arabic on the other hand, has many words that describe relationships and feelings. While in English we talk about the feeling of depression, Arabic has many words to describe the actual type of depression one is feeling. Thus language has a profound impact on culture. How can the new worker relate to his audience and come across as a credible messenger if he does not understand the culture?

In the second part of this book we will examine more closely some universal cultural patterns expressed in terms of guilt-based, fear-based and shame-based common ancestral worldviews.

Credibility

Again, when we find ourselves in a new situation we struggle with a credibility problem. Why should anyone listen to us? We know little of the language, culture, the local situation and the struggles that the local people are going through. The farther the target culture is from our own culture, the greater this problem becomes. This was impressed upon me during our time with the nomadic Bedouin of Arabia. How could I, a Westerner from Canada speak into their situation? I knew nothing of the desert, herding animals, and inter-tribal situations. I came to them, thinking of myself as a messenger, but they saw me as an outsider whose message wasn't relevant to their situation.

In order to bridge this gap, we as Christian messengers must address several issues. A number of these are listed below.

Know who you are and your role in society

Are you a missionary? Does your target audience know what a missionary is? Do they see you as a professionally trained church worker or are you simply a Jesus-loving fool from a foreign country who happens to live next door to them? Very often we ourselves are not clear who we are and we communicate a confusing message to those who are observing our lives.

This problem is compounded if we are 'tentmaking' missionaries. The bottom line, however, is that of integrity. Are we who we say we are? All around us will be neighbors and colleagues who will be trying to figure us out and place us into one of their boxes. The problem is that we often don't know what the boxes are. Once, while visiting the USA I discovered that the people I was visiting wanted to label me as a Democrat or a Republican. In their worldview everyone fit into one of those two boxes. As a Canadian, I didn't easily fit into either of these descriptions. My political views were made up of a very different mix of issues. But as long as I clung to my own important issues, I remained a puzzle to my American friends. How was I to explain that I was an evangelical Democrat that held moral views similar to those of Christian Republicans?

Part of the problem was that I didn't know what the issues were that divided Democrats and Republicans. To my new friends, since I wasn't a Democrat or a Republican I was a real puzzle and they couldn't really figure me out.

So, at the beginning, the new missionary needs to discover what the important issues are in his target culture and community. He should listen to people and try to understand and even enter into the struggles that they experience.

Build bridges into the lives of others

As you meet new friends, try and find things that are of common interest between you. If you have no common interests, then develop some. This means that you have to become interested in the things that they are interested in. Over the years I have had to develop an interest in the history, politics, economy, religion, sports and the local issues of my target community. In order to enter into conversations and identify with my audience I have had to expand my areas of interest. When you can engage your audience in conversation about the issues that concern them, you move a step closer to being seen as a credible messenger.

Work at becoming an insider

This is more than having knowledge and the ability to talk about local subjects. Becoming an insider includes living and acting as an insider. It has to do with everything about you, from how you walk down the street to when you eat your meals. The more time you spend with local people, the easier this will become. Being adopted by a local family or tribe is a great help. This usually only happens when we display our weaknesses and ask our friends or neighbors for their help and support. Your weakness in the area of culture and language is often the key to opening up opportunities in the lives of others. Rather than approaching people as a teacher, approach them initially as a learner. If you are willing to learn from them, they may later become willing to learn from you.

Allow others to see godliness in your life

What are the evidences of godliness, as seen by people in your target culture? For instance, a religious Muslim man would attend ceremonies, read

8

and chant his Scriptures, have special clothing, perhaps a dash of red dye in his beard, and possibly wear only sandals like the prophet Muhammad. If religious people are easily identified in your target culture, how are your friends and neighbors going to know you are godly? Why should they listen to you speak on the topic of religion?

As a Christian growing up in the west I heard teachings about hiding our faith, praying in a closet, and not letting the right hand know what the left is doing. I became an experts at being able to walk through life, without anyone around me knowing that I was a followers of Jesus. When I became a missionary, I was faced with the challenge of learning how to be transparent in my Christian life, and allow others around me to see me as a person who was deeply in love with Jesus. Along the way I learned that one of the ways to demonstrate our faith and the things that are within our hearts, even though we may not have yet grasped the language, is to serve others. Start asking the Lord to reveal to you opportunities where you can serve those around you. Your acts of service will speak loudly, and will be remembered long after the things you said are forgotten.

I feel it is vital that new workers on the field concentrate not only on language learning and cultural adaptation, but that they also address the credibility problem, and work towards being accepted as viable messengers who have something of worth to share. Language learning and credibility building go hand in hand and should be pursued together.

Questions for Reflection or Discussion

1. Do people accept you as a credible messenger? Why or why not?
2. Where are you in the language learning process? (beginner, functional, can say most things, mostly fluent, language is not an issue)
3. How many languages have you previously learned?
4. How difficult is the language you are trying to learn?
5. How much dedicated time do you put in each week to language learning? (1-7 hours, 7-21 hours, 21 – 35 hours, more than 35 hours)
6. What can you do to improve your language learning experience?

7. Do you understand many of the do's and don'ts of the culture you are working in? Have you found words or concepts in your target culture that you do not have in your new language? E.g. nouns for something, or words to describe things?

8. Are you seen as a real outsider in your target community or are you accepted in some way into the community? How do you know this?

9. How are you seen in the society around you? (a religious person, a professional, a visitor or some other category?)

10. What are some of the words you might use to describe how others see you? How would you like people to see you?

11. How much do you know about the local people, their history and their culture? Are there ways you can improve your background knowledge so that you can better understand them?

12. What are some ways that you can better build bridges into the lives of people around you? Are there some areas such as news, sports, politics, history, economy, religion, industry, local issues or family issues that you should learn more about?

13. How much of an insider have you become? Do people consider you as an outsider? Can you comfortably walk down the street without people staring at you? How can you improve being an insider?

14. What are some of the evidences of godliness as understood by people in your target culture?

15. If religious people are easily identified in your target culture, how are your friends and neighbors going to know you are godly?

16. Why should they listen to you speak on the topic of religion?

17. Read I Corinthians 9:18-23. What do you think these verses mean? Why is Paul doing this? In what ways can you also become all things to all people among the people you work with?

Chapter Two
Your Toolbox

Every builder has a toolbox. Before he begins a career in construction he is apprenticed and trained in the use of his tools. Then, using his tools and the materials at hand, he is ready to begin construction.

Church planting is similar in that the end goal is the "construction of a church," that is, a community of believers meeting together, feeding each other spiritually, and multiplying themselves. The work of the evangelist is to begin the construction. Like the builder, the evangelist should have his evangelism-toolbox filled with useful tools.

No builder would imagine constructing a building with just one tool, no matter how proficient he might be in the use of that tool. Even two tools would be very limiting. A hammer and a saw might just be sufficient, but construction would be slow and tedious. A box or even a truck full of tools is far better.

In this book, I want to introduce you to three basic principles that must be considered when planting a church. Along with this, in the church planting handbook on the website (http://rmuller.com), I have tried to provide a sampling of some of the tools that are available. Given the right situation, these tools are not only useful, but perhaps essential for the task at hand.

Over the years that I have been involved in ministry in many different countries on several different continents. I have discovered that there are two kinds of tools available. There are the tools devised by academic missiologists and armchair mission strategists. Then there are the tried and true tools developed and used by successful evangelists and church planters in the field. I plan to concentrate on the latter set of tools.

A number of years ago, I observed a team of Western agricultural experts trying to teach Yemeni farmers how to grow crops in dry conditions. They set up their equipment, laid out their fields, and applied their tools and techniques, which had been developed in ultramodern Western universities. Amazingly, the Yemeni farmers got better yields from their fields than the frustrated Western experts next door. True, the Westerners knew some things that the Yemenis didn't know, but the old Yemeni farmers knew what had worked for them, their parents, and their grandparents.

In growing my own garden, I learned from the Western experts that the soil was deficient in potassium, so I added potassium. From my Yemeni neighbors I learned that there was a particular kind and quality of dust found only in certain locations. When that dust was finely sprinkled on my garden it protected the plants from the burning sun while allowing enough light to filter through. My garden looked dusty and dirty but it grew a tremendous harvest.

Like that dust, some of the tools and techniques I will suggest are not glitzy and glamorous. They may seem simple and basic, even dusty and drab. But our goal is the fruit they produce, not their appearance.

I do not consider myself an expert in evangelism and church planting. There are very few experts. However, in the last thirty years of ministry I have observed a number of successful evangelists at work. At first I was amazed at their success, but then I realized that some of their success lay in their toolbox and the techniques with which they applied these tools. As a result, I've made it my business to dig around in other folks' toolboxes asking silly questions like "What is this?" and "How do you use that?" and "What else do you use?" I then added some of these tools to my own toolbox, and started to train and encourage others in their use.

Now there is a danger here. You might assume that once you have the right tools and some experience in how to use them, you will automatically become a successful evangelist and church planter. Nothing can be further from the truth. The Bible clearly teaches us that "Unless the LORD builds the house, its builders labor in vain" (Psalm 127:1, NIV). We are God's workmen, and thus should be trained in the use of the Scriptures and "always be prepared to give an answer to everyone who asks you to give the reason for the hope that you have." (1 Peter 3:15). It is the Holy Spirit that does the real work in drawing men to God.

Never assume that you can make someone a Christian. Only the Holy Spirit can lead anyone to Christ. Only the Holy Spirit can open eyes to make them see truth. Only God can tug at a heart's door. It is God who stands at the door and knocks, not the evangelist. Our role is to be obedient to God and be available to Him as He does his work.

Success in ministry does not come from simply having and using the right tools. We can have the right tools, use them well, and yet still not see results. Results come from God and have a lot to do with the gifting of the evangelist, the grace of God at work at the time of witnessing, and also God's timing in the situation, for the Spirit blows when and where He chooses. We must be prepared as workers, and allow God to order the events of our lives to bring us into situations where He can use us.

What then is our role? Our role is to be a worker, equipped and ready for work. We should have our toolbox ready, be trained in the use of our tools, know the Scriptures well, and be available to the Holy Spirit. When people are seeking, God usually leads them to those who have prepared themselves to be useful. The evangelist must prayerfully listen and consider the situation. Then, at the prompting of the Holy Spirit, he opens his toolbox and chooses the appropriate tool. If he doesn't have the right tool, the evangelist should arrange the situation so he can get help from his fellow workers.

It is well to remember that style and technique are often as important as the tools themselves. Certain tools fit certain personalities. The outgoing evangelist standing on your doorstep needs different tools than those who counsel children. It would be impossible to review all the different tools available to everyone in every situation, so I have chosen a small sampling of the tools that are available and placed them in the church planting handbook on the website. The real secret to success, however, is not which tools you choose, but rather, the principles that lie behind the tools.

Along with tools, we must also look at the spirit in which the tools are used. A tool used without love is useless. Paul reminds us in 1 Corinthians 13 that whatever we do, we must do it in the spirit of love. The first verse could perhaps be rendered: "Even though I speak the language fluently, and have perfectly prepared my presentation, and understand all there is to know about culture and worldview, and can discern the personal perspective of the person

I am talking to, if I do not have love, I can do nothing."

Love encompasses more than we realize in our cultural context. It means more than not hating, it means more than being generous or long suffering. It may also be expressed by language learning and long-term commitment. As we minister to people, can they see the love of Christ in us and our actions?

Questions for Reflection or Discussion

1. How many evangelistic tools do you have in your toolbox that you can use without much preparation?

2. Have you led people to Christ before? Is your evangelistic experience limited to your home culture or have you also had experience in a radically different culture?

3. Read II Corinthians 5: 9 – 14. What are some of the things that motivated Paul and his companions to witness for the Lord?

4. What motivates you to be a messenger of God's grace and salvation?

5. Examine the Discovery Lessons found in the church planting handbooks and on the website (http://rmuller.com). Do you have any tools such as this in your toolbox?

6. What are some things that your church planting team can do to add to the tools you have in your toolbox?

7. As a team, how can you bring more love, or a more loving spirit into your evangelistic efforts?

Chapter Three
The Making of an Evangelist

In my search for successful evangelists, I became aware that I was looking for more than tools. The gathering of tools was relatively simple; learning how they were used took much more work. But as I researched, I began to notice certain patterns emerging. My excitement grew as I went back over each case, noticing more and more similarities in style and technique. I shall discuss these in the following chapters.

One of the first things I discovered was that there was not one personality type common to these evangelists. The variety of personalities was astounding. Some were bold with outgoing personalities. Some were flamboyant, and some, perhaps the most numerous, were quiet, non-confrontational people.

These evangelists came from a variety of backgrounds and ages. Some were Westerners and some were from the East. Some were believers from a Christian background while others were believers with a Buddhist or Muslim heritage.

However, when I had finished assessing the tools, techniques and personalities behind them, I felt I was still missing something. This bothered me and I began searching again. There was some mysterious quality about these evangelists that made them attractive to nonbelievers, something that was almost magnetic, something that drew people to them.

I was only vaguely aware of this for some time, until God brought it clearly to my attention. The answer came in the form of Harry Young, an elderly missionary who has now passed into glory. We had invited him to come and share with us his secrets of success. Harry and his wife began their ministry in the United Arab Emirates years ago, and later ministered in Birmingham, England. We were delighted with his visit, and benefited from the insights he had to share.

However, one small event during that visit completely floored me. It left me hurt and confused. One evening Harry and I were passing by our local Arab church where I needed to stop for a few minutes to see someone. The youth meeting had just finished and Harry spent a couple of minutes in the courtyard talking with some of the local youth while I went about my business. Most of these young men were on the periphery of the church, attending only occasionally. I quickly finished my business and we moved on to another appointment.

The next afternoon, I had a surprise visit from several of these young men. They arrived at my door, asking for the old man who had been with me. They wanted to visit him. When I explained that he had left the country that morning, they were downcast and commented that they wanted to study the Bible and wanted this old man to teach them! After they left, I sat in my chair amazed. I had lived in this neighborhood for more than a year. One of these boys had helped me find the house in which we were then living. But during that year, none of them had asked me to lead a Bible study. In fact, when these young men were around me, the discussion seldom concerned spiritual things.

Yet, when Harry arrived and talked with them for ten minutes, they were ready to commit themselves to attending a Bible Study. I felt hurt, but challenged. I needed to find out what it was that had attracted them. And the more I thought about it the more I recognized this quality in all the successful evangelists I had met.

Old stories I had heard took on new meaning: the people who "approached the evangelist" in the coffee shop, the rich court judge who came by chauffeured limousine late one night to a fellow worker to ask about God. All of these evangelists seemed to be surrounded by people willing to study the Bible with them. In almost every case, there was something about these Christian workers that made them attractive. People almost wanted to study the Bible with them. It was humbling to realize that I didn't have this quality. It was challenging and almost frightening to find out why.

Taking pen and paper, I began to write out a short list of qualities common to these evangelists. First, these evangelists were intimately familiar with their Bibles. They knew their Bibles, they studied their Bibles. When asked a spiritual question, their first reaction was to reach for the Bible. Each of them loved the Word, and was a student of the Word. People around them had the impression that these were men and women of God. Even in common conversation, references to spiritual things were a normal part of their exchange. It wasn't forced; it flowed out of a life steeped in the Word of God.

This saturation with the Word of God made these people recognizable as men and women of God. I wrote that down, but I knew there was still more to it than this.

I pondered over the matter for some weeks, and then, as I visited with a successful evangelist from the West who was then working in Lebanon, I broached the subject with him. I explained all I had found, but admitted that I was not convinced this was all. There was still a missing component.

He listened thoughtfully, and then he smiled. "I'll tell you what it is." I smiled too, thinking, "Sure, but it's not that easy."

"It's the Cross," the evangelist explained. "Go again and examine every case you are studying. See if there is not some point, or a number of points in each of their lives, where these men or women reached a tremendous crisis, a crisis that destroyed them, a crisis that brought them to their knees, a crisis that stripped them of themselves, in which they died to themselves, and cast their whole lives onto God."

"A cross experience! Death to self! Casting themselves onto God!" The words rung in my ears. Just one year before, my wife and I had faced a tremendously difficult experience. It had brought us to our knees. It had crushed us, almost destroyed us, and had left us asking "Why?" The only answer we could find was that we needed crushing so that our old natures would be destroyed and that Jesus could shine through. In my heart, I knew that this was just the beginning of the work of God in my life. The trials He had taken us through hadn't yet done a complete job and He was taking us through more and more experiences, showing us one thing after another in our lives that needed to be dealt with.

As I sat there re-experiencing some of the pain I had recently gone through, I suddenly realized that this man was right. Each one of these successful evangelists had gone through very difficult experiences. Most of the time, I had considered these experiences as satanic opposition to their work, but now I saw the hand of God at work in their personal lives. The words of Corrie ten Boom echoed in my ears; "God's finest tool in our lives is the tool of suffering."

I didn't know all these peoples' lives in detail, but the Lord brought to my mind situation after situation. Harry and his wife were serving God in the Arab Gulf when their doctor prescribed the drug Thalidomide during Joanne's pregnancy. When their son was born, he was without arms and legs. I had visited in their home several times in years gone by, but somehow I had never recognized their pain until this moment.

One dear brother had been imprisoned, threatened, and lived with uncertainty. Another family had been betrayed by the local Christian community, another family had tremendous difficulties with their own mission organization, while others had been falsely accused of all kinds of evil.

I now saw God's hand in each of these situations. God was at work in each of these lives. I had been looking for successful tools: tools that had been worked on and developed, honed to perfection, tools ready for my use. And all the while, God had been looking for tools: tools that had been worked on and developed and honed to perfection, tools ready for His use. God's tools were people. He was more interested in the character of the evangelist than he was in the tools they were using.

God was looking for lives that He could live in, lives that wouldn't hide him, but would let him shine through. Like the saints in stained glass windows in church, they are beautiful because the light shines through them.

Suddenly I realized that nonbelievers weren't attracted to evangelists, they were attracted to God. People who are true seekers are seeking for God. They may not know it, and might not express it in those words, but when they see God in his beauty being lived out in the lives of his people, they are attracted to him. In order for Jesus to truly shine through a life, the hard exterior has to be broken and removed.

A life broken and used by God is not something that the evangelist has done. It is the work of God. That's why it is often so hard for a new worker to write home about what he has accomplished. Often God is doing more work in his personal life than God is doing through him in the lives of others.

As I reviewed the lives of these evangelists, it was a relief to discover that not all had experienced traumatic events. They were not all "tough nuts" to crack. Some had quietly and obediently submitted to God and had learned to die daily to self. Others, it seemed, needed a more traumatic event to get them moving down the right road. However God did it, he did it in the right way for that particular person or family. You see, it is God who makes a person fruitful. It is not something they have done themselves. God's fruitfulness comes about when God has free rein to work in their lives, and this may involve real suffering. Therefore we should regard disasters and tragedies accordingly, and look for God's hand in them as he works on our own lives.

And so at the beginning I must emphasize the need for each person who wants to have a successful church planting ministry to recognize that his own life is the primary tool that God is seeking to use. He will begin to use your life by breaking it and clearing it of personal rubbish. If you have begun to steep yourself in the Word of God, and are preparing yourself with basic, useful tools to tackle the job of evangelism and church planting, God will, in turn, find places in his kingdom where he can put you to work for his honor and his glory.

Questions for Reflection or Discussion

1. Do you feel that some people have better personalities for evangelism than others? If so, which kinds of personalities do you think are better suited to doing evangelism?

2. List some of the situations in your life that God has used to break you.

3. Do you think brokenness is something to be valued? Why?

4. Would you describe your life as a life filled with God's Word? Does it flow out from you in a natural way?

5. What do you think is meant by the term "Cross life" or "Take up your cross" or "to die daily?"

6. How clearly does God's light shine through your life? What things in your life might be limiting or negatively affecting God's light shining out to others?

7. Read Matthew 5:13 – 16. What is the Bible teaching us about using our lives to witness for Christ?

Chapter Four
Teacher-Based Evangelism

In analyzing the various successful evangelists, one of the first common denominators I noticed was that none of them majored in using the "friendship evangelism" approach that is commonly practiced by many of today's evangelists and church planters. While none of these evangelists was opposed to making friends or building friendships with those they were trying to reach, most of them mentioned that they did not see friendship evangelism as a missiological strategy that should be exclusively followed. In fact, there were those who were quite adamant that friendship evangelism was woefully lacking as a missiological strategy. They felt that too much emphasis was put on this approach when other approaches might work better.

Friendship Evangelism
Whenever I bring up the concept of friendship evangelism with my church planting colleagues, I have discovered that each person has a slightly different view of what is meant by this term. In pursuing this further, I have also discovered that few missionaries have thought through the biblical basis of this approach, and most seem surprised that I would even question its validity. What surprises me more, however, is that so many of these same people seem to agree that friendship evangelism is the correct and accepted method for reaching Muslims, Buddhists, Hindus and others. What Western missionaries often miss, as it pertains to these cultures, is that friendship is a lifelong commitment, not simply a missiological strategy.

At this point, I must admit that my own thinking has also been challenged over the years. When I set out on my missionary career I was well aware that the traditional methods of evangelism, like door-to-door outreach or tent meetings, had proven very offensive in Muslim countries, and so I, too, had accepted friendship evangelism as the only viable alternative.

I first became aware of the concept of friendship evangelism in the 1970s when a veteran missionary couple spoke in glowing terms of "gossiping the Gospel" over the back fence with Muslim neighbors. It sounded interesting and intriguing. As a young man, I had been involved in door-to-door evangelism, coffeehouse evangelism and crusade evangelism in Ireland. Now that I was entering ministry in the Middle East, I was interested in learning what would work in a Muslim setting.

When I arrived in the Middle East and started my language study, I began to look around for experienced workers who could tell me "how to do it." It soon became evident that there was a woeful lack of converts from Islam. Few workers had won any Muslims to Christ, so we new missionaries had few role models to follow.

Once I had acquired some language skills, I began using the friendship evangelism approach that everyone was promoting. Perhaps we didn't really understand what friendship evangelism was all about. Some of my fellow students and I had arrived at the conclusion that all we needed to do was to develop a close friendship with a couple of Muslims. Once a friendship was firmly established, we would then be able to share Christ with them.

As with all evangelistic attempts there were some successes, but most of us never really got around to presenting Christ to our friends. After all, having spent so much time and energy developing the friendship, we were loath to destroy it by saying something that might offend our friends. Only a few workers, with special gifts in evangelism, had any measure of success.

What concerns me is the large number of people around the world who still exclusively use this approach with little, if any, success. Several things may be happening. First, making close friends in a cross-cultural situation is very difficult. In many cases, new workers discover that the target people who try and befriend them usually do so for a reason. A frustrated young missionary poured his heart out to me one day. The young men who had befriended him on the street and in the market place were always looking for something from him. Within a couple of days they would be asking about any sisters he might have, or searching through his apartment for pornography, or wanting him to help fill out applications for a visa. There were very few people out there simply looking for friendships with foreigners. Friendships take time and usually require long-term commitment.

This young man had also discovered that when he did finally make friends, their concept of friendship was different from his. On the street below his apartment were a group of unemployed young men who hung out together. They were open to him joining their little group as they sat and drank tea, or wandered in the market, or just stood talking in the evening. However, it soon became plain that if he was to join their group, he would be expected to be with them all the time. These young men saw each other every day and stayed together until late at night, every night. The young missionary realized he could not give that kind of time just to maintain this kind of friendship. When he told them he had other commitments, they basically said, "Fine, it's us or them."

This left him in a quandary. Should he drop his other commitments, even church-related activities, in order to spend all his time with four or five young men? What about making friends with others? Was his ministry to focus on this small group alone? So far there had been very few opportunities to share the Gospel with them. How long should he be a friend before he shared? What if they rejected his message and him? Was there another strategy he could use?

The concept of friendship evangelism is a strange contradiction for many cultures, as friendship evangelism aims to focus only on several individuals and not broad-based evangelism. Somewhere at the root of friendship evangelism is the desire and pressure for the missionary to be successful in ministry. But how do you report successful friendships? Eventually you must wake up and realize that friendship-based evangelism isn't primarily aimed at making friends, converts is the ture aim.

During my years of ministry as a church planter, I have had many opportunities to observe, and to use friendship evangelism. I've seen well-meaning missionaries give their lives to a few close friends. They've taken years to build friendships within these families. When they write their prayer letters, they describe the friends they are making, the family events they attend, and some of the individuals they are closest to. But many of these workers have told me how terribly difficult it is to share the Gospel with their friends. Having built a good friendship, they feel that if they now share the Gospel they will betray the friendship. It's as though they've used these people, befriended them for a reason, and now months or years later, the reason becomes clear.

These are the good situations. In some of the poorer ones, the workers, having discovered the difficulties, have resigned themselves to the fact that their lives will have to reveal the Gospel as they are never going to get around to having a good talk about it. In some cases, those who depend on friendship evangelism end up with something that is neither friendship nor evangelism. Some of their contacts get friendship, some get evangelism, but many get neither!

As I observed this phenomenon, I have wondered why we have so quickly embraced friendship evangelism as a good missiological strategy? No one I know of is pointing to any wildly successful "friendship evangelists", although there certainly are those who have led some to Christ using it. In thinking this through, the conclusion I have reached is that friendship evangelism actually offers several attractions to the expatriate Christian.

First, it is a comfortable, secure kind of ministry. We often spend a lot of energy, time, and money on being comfortable. We want a home that is pleasant to live in. We need a place where we can get away from the hustle and bustle of life around us and unwind. We want comfortable places to relax in, some familiar books and videos to tickle our fancy, and some familiar foods in the refrigerator. So while the culture around us is unfamiliar and uncomfortable, our homes become an important refuge to us. Likewise, since friendship evangelism is the most non-threatening form of evangelism, it nicely fits into the kind of comfort and security we want to enjoy.

Friendship evangelism is also a readily available option. Door-to-door work, street meetings, crusades and the like are very difficult, if not totally impossible in many cross-cultural settings. Only a specialized few can get involved in producing videos or literature, so for most of us wanting to witness, friendship evangelism is often the only understandable option we know of.

In addition, it fits our active lifestyles. After all, evangelism must somehow fit in between the kids' schooling, their after-school activities, team meetings, shopping, and any expatriate gatherings that we attend. We may find that two or three friendships are all we can comfortably handle while still giving our supporters the impression that we are actually doing something of spiritual value.

Many find that friendship evangelism fits with the modern concept of tentmaking. In most closed countries, tentmakers shy away from projecting themselves as trained religious workers in order to maintain a secular identity in the community. Friendship evangelism then becomes the desired strategy for reaching people both on and off the job.

Since few tentmakers ever reach a high level of fluency in the language, we often find that we function best as we chat with people on a friendship basis. Thus, friendship evangelism often fits our level of language ability as well.

Now, I'm being very hard on everyone, including myself. Nevertheless, I found that the successful evangelists had a totally different approach to life. While they made friends with their neighbors and colleagues at work, these friendships were true friendships. If their friends ask them about their religion and their beliefs, they were happy to share with them. Often conversations about faith flowed out of a mutual closeness and concern in their relationship. But these evangelists never made friends with the intention that evangelization was the goal of that friendship. Their friendships were true friendships, open and clear of any ulterior motives.

In almost every case, these successful evangelists did not use friendship evangelism as a missionary strategy. They all used something I will call "teacher-based evangelism." Most of these successful evangelists never put a label on what they were doing, but after observing all of their ministries, I felt this term best describes their approach.

Teacher-Based Evangelism

First, let me state that in every case, the successful evangelists had the reputation of being spiritual people - men and women of God. They knew the Scriptures and they knew how to communicate them in a way that can only be summed up as teaching. I often found it amusing that their unsaved neighbors and colleagues would tell me that if I wanted to know about spiritual things, I should go and ask that person.

This, I believe, is the key point. In my own life I discovered that people, especially Muslims, who did not know me well would often engage me in religious conversations in order to convert me to Islam. To my frustration, they assumed that I was a secular Westerner and they therefore set out to inform me of a better way of life.

Most of us start out on our missionary careers feeling that we are the spiritual ones. Our schoolmates, our fellow churchmen, and often our families have lifted us up to great spiritual heights. To them we are sacrificing both our futures and our security to travel to far-off parts for the kingdom of God. Unfortunately, we sometimes believe their platitudes, arriving in the country of our calling, feeling that we have sacrificed a great deal, and thus are wonderful spiritual beings.

Hopefully, arrival on the field shocks us out of our self-deception. As we struggle with strange languages, cultures, and loneliness, our real self comes out. In dealing with newly arrived workers on the field, I have often termed their initial struggles as "self shock" rather than culture shock. Most western cultures have insulating activities that shield us from ourselves. We fill our lives with music, sport, or friends, and seldom spend time alone with ourselves. Once we arrive on the field, however, we are stripped of all the insulating factors. We come face to face with who we really are, and often we don't like what we see. Added to this is the struggle with language and culture, and suddenly the newly arrived worker feels less and less spiritual, and more and more needy. As a result it is often much easier for the new worker to concentrate on friendship evangelism than it is to try to discover how to portray himself as a person of God, especially if he doesn't feel very spiritual at the time. The challenge is doubly hard as we struggle to maintain personal spiritual momentum and also establish ourselves as a spiritual resource for people around us.

Some of the more radical evangelists I surveyed, had in time, established themselves as formal religious teachers. They adopted the forms and roles of a culturally accepted teacher and ministered from this point of view. The less radical ones nevertheless moved every contact towards a place where they could sit down with them, and teach them the Scriptures. Some had formal lesson plans, some had a general idea of where they were going, and some used a day-by-day mentoring approach. But all played the role of a teacher, imparting spiritual knowledge and truths.

Another important point I observed was the awareness of agenda. The key to many successful evangelistic efforts is the development of the evangelist's agenda. I discovered the importance of this, years ago while doing door-to-door evangelism in southern Ireland. When someone opened the door and asked, "Yes, what do you want?", I needed to have a well-prepared answer. I knew where I wanted to start, what I wanted to say, and where I wanted to end up. And I was perfectly willing to deal with any questions, objections, or distractions as they came along.

The situation in the Muslim world is quite different. In the early days evangelists arriving with their well-worked-out agendas quickly discovered that the Muslims already had their own agendas. No sooner would the evangelist get started on his agenda when the Muslim would make a comment, "Oh yes, your Scriptures have been changed, haven't they?" or perhaps "How could God have a son?" Many conflicts arose when these two agendas clashed.

As a result, when the western Christians started talking about friendship evangelism, there were many sincere workers among Muslims who thought that this approach held great promise. If the missionary had no other agenda than making a friend, and in the process, slipped in some quiet discussion, then the clash would disappear. However, since the missionary had no agenda for presenting a clear picture of what salvation, and ultimately what the Christian faith is all about, he seldom got around to doing this. Most of the religious discussion now centered on the Muslim agenda. Although Christian workers still had the goal of wanting to see their friends saved, they no longer had a clear-cut agenda to lead them step by step to the cross and ultimately to the foot of God's throne.

Now, this is troubling. Since the missionary often feels that he is accomplishing little, any religious discussion is considered a success. Many of us share with each other about the "good conversations" we are having with our Muslim friends. However, on closer examination, I have often noted that the focus of these discussions has been the Muslim, not the Christian, agenda. This also holds true for ministry to Hindus, Buddhists, and even secular humanists.

Some have commented that once the other person's agenda has been dealt with then the discussion will naturally go on to Christian things. There are two problems with this. First, the other person's agenda can go on and on and on. Muslims like Ahmed Deedat and others have worked hard to expand the Muslim agenda. Second, Satan is also busy contriving lies and rumors to add to the agendas of others. Suddenly we can be dealing with Muhammad in the Bible, or the alleged stories of astronauts in space hearing the Muslim call to prayer, or the sordid lives of television evangelists, and other things.

Most missionaries have a real struggle switching from someone else's agenda to presenting Christianity. Many of those I've talked with really have no agenda other than "gossiping the Gospel." They have never consciously thought through the issue of the best way to present the Gospel to their particular audience, be they Muslim, Buddhist, animist, secular humanists or whatever. Perhaps they never expected to be given the opportunity. Perhaps they never had the opportunity because they were so busy making friends or dealing with the other person's agenda.

When studying the successful evangelists in the Middle East, I discovered that they all had their own agendas. Each one had, over time, worked out various ways to present the Gospel. When they met someone, their ultimate goal was to start on their Christian agenda. Along the way, they dealt with the other person's agenda. If the Muslim objected about the Scriptures, they had an answer. That answer invariably ended with an invitation to look into the Christian faith. If the Muslim objected about the son-ship of Jesus, the evangelist had an answer that again ended with an invitation to study Christian doctrine. Given the least opportunity, the evangelist took it, and began his own agenda of presenting a clear and understandable picture of Christianity.

These evangelists had an advantage. The people to whom they were witnessing realized that they were sitting at the feet of a person of God, who could speak with authority, and communicate effectively. These people of God personified teacher-based evangelism.

Biblical Basis for Teacher-based Evangelism

Is teacher-based evangelism biblical? Can it be supported from the Word of God? Years ago I read *A Practical Approach to Muslims* by Jens Christensen and was challenged with the biblical support for openly proclaiming Christ.

Rather than doing a detailed study of styles of evangelism in the Bible, a quick overview of the concept of teaching should suffice at this point. The words *preach* and *teach* are used in relation to Christ many times. The whole picture of Jesus given in the Gospels is one of a teacher. Along with this, it is good to notice the identity Jesus had among the people. What did they call Him? Names like *Rabbi* and *Good Teacher* are at the top of the list. The very person we are to emulate in our lives personified the teaching lifestyle. Fifty-two times the New Testament draws our attention to the fact that Jesus was actively teaching. He taught in the synagogues, in the temple, in boats, in the street, in the desert, on a mountain, in cities, and in villages.

As Jesus discipled His followers, especially the inner core of twelve, He taught them to become fishers of men. His teaching included things like: "As you go, preach" (Matthew 10:7, NIV); "proclaim upon the house-tops" (10:27, ASV); "preach the good news to all creation" (Mark 16:15, NIV); "this gospel of the kingdom will be preached in the whole world as a testimony to all nations, and then the end will come" (Matthew 24:14, NIV).

The Bible tells us that after Jesus' ascension into heaven the disciples "preached the word wherever they went" (Acts 8:4, NIV). When Peter and John were taken before the Sanhedrin, the court "commanded them not to speak or teach at all in the name of Jesus" (Acts 4:18, NIV). When the disciples were imprisoned, and an angel released them, the angel instructed them, "Go, stand and speak in the temple to the people all the words of this life!" (Acts 5:20, 21 KJV) So the apostles entered the temple about daybreak and immediately began teaching.

Paul, writing to the church at Corinth, begins his letter by pointing out the differences between human wisdom and godly wisdom. The whole chapter is steeped in wisdom about how to teach, not with clever answers and arguments, but rather, in brokenness and humility, the "message of the Cross." Paul emphasizes that he was not sent to baptize but to preach (1 Corinthians 1:17). He points out that he knows "For the message of the cross is foolishness to those who are perishing," (1:18, NIV). However, "in the wisdom of God the world through its wisdom did not know him, God was pleased through the foolishness of what was preached to save those who believe." (1:23, NIV).

There are two important points here. First there is "human reasoning," and secondly there is the "foolishness of preaching." In my years of service, I have seen many examples of human reasoning, when Christians tried to answer Muslim objections. The strength of the Christian argument is logic; the strength of the Muslim argument is ultimately submission to what he considers the will of God, whether it makes logical sense or not. Seldom is there a winner. Paul, however, points to something beyond human wisdom: the proclamation of the truth. As the cross of Christ is proclaimed, the Holy Spirit can work in the hearts of men and women and draw them to Himself.

Paul highlights this in Romans 10:14 when he asks: "And how can they believe in Him if they have never heard about Him?" If we spend all our time in human reasoning, we can be distracted from proclaiming the good news of the Gospel. It is not enough to only answer objections; we must move on to our agenda and proclaim Christ.

Teaching is the core of our work as evangelists. It may seem foolish to those who are listening, it may seem foolish to us, but it is the method chosen by God. The pattern laid down in the Scriptures is that God leads us in our proclamation. The Holy Spirit also takes the Word of God and speaks it into the hearts of those who are listening.

Another struggle is that many well-meaning Christians today have little or no idea of how to go about the business of actually proclaiming Christ so that a Muslim mind can comprehend it. We err either on the side of being too quiet, or being too forthright. Under colonialism some Western missionaries abused their privilege as teachers of the Gospel, and began to teach Western culture and lifestyle rather than simply presenting Christ crucified.

During my short lifetime, I have had the privilege of spending time with several successful Christian workers from various places around the world. While they worked in different languages, cultures and situations, there was one thing I noticed about them: they were all preachers and teachers. They were always ready and able to speak about Christ in a whole variety of settings: Sunday School classes, church services, after a meal, in a home, on a bus, or in an airplane.

My friend Harry Young was a good example of this. Harry was always preaching. Everywhere he went he was taking out his Bible to share from its pages. Indeed, all the older, successful evangelists I've known were quick to preach and teach. People knew them and recognized them for what they were: Christian teachers who could speak with authority.

We've lost much of that today. Perhaps we don't want to appear to be forcing ourselves on anyone. In our timid attempts to be subtle in our approach, we can be completely misunderstood in a culture that is very up-front.

When Harry visited us on the field, he shared with us his "toolbox." In his wallet he had some slips of paper. On the papers were his teaching outlines and references. As he was getting older, his mind was getting slower and more forgetful, so he carried these outlines around in his pocket. And at the right opportunity, he pulled out an appropriate tool.

In 1980 my wife and I had the privilege of working with Harry in Birmingham, England. Harry's ministry was among Muslims living there, so he took us with him on his visits. At some point during his visit, he would take out his Bible and ask politely if he could share something from the Injil (Gospel). Then, to our amazement, he would stand up, open the Scriptures, and deliver a lesson. At first, we found ourselves astonished by his approach, but we soon realized that Harry was one of the few people we knew who was successfully proclaiming the Gospel message to Muslims.

Other Styles of Evangelism

In talking with other missionaries, I discovered that many people considered Harry's approach to be confrontational. They felt that Harry, and others using this method, were deliberately looking for opportunities to confront Muslims, and argue with them. In speaking to Harry about this, I came to realize that he was aware of this danger. Like most teachers, he struggled to keep a balance in his teaching style, but he chose to err on the side of confrontation, rather than miss a chance to proclaim Christ.

There have always been those who simply proclaimed Christ to the Muslim masses, exactly as they would have preached to any crowd at home. They had little imagination, little empathy, and succeeded only in clashing with their Muslim audiences. While there is a place for confrontation, (such as organized debates), it is not the sole or even the best form of evangelism. On the other extreme, some people feel that since they do not want to clash with the Muslims, they will simply live their lives as examples of what a Christian should be like. This is called lifestyle evangelism. All of us are involved in lifestyle evangelism as others look at our lives. But lifestyle is not enough. Many times we are misunderstood, especially if we are from another culture. Below I have charted a spectrum of various evangelism styles as I see them, moving from the least offensive on the left to the most offensive on the right. Proclamation includes literature, media, and other forms of communication. You will notice that teacher-based-evangelism fits into the middle position.

All of these styles of evangelism are useful, and should be used at the appropriate time. I believe that the central method, teacher-based evangelism, should be the most commonly used one as it fits squarely between the extremes of lifestyle and confrontation. Work your way through the following questions to explore more about these five styles of evangelism.

Lifestyle -- Friendship -- Teacher-based -- Proclamation -- Confrontation

Questions for Reflection or Discussion

1. What do you think is meant by the term "friendship evangelism"?

2. Have you had any success moving from a friendship to a relationship where you could freely talk about Christ? Describe what happened.

3. Do you feel you have gifts in evangelism? Has it been quite easy to lead people to Christ?

4. Do you have teaching gifts? Have you ever used this gift to lead someone to Christ?

5. Do the people you work among already have a spiritual agenda for you? Do they want to reach you with their religion? What are some of the things that are on their agenda?

6. How will you move from their agenda to yours?

7. How comfortable are you in a teaching/preaching situation? Do you need more experience in this area? What are some ways you can get this experience?

8. Can your team set up times when you practice teaching through a set of lessons with each other?

9. Have you located a number of good teaching outlines or lessons? Can you list three or four of them that you would use with seekers?

10. Can you think of any confrontation evangelism methods that might work in your ministry? One example would be debates. How would these be best used?

11. Can you think of some proclamation methods that could be used in your ministry? What are some of the good methods of getting the message out to large numbers of people?

12. What keeps you from using these methods? fear, finances, available time, language ability or other things?

13. Are there times in your ministry when your life must be your main witnessing tool?

14. How do you think people perceive you? Are there ways that they might be misinterpreting your life?

15. In the following verses, describe the evangelistic situations, and classify which type of evangelism style is being used: John 3: 1–21, John 4: 3-30, Acts 3:1-26, Acts 8: 26-39, Acts 17: 1-33, I Thessalonians 1:5-10.

16. What are some forms of evangelism that you would like to work at to better your skills?

Chapter Five
The Art of Teaching

How long does it take to explain the Gospel to someone? Could you do it in ten minutes or less if you used the Four Spiritual Laws? At one time in Yemen, I tried developing a "Gospel in a Nutshell" for Muslims. As I tried different approaches I discovered that nothing seemed to work. No matter how carefully I worked at my plan, I found in practice that I needed a lot more time. There were so many misunderstandings, such a completely different worldview, and incredible language problems (in which the Muslim Arabic language did not contain the words or concepts I sometimes needed), that there was no way I could package something together that would work in a single presentation.

Realizing that I couldn't do it in ten minutes, I began wondering how long it would really take. This was one of the burning questions I had as I visited these evangelists. What does one include in a Gospel presentation?

Over the years of watching them at work, I realized that these successful evangelists had all developed a pattern, but they were different than what I had expected. As I watched and listened, I soon realized that they never once tried to explain the Gospel in a single sitting. They would attempt to communicate some spiritual truth to meet people at their level of spiritual understanding. These evangelists were always meeting new people. Sometimes it was through their work or through an evangelistic program, but in most cases it was through the normal course of life, as they met neighbors, friends of friends, and business people. While each of them had developed their own approach, the underlying principle was the same. In every case, the evangelists would bring up spiritual things and then judge the spiritual interest of the new person. They would then deal with each one differently, according to his place on the spiritual progression chart below. Some of them never thought it out in the terms that I describe in the chart, but this is, in essence, the kind of philosophy they followed.

This chart may seem very simple. The concept behind it is simple, but the impact on people's lives can be profound. In effect, the chart gives us six broad steps to spiritual maturity, starting with those who are not interested in the Gospel, and ending with those who are Christian leaders. The classifications and titles are my own, but the principles were gleaned from these Christian workers. Please remember that the terms that I use are not an expression of any particular theological position. Rather, they are an attempt to analyze what is happening in the heart of the person you are trying to deal with.

Six Steps of Spiritual Development
1. Not Interested, even hostile (NI)
2. Somewhat Interested (SI)
3. Seeker (SE)
4. Convert (CV)
5. Disciple (DS)
6. Leader (LD)

Whenever these evangelists met someone, they began to assess his or her spiritual development, and target their ministry accordingly. Their aim was not so much to immediately lead the person to Christ, but rather to move him or her along from one stage to the next. They often felt excited as they saw a person move forward from one spiritual plane to the next.

Not Interested, perhaps hostile (NI)
NIs are people who believe they are not interested in what Christians have to say. The West is filled with NIs who are not interested in religion. They simply want nothing to do with what they perceive as established religion, although those with post-modern leanings may discuss spirituality. On the other hand, most Muslims are interested in religion, but not Christianity because they think they know all about Christianity and are convinced that it is wrong. Lies, misunderstandings, self-righteousness, and pride often blind them in their ignorance. Whatever the reason, the evangelist will come across many

people who are not asking for the Gospel, and respond negatively when he tries to draw them into conversation. If people are not interested in our message, we need to consider carefully how we are packaging that message, and what sort of impression we are making on our audience. Everyone seems to have opinions about Christianity, but many Muslims, Hindus and Buddhists have never had much interaction with a real believer. The evangelist must seek to interact with these people by challenging their opinions, worldview, and their closed thinking about Christians.

Sometimes it is ministry to their physical or emotional needs that awakens an interest within them. Sometimes it is the realization that they have been misinformed about Christian things. Sometimes it is the life of a Christian that speaks to them. Whatever it is, the evangelist seeks to challenge them out of their complacency. Most of us hesitate to speak about prayer, fasting, or our relationship with God. However, the successful evangelists I observed were always bringing spiritual topics into their conversation and saying things to catch people's attention and challenge their thinking.

This is similar to the approach Jesus took when he used parables and proverbs to speak to people. (This is covered more fully in chapter 6.) Surprisingly, he often did not explain them. He spoke in order to make people think. He would simply say things, and wait for people to come to him later for an explanation (Matthew 13:34-36). Few of us would ever imagine dealing with people in this manner. We want to give a short, concise, complete presentation of the Gospel such as we find in the popular Four Spiritual Laws. This however, should not be our goal with NIs. Rather, we should seek to provoke questions, rather than answer them.

Many NIs never move on to the next stage. I was surprised at the number of successful evangelists who were quick to abandon their work with a particular NI, stating that when they saw that God was investing his time and energy in that person's life, then they would follow suit. They would continue to challenge that person's complacency whenever they met him, but they wouldn't pour their life's energies into someone who was not interested.

Most of these evangelists felt that those engaging in friendship evangelism spent far too much time with NIs and in doing so wasted time they could have used to seek out, pray for, and work with more receptive people. Rather than visiting a few select people, these evangelists visited many people in the community. They spent time talking to shop owners, hairdressers, neighbors and people whose homes were open to them. Wherever they went, they were quick to share something of the Gospel, often using parables or proverbs, or short pithy statements. (In the following chapter we will take a more detailed look at this approach.) When they saw a spiritual response in some, they invested more of their time and energy to pursue that person.

When a person comes with a spiritual question, he has started to move to the next spiritual stage. The evangelist can rejoice at this, because a spiritual battle has been won. Such a person is now moving on to being somewhat interested (SI)

Somewhat interested (SI)

When someone who was not interested begins to show an interest in learning about Christianity, he has moved on to becoming somewhat interested (SI). This is often a real work of God. Many people, once they become interested in knowing more about Christianity, slowly become aware of their own spiritual needs. They may compare their lives to that of a Christian. They may compare their lives to what they feel is their own religion's goal of spirituality and perfection, and start seeking ways of attaining this.

Often somewhat interested people bring up objections or misunderstandings about Christianity. Not interested people may also voice objections, but they do this in order to push the evangelist away. Somewhat interested people usually want to know if the objections are true or not. It is important that the evangelist gently answer their objections, and encourages them to continue to pursue the questions that come to them.

Sometimes SI people begin to delve more deeply into their own religion, as a response to the claims of Christ. At first glance, this can look like a spiritual step backwards, but it is actually the natural outcome of their spiritual hunger. If you as a Christian turn to your Scriptures when challenged, shouldn't we naturally expect those of other religions to turn to their own religion to seek answers? Seekers usually start in the places where their families and religious leaders tell them they will find answers. The evangelist should assure their inquirers that they are free to look anywhere to seek out the answers, but they are also available and willing to discuss these things. Once an SI has turned their attention to Christianity to see if it has answers, this person has moved much closer to becoming a seeker (SE).

Seeker (SE)

A seeker is someone who has heard parts of the Gospel message and now feels that he must reconcile the difference between his own position and the claims of Christianity. I am not using this term as a theological statement of any kind. I am simply trying to represent the mind set of those who have arrived at the point where they are wrestling with what they know of Christianity on the one hand, and the teachings of their own religion on the other. They obviously cannot both be right. This term signifies that the contact is taking the initiative to find the truth. An NI takes little initiative and the messenger must work at penetrating the walls that the NI has put up. The SI also takes little initiative, but is more responsive, perhaps expressing commonly held opinions, or speaking in response to prompting by the messenger, and thereby entering into dialog. The SE however, now takes the initiative and strives to discover which of the two viewpoints is the true source of truth. When the messenger feels that someone has become a true seeker, the messenger should work hard to arrange the circumstances so that the seeker can learn more in a student-teacher relationship. There are two options here. One is that the evangelist takes the seeker to a teacher, the other is that the evangelist himself moves into the role of teacher. Whatever the arrangement, the teacher needs to be able to spend sufficient time with the SE to give him a clear presentation of the Gospel.

If this change or roles puzzles you, then you need to consider the situation from the other person's point of view. Remember that many cultures (e.g. Muslim, Buddhist, animistic) are as a rule oral cultures. Very few people read much more than the morning newspaper headlines. Therefore if you need to know something you turn to those who have knowledge. Everyone has opinions, but only those who have studied have knowledge. As the world is full of rumors and lies, information should not be trusted unless it comes from a trusted source, such as a teacher.

When witnessing, personal testimonies are useful in that they are accounts of what has happened in an individual's life. There is no greater expert on a life than the person living it. However, when the topic moves beyond personal experience to that of truth or theology, the seeker usually wants to get his information from an established source. Therefore the messenger must either be able to present himself as an authority, or introduce the seeker to someone else who is. The latter is often easier, unless the seeker already sees the messenger as a religious authority. From our own point of view, we must never consider ourselves to be an authority on Christianity, but must always be careful to reveal that our authority is based on a higher authority: the Word of God.

It is important for the teacher to have two things in place. He must have a sense of direction whereby he can systematically cover the basics so that the contact gets a complete picture of Christianity. He must also demonstrate that the Bible is the source and authority on the Christian faith. The seeker is looking for answers and he wants them from an authority.

It is our moral duty to give the seeker the best Gospel presentation possible; something that is both understandable and speaks the Gospel clearly. There are a number of tools available, some of which can be found on the Internet site: http://rmuller.com.

Converts (CV), Disciples (DS) and Leaders (LD)

These last three stages on the Spiritual Development chart will be taken up in the latter sections of the book when I deal with friendship discipling and church planting. However, we must be prepared to move people through these stages quite quickly if the Holy Spirit is promoting us to do so. Many ministries plan to take years in order to develop leaders. Others move new converts into leadership in two or three years. Most successful instances of rapid church growth or church planting movements have had to quickly develop leaders in order to keep the momentum moving.

Evangelizing Through Teaching

Outsiders who assume the role of a teacher in a society foreign to them sometimes struggle to know how to act as a teacher in that particular culture. There are subtle things that have to be learned or changed. What does a teacher act and look like in the target culture? What are the things that a person should do, or not do, to enhance and reinforce the lesson material? What should the teacher expect of the student? What do students expect of their teacher?

We should never assume that we understand communication and teaching. Learning to be an effective teacher in another culture is a life-long process. As we learn more of the culture, we should readily adapt our teaching style to become ever better communicators. When I have had opportunity to expose new workers to situations in which I wanted them to make observations, I am often struck with how little they see. Although I observe and analyze instinctively, many others do not, or cannot, because they have not developed the basic framework from which to begin to analyze. This is one of the reasons we introduce the concept of worldview as a church planting tool in the second part of this book. Without an understanding of the wider situation, it is very difficult to make the connections and correctly analyze a local situation.

To be an effective teacher in another cultural setting it is important to expose yourself to local teachers. When doing so you may recognize that much is done for outward appearances to impress men. That is not the way of Christ. There may be, however, some aspects of behavior that one must adopt in order to be recognized as a teacher. Get to know some local teachers in your community. Visit some local schools and observe how the teachers behave. If you cannot visit, simply stand near a local school and observe or listen. Remember that these are teachers teaching children. How can you observe teachers teaching adults? Do they teach differently at a college or university? What about the mosque or temple? Perhaps you can watch lessons being taught on television. What makes a teacher successful? What does he do to get and command respect? How does he control his class? Remember that an excellent teacher holds the attention of the class, and probably does not struggle with control. How can you become such a teacher? Ask around the community. Discover what people think are the characteristics of a good teacher. If you are to be seen and accepted as a teacher, you should be well aware of these characteristics, and carefully pray through which of them you will adopt in your own life.

Below is a list of several things to look for when assessing how a teacher acts and what he might look like. Consider each of them carefully, as the total image you portray is critical to the success of your efforts.

Culture & Language

Culture is important. Study your target culture carefully. There is a reason for everything people do. They may not know the reasons, but there are always reasons. Delve into the culture and seek to understand how people act and how they relate to each other. If it is impolite to point the bottom of your feet at someone, then never do it. Try to be conservative. Watch and listen. Try imitating another person's actions. What makes you uncomfortable? Why? Seek to understand the principles behind actions. Then try and fit in.

On one occasion I dressed as an Arab and wore sunglasses. I decided to walk through a Middle Eastern bazaar as an Arab to see what it would feel like. I was amazed that people still stared at me as they would at any foreigner. So I decided to follow a group of young men, and try to imitate them. It was terribly upsetting. They walked so slowly, and looked at things I would never look at! But once I slowed down, and tried acting like them, I started to fit into the crowd and become one of them, thankful that no one was staring at me.

Dress

Dress is important. Teachers often hold an honored place in society. One who does not dress appropriately will soon lose the respect of the students and others in the community. How you dress on the street is important. How you answer the door is important. You might even have to abandon your favorite forms of dress (like shorts and a T-shirt), and adopt something more formal. Watch carefully how the local people look at you. What do they look at first? In the culture in which I presently live, people often judge others by their shoes. So, I have taken to wearing formal shoes most of the time, keeping them polished and presentable.

Styles of Teaching

Most of us have been well educated in our home countries and have preconceived notions of what makes a good teacher. Yet our opinions are based on our culture and philosophy of life. Study the styles of teaching used in your target culture, and adapt these to your use. Visit a local school or observe teaching taking place on television, such as from a mosque or temple. In some situations you might decide that the teacher portrays too much pride. Consider how you can portray yourself as knowledgeable without coming across as proud.

Use of Notes

Have you ever noticed that Eastern teachers seldom, if ever, use notes? The use of notes indicates two things to the audience. First, the speaker doesn't know his material well enough to speak without them and, secondly, the notes are the authority.

One evangelist pointed out to me that when he tried to use written material other than the Bible, the seeker wanted to get a copy of the notes, and then, having obtained the authoritative document, didn't return for further lessons. As a teacher of the Bible, it is vitally important that you use the Bible and the Bible alone. Therefore, you want to communicate that the Bible is the sole source of your authority. You want the seeker to seek God in the pages of His Word. Don't introduce another authority and refer to it more frequently than you do the Bible. If you must use notes, then write them on a small card and slip it into your Bible where you can refer to it occasionally.

Seating

If you have never attended a teaching session in a temple or mosque I would suggest that you make it a point to attend, or observe one on television. Notice that teachers often sit, but are elevated above the audience or in a place of authority. Study your local culture so you can immediately see if there are "seats of honor" or places in the room that command more authority than others. You will need to decide for yourself if you want or need to make use of this cultural aspect of position. You may want your guest to sit in the place of honor. After all, Jesus taught His disciples to take places of lesser authority and asked His followers to do likewise (Matthew 23:5-12).

Handling of the Scriptures

How does a religious teacher handle the Scriptures? If the Scriptures are your sole authority and if they are the holy Word of God and you love and respect them, then treat them accordingly. Don't place your Bible on the floor;

don't place other books on top of it, don't put it in your back pocket and don't write in it. Having said this, there are exceptions. I have seen Muslims marvel at a well-read Bible, which has been carefully marked. The worn, marked Bible can show the seeker how much you love and study its pages. That said, the general rule is: treat your Bible as a precious or even sacred object if you expect others to respect it as well.

Refreshments

It has been our experience that it is best not to serve refreshments during the teaching time, especially if you are struggling to assert yourself as a teacher. Refreshments can be distracting; besides, most students don't drink tea, during a lesson. It is possible to offer a cup of tea before the lesson but then consider clearing it away. More can be offered after the lesson.

Location

Whenever possible, teaching should take place in a neutral place. While it is possible to teach in a restaurant or public place, this can be fraught with difficulties and distractions. The seeker himself may be nervous about meeting in such a public place, and if he doesn't show up, the teacher must wait around for a considerable time in case he has been delayed.

If there is no suitable, neutral location, then the teacher's home is often the best place for him to meet with his students. It is important, however, to have a place where you can sit and teach, rather than informally lounge around. Some people object to the idea of bringing a seeker into a foreigner's home, as there may be cultural things that will overshadow the lesson, but the teacher's home is private and the number of distractions can usually be controlled. If possible, the sitting room should be as similar as possible to those found in other local homes. Often Westerners fill their sitting rooms with books, pictures, and other paraphernalia that make them feel at home, but make their visitors feel on edge. A good teacher or evangelist should have prepared an easily accessible room that resembles a typical sitting room or teaching location for people from your target culture.

Number and Length of Sessions

One of the greatest difficulties you will face is getting the student to attend all the sessions. This is one reason why introducing another teacher to the seeker is so useful. The teacher demands greater respect from the students because he is making an effort to come and teach. In the best situations we have used national teachers. They are usually men of standing (such as a pastor, engineer or medical doctor who traveled into our location when we invited him).

When a national teacher is not available have used *vice-versa* teaching. In this case two Christian workers, usually in different locations, help one another, each one serving as the teacher for the other's contacts. Thus each evangelist tells his contact that he has a friend who is a religious teacher. This teacher is willing to teach a short course on understanding Christianity (or the Gospel). If the seeker is interested, the evangelist arranges to introduce his contact to the teacher. If the seeker is not interested, then they continue their relationship, talking about issues, with the evangelist occasionally repeating the invitation to meet with a teacher. The strength of this approach is that the evangelist can act as a sounding board after each session. The evangelist can also ask his contact questions and encourage him to attend the next lesson, offering to go with him, if needed. This creates a triangle, with the contact, evangelist and teacher all relating to one another.

In my opinion, it is best if the teacher is a national who can speak the local language well, and relate from the same cultural and religious background. On the other hand, in a Muslim setting it is sometimes better if the evangelist is from another culture. Any Muslim seeking truth outside of Islam would be immediately confronted by his family and neighbors. Thus talking to a foreigner may seem safer to a Muslim seeker because the foreigner is not connected to his immediate circle. If this is the case, the evangelist may find it advantageous to circulate through the wider community, finding those who are interested in learning about Christianity. Then, as seekers emerge, they could be passed over to a local believer (or another evangelist) who would act as the teacher.

As for the length of the lessons, evangelists over the years have struggled with the questions of *how much* and *how soon?* The author of the *Discovery Lessons* (see the resources at http://rmuller.com) found that he could not cover the basics in less than six hours. When seekers were invited to attend a "Bible study" they often shied away, simply because of the open-endedness of the commitment and because of the thickness of the Bible. Usually students are more read to commit themselves to attend a study if they know that it is limited to a certain time length. Six one-hour sessions seem more palatable than an open-ended commitment.

While six one-hour sessions can be covered in a week, it is often wiser to leave a longer period of time between the sessions. The student is covering so much new material that he needs time to think about it and assimilate it. In some cases, however, teachers have successfully used three two-hour sessions. You, as the teacher, must decide with the student regarding what commitment he can make.

Repetition and Memorization

There is an old Arab proverb that says, "Repetition leaves its mark, even on stones." Memorization is a learning tool often used by Africans and Asians, so don't be afraid to encourage memorization. Students can memorize Scripture verses as well as the broad outline you are covering. I once saw an Arab give the 70 point outline for the Old Testament series of Walk Through the Bible. He reveled in the use of memorization and weeks later knew it all word for word. So don't be afraid to ask your students to memorize. However, don't rely solely on memorization. Many other mediums can be used. When working with the Bedouin we discovered that songs, drama and narratives are also useful tools. But they are only tools, and should be combined with other forms of learning so that understanding and application happen.

Adaptability

As you progress through the material, you will begin to assess how interested the seeker is, and for what reasons. If he is merely seeking to gain knowledge, but is not personally interested in Christ, then the material can be presented simply as a course on Christianity. If the student begins to respond to the material and you can see evidence of God's work in his heart, then the material can be made much more direct. Try to be sensitive to the seeker's questions. A Muslim seeking to trap you may ask you questions about

Muhammad or the Qur'an, or even some other Scriptures or teaching. Gently remind the student that these are lessons about the Christian faith, and return to the lesson material. You need to trust God to guide the student as he forms his own opinions about his own religion.

Keeping to the point

Know and communicate the material for each lesson and only have two or three sub points. That's all! Memorize the outline and resist the temptation to teach too much material in one session. Remember that many of the concepts you are teaching are totally new to the student, and may be hard for him to grasp. Sometimes one simple thing you say may require hours of consideration before the student can accept it. For the Muslim, simply grasping the concept that God created a perfect creation may be overwhelming. But it is a necessary lesson, for if creation isn't broken, then it doesn't need fixing. This is why the entire first lesson of the *Discovery Lessons* is about the perfect creation.

Who should be present?

This may vary according to the culture you are in. In a Muslim setting, most teachers agree that the best situation is one-on-one with the teacher and the student, or the student and his Christian friend (if they are doing vice-versa teaching) and the teacher.

If more people want to attend the study, then there are several things that should be considered. Some teachers mentioned that in teaching a group, the students should outnumber the Christians so that it doesn't appear that the Christians are ganging up on them. This, in reality, is often hard to arrange. Often the teacher will want to apprentice a new teacher or a Christian observer will want to sit in on a lesson. If this is the case, then the observer should act as an observer and a silent prayer partner He should refrain from entering into the discussion unless invited by the teacher. When the teacher is waiting patiently for an answer from the student, it is often hard for the observer to resist the temptation to help by answering the question for the seeker.

The dynamics change when there is more than one student only. All the evangelists agree that they would prefer to deal with two or more students if these are already the best of friends. If they are going to think and act as a group (see chapter eight "Honor and Trust"), then it can be helpful to deal with them as a group. This takes more skill, as the students can hide behind one another's responses, defend one another, and create an argumentative atmosphere. If everyone in the group is a really a seeker then it may be possible to move them as a group closer to Christ.

Almost all evangelists agree that the presence of persons of the opposite sex should be avoided and that female teachers should deal only with female students and male teachers with male students. The only occasion when students of the opposite sex should be together is if they are a married couple. In most cases it is unwise to teach an engaged couple together, as it may appear that this is an occasion for courting rather than study. Even teaching a brother and sister together should be avoided unless they are either young children or older, respected members of the community.

Questions for Reflection or Discussion

1. What would you want to include in a gospel presentation? Can you write a short outline of things you would share if you only had a short period of time, say fifteen minutes?

2. Make a list of your closest national friends and decide where they are at in their relationship with Christ. Categorize them as NI, SI, SE, CV, DC, or LD

3. How many not interested or hostile people do you deal with on a regular basis?

4. What are some creative ways that you can demonstrate to them the love of God?

5. Do the not interested people see you as a spiritual person? Start praying about ways that you can demonstrate or verbally share something of your spiritual life with the not interested people in your life.

6. Are there any somewhat interested people in your life? Who? What sort of things do you talk about? Are you always answering their challenges, or are they open to discussion?

7. What are some ways that you can continue to encourage conversations with somewhat interested people, and lead them to more questions, without you always being the one to initiate the religious conversations?

8. How does this chapter describe seekers? What makes them different from somewhat interested people?

9. If a person wanted you to tell them what the Christian faith was all about, what would you say? Do you have a plan?

10. If you needed a teacher, who could you call on? Think of both missionaries and national workers. Can you trust them to do an excellent job in clearly explaining the gospel to someone from your target group?

11. Do you appear as conservative or Western to your national friends? How could you find the answer to this question?

12. Observe a local teaching situation. Visit a school or observe teaching on television. What do they do differently? What makes you uncomfortable about their teaching? What could you adopt from their teaching style?

13. Is your house different from the people you want to reach? What might make your living room comfortable or uncomfortable for them? How are their living rooms different from yours? Are there things you can change to make them feel more at home?

14. Do you have any seats of honor in your house? What is Jesus teaching in Matthew 23:1-12?

15. In your culture, is it best to separate genders at a Bible Study? Why or why not?

16. Can you list two or three people that you would like to encourage to sit with a teacher?

Chapter Six
Parables, Proverbs, & Prayer

How does one go about impacting a community for Christ? Many modern missiologists tell us that the secret to impacting a community is through its leaders. In a sense this is true, but I feel this is a simplistic approach to what may be a very complex community.

Some have suggested that in many settings, the evangelist should focus on heads of families; once these come to Christ the rest of the family will follow. This too is true, but in practice, due to their busy lifestyles, it is very hard to find heads of families, and sometimes even harder to win them to Christ.

I would like to suggest a slightly different approach. The Bible calls us to be salt and light in our witness to the world. When salt is added to a pot of boiling potatoes, the salt affects everything in the pot. And so a salt-type witness is one that affects the whole community. Light, however is different. It shines into the darkness, penetrating only the small area the light is pointed at. I believe that light-type witnessing focuses on a few individuals, endeavoring to share truth in a way that brings light into their lives. Then there are two lights, then three, and so on. Our witness to the world should include both of these kinds of witness.

Salt-Type Ministry

As I worked in our community, I developed a desire to see the whole community come to understand what faith in Jesus really means. This would have three major impacts on the community. It would make the not interested people (NIs) aware that there is another way of thinking other than the way they have always thought. It would open doors for somewhat interested people(SIs) to ask questions more openly. Third, it would lower the resistance of the whole community towards converts (CVs) as they come to Jesus.

Impacting a community takes time. Many evangelists think only of working with people one-on-one. Trying to impact a community of any size through the one-on-one method would take a long time. Another alternative has been to utilize mass media tools that work as salt. Mass media tools such as newspaper advertisements, literature and video distribution, radio, and TV, can all work as salt, influencing a community in general. These are greatly used of the Lord, and I would never want to minimize their impact. There are, however, other tools that may be available to us.

Some of the evangelists I have watched had a particular interest in moving their whole community towards a greater awareness and understanding of the Gospel. They had a salt-type ministry which was really very simple, so simple that many workers have overlooked it, and concentrated on technological tools.

I discovered that the daily chores that are part of everyday life are actually opportunities to be salt to the community. A visit to the shops, the mechanic, the park, and to neighbors are all part of being salt. These evangelists sought for and used opportunities to speak in simple ways that made people think.

I first saw this in the life of an evangelist who came to visit us while we were ministering in Yemen. This man had an amazing gift of speaking to people along the path of life. I watched this young man turn almost every conversation towards spiritual things. He would then say things that would make the listener think.

On one occasion, a Yemeni man asked him about the price of a bride in his country. The evangelist thought for a moment and then replied that the price of a bride was very great. The Yemeni was shocked. This was obviously not the answer he was expecting. The evangelist took the opportunity to teach a short lesson. He explained that in Yemen a bride only costs money. In his country, bride cost much more than money. The man needed to give his heart to the bride. He would have to promise to love and cherish only this one woman. The price was very expensive, he told the listener, because when a man gives his heart to his bride, she gets everything in his life. The evangelist paused, then looked the Yemeni in the eye and continued. He pointed out that this is exactly like God. God doesn't just want our money, or our prayers. He wants our hearts. And when God has our hearts He has all of us.

The story was very simple, but it caused the Yemeni to think. The evangelist's objective was not to convert the Yemeni, but to make him think about a fundamental truth of the Gospel. It was an excellent example of how to minister to an NI individual.

As soon as I realized that this was a significant missiological tool, I too tried my hand at it. Like every skill, it took time to develop, but the results, both in ministry and in personal satisfaction, have made it very worthwhile.

On one occasion a member of our community offered me a cigarette. I politely refused, and then a few moments later asked him if he knew why I didn't smoke. He didn't, and asked why. I told him: God has given us two important things in this life, a body, and time. When we reach Judgment Day He will ask what I did with the body He gave me, and what I did with my time. If I misuse my body, I will need to answer to God for it. The man was quite surprised with my answer, so I continued, "So many people in this part of the world think that God will only judge them about things like prayer or fasting. But God will want to know what we did with our bodies, and also with the time we have on this earth. Many of the prophets spoke of these things. There will be lots of surprises on Judgment Day." The object of such a conversation was not to witness, but rather to spread salt. Many Muslims pride themselves on being more religious than others. I tried to shift the conversation from a physical topic to a spiritual one. As most Arabs smoke, I discovered that there were many opportunities to share on this topic. Whenever the conversation allowed, I would try and share how a Christian's outward actions need to be a response to Christ changing us from within.

In trying to be salt to the community it is important to speak provocatively, as the two stories above illustrate. It is also effective to use parables, proverbs or stories to communicate a truth. Once I heard a missionary to Muslims say, "Imagine a truck load of ceremonially clean meat. What would happen to that whole truckload of meat, if I mixed in one teaspoon of pig meat? Sin is like that. We think the small things don't matter very much!" In saying things like this, we not only communicate to those who are listening but the stories and sayings will also make their way around the community. On some occasions my wife has reported to me that the group of ladies she was visiting was discussing some of the stories that I had told to men in another part of the city.

The advantage of good stories is that they are easy to pass on. In our community, people spend a lot of time visiting each other. They often rack their brains trying to think of good and clever things to say to stimulate the discussion and keep it going. Stories, parables, and provocative sayings about the Gospel will be passed around the community, and the effect is a kind of Gospel salt that influences the general attitude and understanding of the community about Christian things. This is important because a salt-type ministry helps prepare the community for the presence of the church that will one day exist there.

Light-Type Ministry

Ministering light is another skill. Since light is usually focused on those who are seeking the truth, those endeavoring to minister light need to know how to make a presentation which will communicate the message of the Gospel clearly to the mind of the contact. This type of ministry is generally focused on those who are seekers, or at least somewhat interested, and usually takes the shape of some form of teaching.

I believe that the Christian worker who is ministering light into a situation also needs to be able to use proverbs, parables, and stories. Rather than saying something short and provocative, the person ministering light uses these proverbs and parables as illustrations to sharpen and focus the conversation.

Hostile and Not Interested People

It is a common experience for missionaries to become discouraged in the face of hostile or uninterested people. The missionary wants to share the gospel and lead the person to Christ. The listener seems to reject what is presented and missionaries often give up at this point. Instead of giving up, the missionary needs to find ways to challenge the thinking of the listener.

Jesus faced many kinds of people. Some came to get something from Jesus and then went away. Some came to hear his teaching, but many times people came to oppose him and find fault in him and his message. When facing opposition, Jesus used proverbs, parables and prayer. These same three tools still work today with hostile and uninterested people.   51

Proverbs

People of every race or culture have their own ways of communicating among themselves, as in music, art, and drama. By far the most commonly used mode is verbal language. There are different forms of verbal language; for instance, common language, idioms, secret or esoteric language, and proverbs. Proverbs are common in every language. One of the signs of a wise teacher is his use of proverbs or local wisdom. Anyone wishing to be recognized as a teacher should be skilled in the use of parables and proverbs.

Proverbs are normally short sayings which contain wisdom and experiences of the past and can be used to illustrate a truth, usually by contrasting two situations. Although there are long proverbs, which look more like short stories or poems, the overwhelming majority of proverbs are short, direct statements.

Proverbs usually have two meanings: the literal or primary meaning, and the deeper or real meaning. The real meaning of a proverb is not always apparent. Often the proverb is a play on words, or a saying with a special twist to make it complicated. Its meaning is usually not fixed, and so can be modified. The user, therefore, is free to reconstruct a proverb in order to make it appropriate to the particular context in which it is being used. He may delete, paraphrase, elaborate, or transfer elements in it.

For a proverb to be appropriate when cited, the situation depicted in the primary meaning, as well as in its deeper meaning, must match that of the context and situation to which it is being applied.

Likewise, the hearer must be smart enough to interpret and grasp its meaning. Understanding a proverb correctly, calls for discernment. This is because the truths and advice expressed in proverbs are not always stated in plain language but rather in figures of speech, metaphors, and images. Sometimes things that are alike or opposite are compared and contrasted. Reason and the use of the imagination are needed in order to get the real meaning.

There are thousands, perhaps millions, of proverbs in use worldwide. A number of useful proverbs are listed on the Roland Muller webiste.

The best way to learn proverbs is to ask wise people in your community to teach you some. If you visit a lot in the community, you will hear proverbs being used continually. Write them down. If people know you are interested in collecting proverbs they will often be willing to help you discover more. New proverbs are always being composed, and old ones are adapted or given new meanings to suit new situations. Anyone who is creative and observant and has the ability to reflect and deduce a moral lesson from common happenings can compose a proverb.

A close look at traditional proverbial sayings shows clearly that the main concerns expressed relate to every aspect of human life and behavior. They touch on wealth and poverty, health and sickness, joy and sorrow, marriage and childbearing, occupations, and all kinds of activities. There are proverbs which speak to and about all manner of people: kings and citizens, nobles and slaves, men and women, adults and children, craftsmen and apprentices. Some proverbial sayings contain historical statements or facts about the people, while others contain information about their culture. A great number of them express philosophical thoughts, religious beliefs, and values.

The ultimate purpose of proverbs is to teach wisdom. Thus they are used to convey moral lessons and advice on how to live life. They embody observations and good counsel against undesirable vices like anger, backbiting, greed, ingratitude, laziness, lying, pride, procrastination, selfishness, and stealing. Others praise and advise people to cultivate virtues such as circumspection, cooperation, gratitude, humility, patience, perseverance, prudence, respect, and unity that promote progress, ensure well being and promote peace.

In rural settings, a person rarely speaks more than a few sentences without quoting a proverb. For the initiated, the citing of proverbs comes naturally without any conscious or special effort. Since a proverb can have several meanings it can, therefore, be applied to different situations. This is as true during ordinary conversation as well as formal and solemn discourse.

Proverbs, then, are a literary device used to embellish speech and increase understanding. Many of the idioms of a language are embedded in its proverbs. They are cited to confirm, reinforce, or modify a statement, to heighten and attract attention to a point or message, or simply to summarize a speech. Sometimes they are used to communicate a fact or opinion which might be impolite or even offensive if stated in direct speech or plain language. When dealing with a difficult theological issue, the use of a proverb can bring light to the listeners, add a humorous twist, and defuse the tension.

Although all these uses are important, they are, in fact, only a means to an end. The ultimate purpose of proverbs is to impart wisdom. As a result, proverbs can be extremely useful and effective as a tool for teaching. They are short, easy to remember, and are often popular for their humor. They provoke vivid images in the mind. Things that are otherwise abstract and difficult to grasp can be relatively easy to understand when explained with a proverb. They are, as it were, sweeteners to effective communication. It has been said that speaking without citing proverbs is like eating soup without salt. Since proverbs are important tools in communicating wisdom, we need to ask God's help in learning how to use and apply proverbs in our daily communication. James 1:5 tells us, "If any of you lacks wisdom, he should ask God, who gives generously to all without finding fault, and it will be given to him."

Biblical Proverbs

Proverbs and proverbial sayings have been used in both the Old and New Testaments. They can be found throughout the Bible, "Like mother, like daughter" (Ezekiel 16:44), "The parents have eaten sour grapes, but their children's mouths pucker at the taste" (Ezekiel 18:2), "A dog returns to its vomit" (2 Peter 2:22). The best known, however, found in the book of Proverbs.

The Hebrew word for "proverb" comes from a word which means "to be like" or "to be as." Thus, in the book of Proverbs the message is often given by comparing two things and showing their similarity in some respect, "Timely advice is as lovely as golden apples in a silver basket" (Proverbs 25:11), or "A person who doesn't give a promised gift is like clouds and wind that don't bring rain" (Proverbs 25:14).

Another style commonly used in Proverbs is that of contrast, showing the difference between two things. This is common in chapters 10-15, "Wise people don't make a show of their knowledge, but fools broadcast their folly" (12:23). Sometimes conditional statements are used. For instance consider these proverbs, "If you repay evil for good, evil will never leave your house" (17:13), and "Plans succeed through good counsel; don't go to war without the advice of others" (20:18).

The book of Proverbs does have its problems for us. First of all, since a proverb is often a play on words in its original language, it can be very hard to translate it into another. I found this true when living among Low-German speaking Mennonites on the prairies in Canada. They would often quote a proverb, there would be some laughter, and then someone would try to explain it to me. Even after I understood the meaning of the words, I still did not understand the meaning of the proverb. It was only after I understood the context in which it was used and the background material to which it referred (usually farm-related things, especially animals), that I began to understand a bit of what was meant.

Many evangelical Christians in the West seem to have discarded the use of biblical proverbs and tend, at best, to use clichés. Perhaps our struggle with them comes from our struggle to understand Hebrew proverbs translated into English. This, however, should not discourage us from using proverbs with those we are trying to reach, since proverbs have an important role in their own cultural and literary backgrounds.

Possible Objections to the Use of Proverbs

Not all Christian workers like the idea of using proverbs in preaching the Christian message. Some feel that since proverbs are part of traditional culture, Christians should not use them. They may be reluctant to use proverbs in case they overshadow Biblical texts or themes, since some are so vivid that they may be more easily remembered than the Biblical texts they are meant to help explain. These Christians may also be uncomfortable with using traditional proverbs for fear that some of the teachings they contain may conflict with the teachings of the Bible.

These are well-founded fears. We must be careful, as Christians, to choose our use of proverbs wisely. Many proverbs teach good moral values. These are of use. Teachers must never build their teachings around proverbs, however. They should only be used only to explain, illustrate, or reinforce biblical truths. They should be chosen carefully, especially since some hidden meanings may not be readily apparent. Proverbs that teach opposing values to the Bible teaches should not normally be used, but they may be cited if the intention is to show a better way through biblical revelation. Jesus did a similar thing when He declared, "You have heard that ... But I say...." (Matthew 5:21-22, 27-28). Of course, for the Christian, the Bible is the revealed Word of God and must remain the highest authority.

Parables

Parables can be frustrating to Western Christians who have a strong desire to communicate truth. They struggle to tolerate loose ends but it is obvious that Jesus himself, along with other Biblical authors who used parables seemed to have no problems with loose ends.

Parables are stories. They are fiction, not true stories. Often we so desire to share truth that fiction has no place in our teaching. Most of us don't want to risk making up stories so we rarely use parables unless they are directly from the Bible. Telling parables, however, is a biblical skill that we need to develop. It usually doesn't come easily to us.

It must be remembered that parables are stories that get attention, bring involvement, produce emotion, and speak to antagonists in a way that causes less offense.

Most of Jesus' parables did not hide truth from his antagonists (Luke 15:3, 20:19) or at least that does not seem to be the intention of the parables. Further understanding of truth was hidden from those who did not accept what they already understood. When we compare the parallel passages in Mark 4:10-12 and Luke 8:9-10, we see that the disciples actually asked two questions at this time: What does the parable of the sower mean and why speak in parables?

So Jesus' answer in the following verses addresses both questions. Whoever responds appropriately will be given more - applies to the meaning of the good soil and also to the understanding of parables (see Mark 4:13). Whoever responds inappropriately, even what he has will be taken from him - applies to the bad soils (particularly the path) and to the understanding of parables. One's response to the parable determines one's understanding.

Were the parables designed to hide secret meaning? On the basis of Mt. 13:10-13 and Jesus use of Is. 6:9-10; many have believed that the parables have secret meaning for believers, but that they only serve to harden unbelievers. Unbelievers think they are just simple stories, and cannot see the real meaning. His enemies could therefore find no direct statements to use against him.   Although there is some truth in this understanding, it is an imperfect understanding of the purpose of parables, and does not at all apply to some parables. Isaiah did not preach in a way so as to hide his message. His message was hidden because people refused to believe that which he plainly proclaimed, and so their condemnation was even greater. The same is true in Jesus.

56

When dealing with sensitive issues parables can be used to minister to those at the NI or SI stage without causing offense. Jesus used many parables in this way. The crowds that followed him were made up of many types of people. Through his use of parables and proverbs, everyone heard him and thought about what he said, but Jesus knew that the true seekers would return and ask him personally about the parable's meaning.

What do parables do for us?

Why would we want to use a parable anyway? Why not just speak the truth? In watching my evangelist friends at work, I've come to realize that parables are very useful for illustrating a point, bringing things into contrast, sifting and drawing people out, giving people something to ponder, appealing to reason, and particularly ambushing listeners. Ambushing includes setting up a story, developing a thought that people identify with and then hitting them with an unexpected truth. We can see this, for example, in Nathan's parable to David (2 Samuel 12:1-7) and in the story of the Good Samaritan (Luke 10:25-37).

Parables are especially useful when dealing with people raised in an oral tradition. In Yemen, I tried using a nutshell presentation of the Gospel. It never worked. No sooner would I say something, then people would start with their objections. So I, with some of my colleagues, thought and prayed about it and searched the Scriptures to see what Jesus would have done. We discovered that he told parables. We knew this all along, but somehow it never occurred to us to use parables ourselves.

The amazing thing was that when Jesus told a parable he didn't bother to explain it! He allowed those who were thinking and seeking to ponder over the parable, and then approach him later. Some, like Nicodemus came at night to ask what Jesus' teaching meant. The hostile and not interested people never came and asked, but the somewhat interested and the seekers returned! Once we realized the importance of this we decided to begin using parables.

When two of my colleagues visited a village, they introduced some basic Christian concept in their conversation and illustrated it with a parable. They gave no further explanation. At first they felt this was the wrong way to communicate. They had been trained in Bible college to give three-point talks, bring people to a conclusion, and then ask for a decision. When these villages were visited some months later, they discovered that the people had thought about what had been said, discussed it together and now they wanted to know more. So another teaching was added, a parable given and the team left again. In this way Christian thought and teaching were slowly introduced and taught in a number of villages.

Sources of Parables

From the parables of Jesus, which are forms of extended proverbs, four sources can be discerned:

First, there are observations from the world of nature: for example, the parable of the sower (Mark 4:1-9) and the parable of the seed growing secretly (Mark 4:26-29).

Second there is knowledge drawn from the familiar customs of everyday life and events; such as the parable of the yeast (Matthew. 13:33) and the parable of the ten virgins (Matthew. 25:1-13).

A third source comes from well-known events in contemporary history: for example, the parable of the high-ranking man who was about to be made king although he was hated by the citizens, and upon his departure gave gold coins to his servants to trade with (Luke 19:12-27). (Historians have identified the activities of this person with those of Archelaus, son of Herod the Great.) Imagine doing this today, starting your parable with: "There once was a president of a great nation, who decided to invade a smaller nation that offended him." You would immediately have the attention of your Muslim listeners, and maybe many others as well.

A fourth source is from normal, probable events, as in the parables of the laborers in the vineyard (Matthew 20:1-16), the prodigal son (Luke 15:11-32); and the unjust judge (Luke 18:2-8).

Another feature of parables is that behind what seems to be a general truth can lay another deeper hidden truth. Jesus used this kind of story. He said that the kingdom of heaven was as valuable as a piece of land with hidden treasure. This parable really described the need to sacrifice everything else in order to possess the kingdom of heaven (Matthew 13:44). In the parable of the wedding feast (Matthew 22:1-4) Jesus clearly explains that if you want to enter the kingdom of God, you must not defer the decision to accept the invitation.

Today many evangelists use parables as stories that illustrate redemption. These are called "redemptive analogies."

Problems with Parables

There are a number of difficulties that a would-be storyteller will encounter. One must understand the language well in order to be a good storyteller. One must understand the local culture well in order to insure that the story has punch. One should have some experience or gifting in storytelling. Half of a story is in the telling. Comedians make their living by being able to tell stories and jokes better than the average person. Everyone, especially in an Islamic setting, appreciates a good parable teller.

Second, parables don't work well outside of their intended setting. Many Biblical parables lose their punch, or even their meaning because we or our intended audiences don't understand the context or the cultural setting. If you have never seen a vine, how is it helpful to have to explain what one is, before saying what you want to say? Because the Bible is holy scripture, many missionaries expect Biblical parables to always communicate in every setting. Believing the Bible, sometimes means following its example by making up new parables, rather than quoting archaic parables. Perhaps it means changing the parable to suit the culture.

Every good evangelist should have a collection of proverbs and parables, and an understanding of situations where they can be applied. As these can vary from culture to culture and language to language, we have only given a few examples in the church planting handbook.

Prayer

When dealing with not interested people, or even hostile people God sometimes provides opportunities for us to pray with them. As we interact with people around us, we may learn of some difficulty in their lives. Most of the successful evangelists I know seek out these kinds of opportunities to ask people if they can pray for them. Then if it is at all appropriate, they bow their heads and pray aloud. This often takes the host by surprise, but once a sincere prayer is offered, the host is almost always appreciative. In some cases I have known Muslims to invite Christians back into their homes again and again so that they will pray for their homes. One family told me that when Christians prayed, their homes were filled with peace and tranquility. Along with this, our prayers of faith give God opportunities to demonstrate his power and ability to transform situations for his honor and glory. Prayer is a powerful way to minister to not interested or somewhat interested people.

Questions for Reflection or Discussion

1. Is your community aware that Christians are living among them?

2. What are some salt-type ministries that your team is involved in to affect your community?

3. Would mass media tools such as newspaper adverts, literature and video distribution, radio, and TV work in your community? Why or why not?

4. How can you compliment or replace mass media? How can your team go about impacting the community at large?

5. What are some key methods of communication in your community? How important is mass media? Do people visit or do they gather in certain places to communicate?

6. Is your language ability strong enough to be able to hear and understand proverbs when they are used?

7. Is there a key person you or your team members know who uses proverbs a lot when they speak? Could you approach this person to start recording and learning proverbs? This is often an excellent way to build bridges with older people. Remember to ask them what kind of situation the proverb applies to. Try and collect proverbs that deal with every area of life: wealth and poverty, health and sickness, joy and sorrow, marriage and childbearing, occupations, all kinds of activities and all manner of people: kings and citizens, nobles and slaves, men and women, adults and children, craftsmen and apprentices. Some proverbial sayings are statements of historical facts while others contain information about culture. A great number of them express philosophical thoughts, religious beliefs, and values.

9. How might you use the following Biblical proverbs? Proverbs 25:14, Ezekiel 18:2, Proverbs 17:13, 2 Peter 2:22?

10. Why do you think Nathan used a parable when speaking to David in 2 Samuel 12:1-7? Did this approach work?

11. Read Luke 10:25-37. What aspects of the parable of the Good Samaritan are only apparent to those who knew Jewish history and culture?

12. If you wanted to illustrate the fact that a little sin is as bad as a big sin, what sort of parable could you tell? Can you make up a parable that might speak to your target people?

Chapter Seven
Contextualization & Community

On occasion I have heard some expatriate workers comment that they fully understood the culture they were working in. Having lived in North American culture as a youth, I have often wondered if I understood my own culture. As I thought through this I realized that there are different levels of how we can understand culture.

On a superficial level, there are the dos and don'ts of the culture. In the Arab culture I'm working in, women don't look men in the eye, you need to drink three cups of coffee at a formal visit; and you never point the bottom of your feet at anyone.

Beyond this you may want to know why they do one thing and why they don't do other things. For instance, why don't women look men in the eyes? Why are there are three cups of coffee? Why does each cup have its own name? Why don't you point the bottom of your feet at someone?

On a deeper level, we must ask ourselves, what these things tell us about worldview. I believe that each evangelist should work towards understanding the worldview of the culture he is ministering in. The evangelist needs to understand the basic philosophies from which principles of life have been developed. While we will examine worldview in more detail in the second section of this book, at this point I would like to look at two important issues: values and convictions. These have helped me understand cultural differences.

Values

What do we value most? What does the target culture value most? Think about your own culture. What are the most important values in your culture? In what order of priority would you place the following? What values would you add to them?

Honesty, Sanctity of life Freedom of movement, Freedom of speech, Rights for education, Equality of sexes, the right to work, the right for quality of life?

As you can see, it is hard to order these. Some of these values are important to some people while different ones are important to others. Only after living and working in a community for a long period of time can one really begin to understand the values of that community.

Convictions

Convictions are different from values. Because society has certain values, it develops certain convictions. It may not formulate them but they are the underlying convictions of the majority. For instance, in some Western countries "More is better" is a general conviction held by many people.

Many North Americans like to shop. So, when in America, the cultural thing to do is to visit malls and spend time shopping. There are two principles that drive this habit: the obsession with owning material goods, and the obsession for options. Once one understands these two convictions, the obsession with shopping becomes clearer, and so do other North American cultural actions. Shopping is driven by materialism, which is simply an expression of "More is better."

We can also begin to understand why North Americans build huge malls because they give more shopping options, thus they are better places to shop. In following the same thought pattern we can begin to understand the high divorce rate: there is a desire for more options in marriage. People switch churches regularly reflecting their desire for more options in church. It may help us understand why students switch university majors two or three times during their studies, and why North Americans switch their careers several times during their lifetime.

But understanding materialism and the desire for options is only a first step. We need to relate these principles to North American worldview where materialism and obsession with options are the natural outcome of the conviction that "More is better."

In the Muslim world, women usually cover their hair. For many years I accepted this, but then I started to ask "Why?" I discovered that in Yemen women were afraid that an infidel might see their hair and as a result they would hang from their hair in hell. I searched the Qur'an and Hadith for references to women hanging by their hair in hell but never found them. Although people in this community do not have a written basis for this belief, it is still a strong tradition in their culture.

The first step towards contextualizing our message is to understand the worldview (as best we can) of the people we are trying to reach. We must also remember that not everyone in a country or even in a given city will have the same worldview. We must be sensitive to ethnic and tribal differences, family preferences, and individual understanding.

When we arrive in a country with the message of the Gospel, we endeavor to make it understandable in that culture. The Gospel is like a beautiful pearl. If it is thrown into the mud, people won't recognize it for what it is, and will trample it underfoot. However, if it is clean, sparkling, and placed on velvet in a beautiful, polished box, they will all stop and admire it. Contextualization is the act of building the box and providing the velvet background.

Removing Cultural Offense

The most important part of contextualization is to present ourselves in such a way that our lifestyles demonstrate and even enhance the message we want to communicate.

If a single woman claims she has been set free from sin but dresses and acts as would a prostitute in the target culture, no one will believe her message. Likewise, if a man says he is a teacher but dresses in shorts, T-shirt, and sandals as if he were a useless young man on the streets, no one will believe he holds such an honored position. Then when he speaks about knowing God as his Savior everyone will assume he is telling lies.

The Offense of the Cross

The danger in contextualizing is that in trying to remove cultural offense, we can take a step too far, and remove the offense of the Cross. We must remember that there is something offensive about salvation. Salvation is not fair. It is a gift to us, but it is not fair to God. Many people struggle with this as they conclude that God did something out of His natural character, in that it damages himself. This is particularly a stumbling block to Muslims. We as Christians need to demonstrate this side of salvation as "the love of God expressed for us."

Our Identity

As we mentioned in the first chapter, we must ask ourselves who we appear to be in the target culture. Often we move around in our own little world unaware of the impact that we are having on others. They watch us and evaluate us according to our dress, our actions, and our words. Experts in communication tell us that as little as 7% of our communication comes from our words; the rest comes from our actions.

So after you enter your target community, people will immediately try to identify what sort of person you are. Below is a simple illustration of what I call the Muslim identity line. This evaluation is quite different from what you would find in a non-Muslim setting.

Fundamentalism <------------>Westernism

In my community, there are two opposite types of Muslims: either Muslim fundamentalists, or Westernized nominal Muslims. Everyone is somewhere between these two. What you wear, how you act, where you live, and even your vocabulary all identify you as being closer to one end of the scale or the other. Most Muslims are moving, either quickly or gradually, towards one side or the other. It's hard for them to stay stagnant in the middle. Since this is what Muslims universally experience, the members of my community judge me by the same standards.

Missiologists often talk about contextualization, or the effort to display and teach the Gospel message within the context of the local people. The object of contextualization is to make our message understandable to people in the culture in which we are working, by stripping off unnecessary cultural baggage from the messenger's culture. In doing so we face a struggle. If we identify too closely with one extreme (the fundamentalists in the illustration above), our Christian message becomes confused: legalism and grace mixed together. Likewise, if we identify with the opposite extreme our message also becomes confused. Permissiveness and grace get mixed together.

Our goal must always be clear communication of the Gospel to the target culture. In order to present clear messages we must be clear ourselves about two issues: our identity in Christ and our identity in the community.

The Goal of Contextualization

There are lots of books written on contextualization. The new evangelist to a foreign culture should read a broad spectrum of such books so that he is aware of the ideas and concepts that different camps are promoting. In working this through in my own life, I have come to categorize various schools of thought, as outlined below.

There are those who try to live a totally integrated lifestyle in order to reach people within their target culture. Years ago I heard of a Western missionary who tried this in India. He dressed as an Indian, ate Indian food, and lived in an Indian house. However, he was disappointed when people called him *sahib* (teacher). So he moved to a very poor part of town, and attempted to identify with the poor. He got a job on a road construction crew, and people still called him *sahib*. He asked the men around him why they called him *sahib*. They thought for a minute and then told him that it was because he used a toothbrush. He got rid of the toothbrush and used a stick to clean his teeth as the other workmen did. And people still called him *sahib*. One day in desperation he asked a wise man why he was not considered an Indian. The man replied, "It is because your mother was white." No matter how hard we try we can never completely identify with those from other cultures; not because of outward cultural issues, but because of unchangeable biological and sociological issues. (This theme is explored in the next section, *The Message*)

There are others who try to enter into their target culture in such a way so that converts will have an example of how they should act. This is highly commendable and thoughtful. However, I have seldom seen it work in a Muslim setting. An outsider simply doesn't have the same responsibilities as the local person. The latter has to relate to his family and community in a totally different way from a socially independent outsider. None of the successful evangelists I met supported this approach, or promoted it among new workers. Instead they encouraged the workers to use their positions as *sahib* or teacher to its best advantage.

A third group seeks to work within a cross-cultural setting, trying to bring the Gospel from one culture to another. They realize that they must remove from their message those things that are culturally offensive to the target culture. They must be very careful not to insist, or even suggest, that something from their culture is more acceptable or preferable. They enter into the target culture as much as they possibly can so as to be able to present the Gospel clearly. They then seek to help the converts discover how they can live a Christian life within their culture, while explaining that they themselves do certain things because this is what their own home culture demands. New converts should be free to work out the Gospel in their own culture while being led by the Holy Spirit.

Despite all our efforts at contextualization, we must realize that we will never ever be able to enter completely into another culture, language group, or religious community. I simply cannot find any biblical justification that this is what we are called to do.

There are two important examples of contextualization in the Scriptures. While there are also others we could look at, we will concentrate on these two: Jesus and the Apostle Paul.

The Lord Jesus

Missiologists sometimes use the term "incarnational ministry" to describe Jesus' identification with mankind. Jesus experienced everything that we experience in life. However, he did not enter into our sin; he lived as a religious Jew and as a religious teacher, under the law. While he demonstrated the inability of the law to deal with sin in the inner life, Jesus did not sin. He did not need to enter into the bondage of sin in order to lead us free from that bondage.

I believe that all contextualized ministries must carefully limit the extent of their contextualization. The line is sin, or the appearance of sin. Islam, Buddhism, and Hinduism are nothing short of religious systems of works bound together by tight codes of conduct. We may try to live and conduct ourselves in ways that are not offensive (practicing contextualization), but we must also be careful not to enter into the system of works, or appear to be in bondage to the system of works. While it is true that Jesus was under the law, He did not abandon the law but demonstrated that inner change was what was needed.

While Jesus does illustrate incarnational ministry to some extent, (he left heaven and adapted to human life), he only ministered within the culture he had been raised in. He learned no languages for ministry purpose and he dropped out of normal life and became itinerant. There was a place of itinerant teachers in his culture, but most teachers were not itinerant. He required his closest followers to abandon their jobs. He operated within the culture in as much as he was raised in it, but he selectively scandalized the culture at many key points. He was not for or against the culture – it was not about culture. He was not doing missiology, and so he is not really a model for contextualization, for he did not ever attempt to move into a foreign culture, nor did he aim to fit into his own. In much the same way, missionaries must not become so enamored with the target culture that they forget to challenge people with the claims of the Gospel.

The Apostle Paul

The Apostle Paul was born of Israelite descent, but grew up in a Gentile city. He studied under Jewish teachers, but was also a student of Greek philosophy and thought. In Acts 23:3 Paul makes his defense in Jerusalem and tells the Jews that he was trained in Jewish law under Gamaliel. This is significant, since Gamaliel trained Jewish men for the Sanhedrin court. Both Gamaliel and Joseph of Aramathia were members of the Sanhedrin. The Bible specifically points out that Gamaliel was known as a :teacher of the law." Paul was a "Pharisee, the son of a Pharisees", who studied under Gamaliel, and thus was preparing to perhaps someday sit on the Sanhedrin. Besides studying the Jewish law, teaching languages would have been one of Gamaliel's other main tasks in preparing Paul for this possible appointment.

The Sanhedrin believed that during a trial everyone should be able to give their defense in their own language. So those training for the Sanhedrin studied seventy languages based on the seventy original languages mentioned in Genesis 10. (Mordechai: The Key to Locked Hearts, Rabbi Avrohom Feuer) If this was the case, then Paul was being prepared by God to take the gospel to the Gentiles even before his conversion on the road to Damascus.

Even with all of this training, Paul still struggled to integrate the Gentile converts with the Christians from a Jewish background. Paul tried to teach and witness in such a way that, whatever the audience, they would accept him and his message. To the Jew he preached as a Jew; to the Gentiles, he preached as a Gentile.

The book of Romans is an excellent example of the kind of teaching that Paul would give to a Jewish audience living under Roman Law. Paul had long wanted to visit the Jews in Rome, but since it was impossible at that time (Romans 1:13-15), he decided to write to them instead. In the book of Romans, Paul quotes the Old Testament and appeals to the Scriptures as his basis for argument. In contrast, we have the sermon on Mars Hill (Acts 17:16-34) where Paul speaks to a purely Gentile audience. The discourses are very different. On Mars Hill, Paul appeals to the Athenians understanding that there was a god they did not know. He then quotes (17:28) from their own secular philosophers to illustrate some of his teachings. His use of Scripture is limited, but he still boldly proclaims creation, salvation, and the resurrection. Paul demonstrates to us that even though he is a Jew, he can bridge the gap between the Jew and Gentile by teaching in a way that is understandable to the Gentile.

Paul could do this because his early childhood in a Gentile city gave him the necessary background, plus his education under Gamaliel prepared him to be a cross-cultural communicator. He understood and likely appreciated many of the values and convictions held by the Gentiles in Greece and Rome as well as those held by the Jewish community and probably spoke many of the leading languages of his day.

As we can see in these two Biblical illustrations, neither Jesus nor Paul aimed to adopt or blend into their target cultures. Paul used itinerant ministry and his refused to restrict himself to either just a Gentile or just a Jewish audience. Jesus and later Paul operated within recognizable roles, but neither was ruled by culture. They were both master communicators, effectively bridging gaps between cultures with a clear communication of the Gospel. Neither, however, tried to totally integrate within their target cultures.

Relationships

Fundamental to functioning in any culture is managing relationships - knowing what is expected and how they work. Most Eastern cultures place high value on relationships. In the Middle East, for instance, holidays are an opportunity to restore broken relationships. During holiday times, families visit every family member that they are well acquainted with, as well as those outside of their immediate group such as friends and work colleagues. The reason for these visits is simply to insure good relationships with all their friends and acquaintances. If someone fails to visit a friend or acquaintance during the holiday season, then the relationship is strained, and the offended party might visit the offender to find out just what has come between them.

Building Relationships

The high value placed on relationships can also be beneficial for the teacher of the Gospel. The whole crux of the Gospel is the good news that Jesus has restored our relationship with God. Through this restoration our relationships with each other can be improved.

The Bible clearly teaches that the world will know we are Christians by our love for each other. However, when one examines the lifestyle of a typical Western Christian, it becomes obvious that Westerners struggle with relationships. They may get so involved in programs, technical projects, and social ministries that they have little time for friends and neighbors. Western culture is ordinarily relationship-deficient and the Western Christian naturally takes this deficiency with him to the field.

Once the Christian worker begins his ministry, he often thinks in terms of weekly Bible-studies, weekly discipleship meetings, and weekly teaching sessions.

The thought of meeting daily or twice daily with a new contact or convert doesn't usually enter his mind. If he is to take on the role of a religious teacher, he must remember that his students may want to develop a relationship with him and not merely sit in on a series of lectures. Students may sit quietly for a couple of lessons, but if no relationship is forthcoming they seldom want to continue. In the Bible, Jesus spent many hours with his disciples as he taught them.

The Muslim Community

Muslim religious scholars often talk about something called the *umma*. The best English equivalent I can find is 'community.' In many cases I have seen the convert from Islam struggling to leave the close support of the Muslim community for the isolationist, individualistic lifestyle of many Christians.

Christian workers frequently want to make the transition to Christianity easier for converts from a Muslim background. They try to strip all the external, non-necessary trappings from Christianity and fit it into the Muslim setting. They dress as Muslims, develop Jesus mosques, and place an Islamic facade on Christianity in an attempt to make it less offensive. But they seldom develop the kind of close community that Muslims experience. Theologically, the new convert is able to see and understand the Gospel; he can exercise faith experience gifts and enter into ministry. What he struggles with most is the idea of leaving community. This topic will be explored in detail in the last section of this book, but needless to say, the key thing here is "belonging." Community is not based on likes, dislikes or what is fun; it is about belonging and security. Those coming out of community feel exposed and vulnerable.

I've discovered that in most settings where large numbers of Muslims have turned to Christ, the common attraction isn't contextualization but rather the existence of a viable alternative community.

Do expatriate workers develop community among themselves? The answer is "Yes." They often meet together. They talk about where they bought things, how much furniture costs and how much they pay for house help. They discuss their jobs, help one another to find jobs, and share corporate and individual wisdom. They meet together for Bible studies, prayer and worship times. They vacation together, visit tourist spots, play, and relax together. They enjoy meeting other expatriate family members and of course their children often go to school and play together. Sometimes missionaries struggle with these kind of gatherings. They want to spend more time with local people. They realize that they have been sent to this foreign country so that they can witness and share the Gospel, but the attraction of the expatriate community pulls them towards other expatriates. It's strong, it's enjoyable, and moreover it is natural.

It has sometimes struck me as both strange and tragic that while so many missionaries struggle with Christian community and want to get rid of it, many converts from Islam struggle with the lack of Christian community and crave it so desperately.

Some years ago I heard a missionary who worked in Bangladesh tell his story. He desperately wanted to reach people for Christ, so he started to dress as a religious teacher. He eventually rented a small shop where he placed rugs on the floor. He sat there and prayed for several hours each day. For two years he sat praying and meditating. People went by the shop and some looked in but at first few came in to him through the open door.

Every day this teacher visited in the community, then returned to his little shop, praying and waiting, ready to meet people. After two years, people started to drop in. Some came for just a short visit, but others came for help with their problems, usually concerning marriage or relationships. The teacher pointed them to Christ. Over time, more and more visitors came to sit and hear his wisdom. Eventually a core group of believers was gathered, a community was formed, and in time, several thousand came to Christ.

I found his story fascinating, because it clearly illustrated both the teaching approach to evangelism, and the importance of community. These people had found each other, and in doing so had formed an identity all of their own.

A Muslim coming to Christ needs to be given a greater sense of joining than of leaving. If a person is always identified with what he has left, he will always feel he has lost something. If he is identified with something he has joined, he will feel part of the group he has joined. Many converts return to Islam simply because they can't shake off the feeling of lost community.

As Christian workers we must be very careful not to refer continually to new believers as converts from Islam, but preferably as new believers or as something with a more generic name. Personally, I would like to see the new movements that have sprung up across the Muslim world develop some form of generic identity with which new believers could identify, wherever they are located. Many years ago I put this challenge to a group of Muslim-background believers. After some thinking they decided to adopt the term in Arabic *mujedadiin*, or "the regenerated ones." More recently others have suggested coining a term from Hebrews 12:23 based on "the firstborn." Others have used the term "disciples." The idea is not to name a certain group of believers, but to simply create an identity that believers from a Muslim background could claim. Christianity, wherever it is, includes new believers from every faith in this world. Our identity is that we are now all one in Christ, not in what we have left.

Questions for Reflection or Discussion

1. How would you rate your understanding of your target culture? (Much is strange, some situations are still puzzling, can function comfortably in most situations, feel totally at home)

2. When thinking of your target culture, number the following values in importance from 1-9 (Honesty, Sanctity of life, Freedom of movement, Freedom of speech, Rights for education, Equality of sexes, The right to work, The right for quality of life, Honor)

3. Western society has some basic convictions that influence how people live and act. For instance, "More is better" or "do it as long as you don't hurt someone else." What are some convictions you feel your target culture possesses? Discuss these with your team members and see if they have the same perception. Why or why not?

4. What are some of the ways that your target culture classifies people? (Success, Religion, Culture, Good Person, Class, Education, Family background)

5. What type of contextualization are you working towards? Are you trying to live a totally integrated lifestyle, or trying to enter into their target culture in such a way that you are understandable, or just trying to bring the gospel from one culture to another?

6. How did Jesus and Paul use or demonstrate contextualization?

7. Which is most important in your target culture? Accomplishment or Relationship?

8. How are you demonstrating that relationships are important to you?

9. Please evaluate your time. Do you spend more time with the people of your target group than you do with others? Who are the others, and why do you spend time with them? Do you feel you have a good balance or would you like to increase your time with your target people?

10. Do new believers in your target group have a greater sense of joining or leaving their old community? Why is this?

11. When people come to Christ do they have a new strong new identity? What sort of identity do they have? Is this a good situation, or should it change?

12. Read Acts 19:20-26. Did the new believers have a new identity or was their identity still tied to their former religion? Read Acts 11:25. What was their new identity here?

Chapter Eight
Honor and Trust

Much of the material in this chapter relates to the situation I faced in the Levant. Yet, a great deal of it is relevant to other areas of the world which have been influenced by Islam or shame-based worldviews (as explained in the next section of this book). As you read through this chapter, it is important for you to consider ways in which this material may apply to your particular situation. It also provides essential background material for the next chapter, and is introductory to the next section of the book: *the Message.*

Nearness

In many cultures, people think of themselves collectively rather than individually. There is an old Arab proverb that states, "I against my cousin, my cousin and I against the world." To one looking in from the outside, these people may appear to be set against each other, but in reality there is a lot of bonding and brotherhood among them.

In the areas where I have ministered, I've come to recognize that "nearness" is an important part of their culture. One day, when I arrived at the small garage I used regularly, I discovered that there was a new employee. This employee quickly discerned that I was a foreigner, and therefore decided to charge me appropriately high prices. However, his boss soon recognized the blunder and explained to him that I was near to them. The meaning was clear, and after that I got fair prices with excellent service. Nearness or belonging is at the core of most Arab relationships.

There are a number of ways that nearness is evaluated and considered, the most important being blood relations, then married relations, adopted relations (those they choose to include), and finally hospitality requirements (neighbors, business).

73

There are a number of other factors that can influence nearness. Religion marks you as near or far. Language can mark you as near or far as well. Arabs make good use of the different dialects of Arabic to differentiate between who is near or far to them. A tutor may be reluctant to teach his own dialect to a foreigner without permission from the family elders and will make many excuses to his student as to why he cannot do so. As a result, foreigners are normally taught classical Arabic. Yet, learning a tribal dialect and being adopted into a tribe can be very powerful in building relationships.

Nearness is also accompanied by an expectation of conformity to the code of ethics and honor commonly practiced by the group. By adopting the dialect or accent of a group or in some other way becoming "near," it may be assumed by the community that you are making a commitment to live in submission to that group.

Honor

Imagine growing up in a system where you are constantly focused on the group or tribe. All your life, the concept of "we" is very important. You interact on a weekly or daily basis with your aunts, uncles, and cousins who often live nearby. You discuss everything as a group - the price of food, appliances, land, job prospects, local and international news. Group knowledge is important and often takes preference over individual knowledge. Everyone knows everyone else's business, and you share what you learn, know, and experience with the group.

In theory, at least, each person in the group helps everyone else and shares in everyone's joys, excitement, sadness, and grief. You wouldn't dream of missing a wedding or even a birthday if at all possible. When a member of the group dies, you sit with his family for several days. You don't need to speak; you just sit near them, sharing their grief.

Weddings are important events. If the couple is from within the group, a great celebration commences. If the wedding unites two different groups, then a great deal has to take place to bring the two groups together, to establish the growing nearness of the two groups. When a young man wants to ask for a girl's hand in marriage, he takes with him those of authority within his group. The family on the bride's side must seriously consider the joining of the two groups together in this way. Then, when the wedding takes place, a number of events occur that illustrate the coming together, not just of two individuals but of two groups. Similarly, when a student is considering which occupation to pursue, he consults the group. His personal preference is weighed in the context of the needs and wants of the group.

Every group seeks to have one of its members in various positions in the wider community, store owners, gas station owners, mechanics, electricians, engineers, lawyers, doctors, dentists, pharmacists, and, of course, members in the police, army and civil service. These people not only serve themselves, or their country, but they are also expected to serve their group. In essence, they act as mediators for their group. For example, before someone gets his car registered or applies for a telephone, he checks to see if he has a mediator in that part of the government to help him.

I once overheard a conversation in which the owner of a new electrical shop expressed amazement that he was getting customers that he didn't know! When he opened his shop, his vision had simply been that of serving his own group.

Sometimes I have puzzled over the presence of two or three hardware stores or pharmacies located side by side. It seemed strange to me to have groups of identical stores bunched together like this. In the local setting however, it made a lot of sense. First of all, you support your own group and go to the store of the one who is "nearest" you. If that store doesn't have what you want, the shop keeper will check with another store only one or two doors away and try and get you what you need.

Value Systems

Against this background, let's look at common value systems. Each of us values rights and privileges in our lives. Most Westerners highly value human life and are shocked when someone is willing to give his life as a martyr. We also value honesty, the right to education, the right to choose for ourselves, the right to move freely, the right to... and so on. In many Eastern cultures, personal honor and the honor of the group are more highly valued than rights.

Arabs strive for honor. They look for honorable jobs, honorable houses, honorable cars, and honorable clothes. The sheer number of Mercedes cars on the streets in many Middle Eastern countries often strikes newly-arrived foreigners. They also notice that many men dress in suit jackets or smart national dress. Everyone needs to appear honorable in order to raise the common honor of their group.

My neighbors liked to consider themselves honored by having foreigners living among them. However, when I put on my old overalls and worked on my car, or when I went out and washed my car in front of everyone, they became embarrassed. They preferred to hire someone to fix and wash their cars, even if they could do it themselves. They didn't really understand my demonstration of independence and ability compounded with meekness, humbleness and a simple lifestyle. Likewise, I didn't understand and appreciate their demonstration of wealth, honor and prestige.

Now while this may be interesting, and may be more or less common in other countries, these observations bring to the forefront two major spiritual issues: trust and honor.

Trust

One of the by-products of this honor-based lifestyle may be the inability to trust outside the group. I've seen people become very afraid when they realized that they had to do something without a mediator. Even trusting someone within the group can be difficult. In many situations I have discussed trust with my friends and they readily admitted that they wouldn't trust a doctor or politician or lawyer or even an employer who wasn't near to them. Even with someone who is near, they might still be wary.

Thus, trust can be a major hurdle for them to cross. If you can't trust people who are near, how can you trust God, who is far away? As Christians we are taught about the love of God and the promises of God. Within Islam, God is far away. He does not act out of love. God is almighty and can do anything He wants, either good or evil. He created both of them.

Hope, in Islam, is placed, not in God or in someone else's actions for you, but on your own actions. You submit and obey and trust that your mediator (the prophet Muhammad) can do the rest for you.

The great struggle that so many seekers face is learning to love and trust God; to take His Word as true promises and to rest in God's work for us. In other words, they have to learn to trust God by faith rather than through nearness.

Group Honor and Dishonor

In Middle Eastern tradition, barbers perform many functions. Not only do they cut hair and give shaves and have the honor of performing circumcisions, but the barbershop is often the center of community and the hub of group information and communication. Looking for a house to rent can be a challenging job. Many landlords only want to rent to those who are somewhat close to them, so few landlords advertise. If you are searching for a house to rent, you not only ask those you know, but you always check with the local barber or corner grocer.

In our neighborhood, the barber also had another responsibility. In a drawer in his shop he kept a pistol and some ammunition. When a gun was needed, he rented it out. Hopefully it was never needed, but if someone seriously dishonored the group, then it was the responsibility of the oldest brother or uncle to become the executioner. For instance, if a girl becomes pregnant out of wedlock, it is the duty of her eldest brother, or eldest uncle, to preserve the honor of the family. This person will secure the gun, and then wait for the right opportunity. He may stand in the middle of the street, waiting until the girl emerges from a store and then announce to all on the street that he is preserving the honor of the group. After shooting the girl he would return the gun to the barbershop and turn himself in to the police. He will probably stay in jail for several weeks or months until the police are sure that there will be no reprisals and that no other tribes or groups are affected.

In the small country of Jordan, during the first six months of 1995, an Arab newspaper reported that there had been over one hundred such honor killings. Each year there are hundreds of honor killings in Iran.

One close friend of mine found himself in an awful position. His sister ran away from home and married a man from outside her group's religion. As my friend was the eldest brother, it fell on his head to kill her. Since he had become a follower of Jesus, he refused. As a result, he became an outcast from his group. His uncles were very upset by his refusal, and offered one of their sons to carry out the killing if my friend's family would pay. Eventually his father stood by his son and his whole immediate family became outsiders. He could no longer visit us in our home since we lived in a house owned by one of his uncles and he was no longer welcome in any of their buildings.

Another family we know well had a brother who was operating a pharmacy. One day a group of men arrived at the pharmacy, angry and bitter. They claimed that the pharmacist had given the wrong medicine to a man from their family group, and the man had died. They wanted to kill the pharmacist in revenge. The whole thing was handled at the group level, not at an individual level, and in the end the pharmacist's family group agreed to pay blood money so that the pharmacist could live.

Obviously a person's group is more than just a support group to get him work, a wife, a house, and a car: it is also his insurance.

Impact on a new convert's life

It can be devastating for a new convert to lose his group! Not only does he lose his whole social support but he also loses his identity. Once someone comes to

Christ, the evangelist needs to help the new convert openly profess faith in Christ without being killed, punished, or banned from his group.

In my research I discovered that each successful evangelist had faced this challenge, and each one had worked out his own answers to the problem. Their general conclusion was that our vision should not be to reach individuals in isolation, but through these individual converts find ways of reaching out to the whole group.

Persecution

Persecution arises when communities conclude that a new convert has dishonored them. For example, in most cultures a son must honor his family; if he does not, both the father and the group may be dishonored in the eyes of outsiders. No matter how nice the young man may be, taking a different and unsanctioned direction is a rejection of paternal authority, and implies rejection of his forbearers. If the group has a strong religious identity such as Islam, then someone leaving the religion of the group is paramount to leaving and renouncing (in their eyes) the entire community. Since they see Islam as superior to all other religions and against all other religions, the act of leaving Islam is a greater outrage than merely being a badly behaved son.

Persecution could come from many corners. First of all, family members would feel dishonored and ashamed in front of others. In the town I lived in Muslims and Christians would taunt each other on the street. "We got one of yours last night" they would jeer, whenever a Christian would abandon his faith and become a Muslim. Along with family, there would also be those who feel that the honor of the religion needs protecting. Vigilantes might rise and take action if the family refuses or is unable to. Some countries consider their nation to be Muslim, Christian or Hindu. In these places government officials may feel compelled to protect the honor of their national religion and the honor of their country.

A major goal of the worker doing discipleship is knowing how to train the new convert to portray his change of heart in an honorable, rather than offensive manner. This will be discussed in the next chapter.

Questions for Reflection or Discussion

1. What are the important groupings of people in your target culture? How important are cities, towns, families, tribes, etc?

2. What are some of the ways people evaluate "nearness" in your target culture?

3. How might your target culture view these Bible verses: (Mark 1:15, Ephesians 2:13, Hebrews 10:22)?

4. Does family honor play an important role in the lives of the people you are working with? How do you know this?

5. How important is trust in your target culture? Do people trust doctors, professionals, or politicians? Do they trust you?

6. What happens to people when they lose the support of their tribal or family group?

7. Is there some way that people can become followers of Jesus, and yet remain in their family and tribe? Have you heard of this being done?

8. Is persecution an issue where you live? Are people persecuted because they follow Christian principles or because they have left the group? Will leaving the dominant religion bring shame upon the individual or the group?

Chapter Nine
Friendship Discipling

When a person accepts the Lord, he is immediately put into a place of tension. On one side is his new Christian faith, and on the other side are his old religion, family, and community. Usually the convert comes to Christ through the witness and teaching of another believer, and as he grows in the Lord, the tension begins to build. Who should the convert relate to? How can a convert from a religion such as Islam or Buddhism relate his new faith to the family and community in which he lives?

Tragically many converts decide that they cannot reconcile the two. The obvious quick solution to the issue is to develop two faces. With one face they welcome Christianity, meeting with other Christians, praying, reading the Bible, and studying together. This is where their heart is. With the other face, they live and relate to their family and community. They have mothers, brothers, sisters and perhaps spouses and children. This is also where their heart is, and so the tension builds. Soon one of five things will happen.

First, the convert may abandon his new faith and go back to what is familiar to him. This may be because of persecution or pressure, but often it is because he feels he cannot exist in a two-faced situation. As long as he has two faces there is always the strong temptation to abandon the Christian face and assume the old one.

A second option is that the convert may choose to completely identify with the Christian face and reject his old one. This was often encouraged by missionaries in the past so converts took on new names, and identified completely with the Christian community. In the most extreme cases these converts emigrated to the West, or to another country, where they could abandon their old face, and live solely with their Christian face. By doing this, they sacrificed their family and community and their ability to witness to them. In recent years, some of these converts have started to rebuild contact with their family and community, but in most cases this is a very difficult road to take and it is a long time before they are accepted again.

A third possibility is that the new convert becomes a secret believer while outwardly maintaining his former life style. Secret believers are often filled with fear that they will be discovered. One man I knew lived in constant fear of his teenage son who would come home from school full of anger and bitterness at the Christians and Jews who, he considered were the source of the world's problems.

A fourth possibility is seen in other converts who are so distraught with the two faces that they eventually become mentally unstable. I know of one such man living in my city. He wanders the streets in ridiculous clothing, perceived by all as crazy. In another case, I know of an Arab convert who claims he is not an Arab but actually a Westerner. He calls himself by a different name, refuses to recognize his family, and claims he is a citizen of a Western country. His mental condition has slowly deteriorated over the years.

The fifth possibility is that through the work of the Holy Spirit, and often with the help of a wise discipler, the convert can learn to unite the two faces, discovering freedom in Christ. He no longer hides behind two faces, but now lives with one face, living freely as a follower of Jesus in his family setting. Enabling this fifth option, I believe, should be the chief and primary aim of a discipler.

The following are what I feel to be the five major concerns of a person who is attempting to disciple a new convert from a major religion such as Islam, Hinduism, or Buddhism: (1) Keeping the convert physically alive, (2)·Uniting the two faces, (3)·Encouraging spiritual growth, (4)·"Coming out" as a follower of Jesus, (5)·Integration into a fellowship.

I have gathered recommendations from various evangelists on these concerns and included them in the material below.

Recognizing the two faces

It is important to recognize that, at the beginning, almost all converts will develop two faces. This is normal and, at first, may be advantageous. At home, and in their community, they continue to be who they always have been. They are often afraid of betraying their family group so they continue to portray their original face. If they are Muslims, they may continue to pray five times a day, and in some cases even go on the Pilgrimage. However they may act with their families, they usually do so out of pressure rather than choice.

Since they are also seeking or have found Christ, they develop a second face. This is the one that the religious teacher and other Christians are most familiar with. When they are with their Christian friends these converts will open up their inner lives a little and ask, seek, discuss, and pray.

Many Christian workers are encouraged as they see the seeker or new convert growing in the faith, learning the Bible, and developing some spiritual maturity. And then, all of a sudden, he is gone, or he dramatically slows down and soon stops seeking or growing. The Christian worker may wonder what has happened. While I cannot speak to every situation, most of the successful evangelists emphasized that successfully uniting the converts' two faces is usually the first step in successfully bringing the new convert to maturity in Christ.

The most effective way to do this is for the discipler to become intimately acquainted with both faces. This naturally requires a lot of work and time.

Discipling cannot be equated with the expectation of meeting with someone one or two nights a week. The discipler must commit himself to spending many hours with the new convert, visiting his family, and demonstrating to him that the Christian life is honorable, even in other religious settings. This kind of "friendship discipling" will require getting to know the individual members of the family, familiarizing oneself with their situations and understanding the pressures and blessings they bring into the convert's life. Even more important than this, the discipler must not permit the convert to live a two-faced life forever. When inconsistencies and lies become apparent, the discipler must recognize these, expose them and deal with them. It is very important that the new believer comes to realize that the strength of the Christian faith is rooted in the truth. Jesus is the way, the truth and the life, and this knowledge needs to be exercised in the target culture where lies are often an acceptable method of disguising reality.

Keeping a convert alive

In some situations, a new convert will be tempted to rush home and tell his group about what he has found. In his spiritual immaturity and zeal, he may even attack his old religion and quickly invoke the wrath of the family group. Sometimes rash converts are expelled from the group; sometimes they are killed. It is imperative that you, the messenger, do everything you can to guide the new convert in the first few days of his new walk with Christ.

Most evangelists encourage the new convert to keep a low profile for a while, at least until they are ready to "come out." The teacher then concentrates the discipleship process on preparing the convert to step out as a Christian, not in a dishonorable and disrespectful way, but in a way that is courageous, honorable and respectful to both the family and God. After all, following Christ is not something that is dishonorable.

Meeting the other face

The key to uniting the two faces is to become familiar with the convert's second face. You must assume that there is another face and then begin to visit the convert in his home observing him in his natural surroundings, in order to understand the key family and group relationships.

There are five goals that should be attempted: 1. Understand how the new believer has related to the family group in the past. 2. Recognize those who will be opposed to the new believer and make them the focus of concentrated prayer. 3. Recognize group weaknesses and sinful behaviors so they can be addressed in discipleship sessions. Don't generalize, but be very specific with the convert in this area. 4. Recognize the new believer's own weaknesses and sinful behaviors. These will also need to be addressed in discipling sessions. 5. Subtly, but clearly, help the new believer understand that he cannot live a two-faced life. Promise, and give him, all the support he needs in working out his new faith in his old surroundings.

Uniting the two faces

Recognizing and understanding the two faces goes a long way in helping the new believer deal with them. Once the new believer knows that you understand him, both in your discipleship sessions and in his family situation, it becomes much easier to identify and deal with issues as they arise in his life. In the past, the convert related all his problems and issues to his family group, and drew from them the wisdom that he needed in order to make wise decisions. Now that he has a new teacher and a new Christian community, he needs to start drawing wisdom from them as well.

The sooner the discipler starts getting to know the other face, the easier the discipling process will be in the long run. If the teacher begins this process even before the seeker makes a full commitment to faith, the seeker will not feel guilty or ashamed of his old religious background and group. If it is left too long, the new believer may feel afraid of rejection by the believing community, because he has only known them as a seeker.

This process is an important one, and takes a lot of effort, especially if the teacher and other Christian contacts don't have a long association with the new believer. The discipler will need to judge how much teaching the new believer has had before he came to Christ, so he will know how much time will be needed for the discipleship process. Don't be discouraged; most of us took years before we were capable of successfully discipling others.

Friendship discipling

Most successful evangelists agree that it is unwise to put all your evangelistic efforts into people who are not interested. A lot of time and energy can be spent building friendships and bridges which may never lead anywhere. However, these evangelists insist that once someone comes to Christ, they now require a serious investment of time and effort. This often means some contact with the new believer every day, and often for extended periods of time. There are three things to recognize here that may be important for the new believer:

1. He needs to feel that he belongs and has joined a new group of friends and support structure.

2. He needs spiritual input every day. He doesn't know how to feed himself. A good thing to talk about is what he has read that day from the Word of God. If he hasn't read anything, it may mean that he doesn't have the opportunity at home. Allow him time to read by himself, and then discuss what he has read.

3. He may want to discuss non-spiritual items. This is an important step in his life, as he learns to relate all of his life to Christ and the fellowship of believers. You will need to make time for this as well.

Spiritual Growth

Momentum in the area of spiritual growth can be maintained by beginning a series of Bible studies that are designed to help the new disciple grow. The difficulty in using most Western-produced course material is that they assume a certain level of basic background (Christian) knowledge.

In designing your own discipling material, make sure you cover fundamental topics. The church planting handbook has examples of the following, Who Is God?, The Different Persons of the Trinity, Biblical Authority in Place of Fear, Characteristics of the Believer, Life and Gifts of the Body, Faith, Praise, The Believer and Suffering, The Kingdom of Christ, Baptism, and The Cost of Discipleship.

'Coming out' and making a stand

Is it possible for a new believer to be recognized by his family and community as a follower of Jesus and still be accepted in the community? Each of the evangelists I spoke with believed it is possible. However, a number of things must be in place for this to occur.

At the beginning the new believer will lose some standing in the community. There will always be those people who will remain suspicious. However, if the community is prepared properly, and the new believers live holy and godly lives, then most family members can be encouraged to accept the changes in his life as positive, not negative.

The whole area of "coming out" can be very frightening for the new convert, and even for the discipler. Much prayer and preparation need to go into the process. Sensitivity needs to be exercised so that the new disciple can recognize God-given opportunities that allow him to open up a little and share with his family.

One young Muslim man I know, whom we'll call Ahmed, was being discipled by a Western believer whom we will call Charles. Every day or two Ahmed would meet with Charles for Bible Study. On the days between they would often meet for coffee, or Ahmed would visit Charles' home. Charles had cut up a small New Testament so that Ahmed could take one or two pages home each day in his shirt pocket. When time allowed Ahmed would secretly read the pages, often studying them again and again.

One day Ahmed's mother was washing clothes and asked Ahmed for his shirt. Without thinking, Ahmed passed his shirt to his mother and went to his room for another one. When he returned, he discovered his mother reading the pages from his pocket. Ahmed was horrified, terrified of being discovered. He quickly snatched the pages from his mother. When his mother asked what they were, he said they were '*nothing*,' and left the house. A short time later a shaken Ahmed related the story to Charles.

When he finished, Charles sat and looked at him. Then quietly Charles said, "So that's what it is. It's all *nothing*?" Ahmed was stunned. This was not what he had meant to portray by the story. Charles continued: "After all this time together, after everything you've said and done... it's all *nothing*?"

"No!" Ahmed protested. "It's not all '*nothing*'. I've met Jesus. He has changed my life. Before this my life was empty. God was far away. But now He has touched my life, He has changed me and I'm His follower. It's not '*nothing*'."

Charles smiled. "Ahmed, that's wonderful. You've just said your testimony. Do you think you could repeat that to your family?" Together they looked into the Word of God, studying what it meant to talk about one's faith and not to be ashamed of the Gospel of Christ.

The next day, Ahmed's oldest brother came to talk to him. He explained that their father had sent him to discover what the papers were that their mother had found. Ahmed paused, and gathered his strength, knowing that Charles was praying for him (the single most important work that the disciple-maker can do for the new believer.) He then shared his testimony with his brother. His brother listened, and then said, "I'll talk it over with our father."

Several days later Ahmed's brother approached him again. "I've talked it over with Dad," he said, "and we've agreed that during the last few months we have seen a real change in your life. You really are different, better than before. We've decided to let you continue to read the writings of the prophet Isa."

That night as Ahmed met with Charles he was amazed and filled with joy and thankfulness. He had made his first step in coming out. The road would not be easy, but now that he had started down it, he was excited and encouraged. Perhaps someday he could be free to love Jesus openly in his own community, and not just he himself, but others with him.

When doing "friendship discipling" it is important that the discipler get to know the family, has having the respect of the family may help. It is certainly better than the family finding out that one of their family members has been listening and following a total stranger. By getting involved in an early stage, the discipler can assist the new believer in his coming out experience. For instance, during the first few months of his new walk with God, the new believer should make himself a model member of the family. After this, he might want to approach the most sympathetic family elder (possibly an uncle or aunt), and explain that he has a problem trying to please God. He could then share some of his experience being careful not to offend or alarm the family. He should stress that he does not want to hurt or dishonor his family, but wants to follow God with his whole heart. The discipler (and his community) should coach the new believer in what he is going to say, and cover him with prayer during this time. Generally the family elder will try and reason the new believer out of his new faith, but if she or he becomes convinced that the convert is virtuous, sincere and honorable, that family elder may take up the role of intermediary with the rest of the family. The fact that the new believer has sought a way to preserve family honor will be a big point in his favor.

Working through the Discipleship Process

Discipleship has two parts. On one side there is growth in intellectual knowledge about the new faith. On the other, there is a change in actions, lifestyle, and attitudes. In the West, too many Christian workers see discipleship as being about accumulating head knowledge, but in reality discipleship is about what you do and why you do it. Jesus hardly ever taught in doctrinal terms. Discipleship is a form of apprenticeship. This is what Jesus did with his disciples. The discipler must communicate clearly to the new believer that what the new disciple does is more important than what he says.

The discipler must consider what changes he would expect to see in a new believer's daily and weekly life as a result of his coming to Christ. He should then consider which of these has a clear biblical mandate, and what should be done about the others. Caution must be exercised to ensure that these issues are really biblical issues and not simply cultural views. It is often good to check these ideas with other Christian workers to get a rounded idea of what is necessary. Working in multinational, multi-denominational teams helps us, as you will get a much wider perspective on this.

Several workers I have talked with have discovered that a catechismal approach to discipleship seems to work well. The new believer clearly understands the teaching and responds well to questions and answers and can memorize a whole catechism given the chance. However, the teacher needs to make sure that the believer understands clearly what the teaching is about, and why he believes it, because his former religious beliefs were simply to be accepted and perhaps not understood.

Beyond the basic elements of faith, we need to be careful how we interpret Scripture. Even though we say the Word is our rule of faith and conduct, we struggle with which parts of it to read literally and which parts to read figuratively, which parts are commands, and which parts are more about heart attitudes. Why do we expect more from new believers?

Additionally, we need to be very careful at this point to let new believers understand the Scriptures in the context of their own background, and to relate them to their own culture in their own way. Much of our understanding of Scripture is dictated by our own culture. It is a irresponsible to burden someone with our cultural baggage. All the converts who come after will be shackled with it.

Take a fresh look at the Bible and discover the tremendous freedom there is in Christ to worship him in many ways. The form that our study and worship takes is less important than the fact that worship and Bible Study do indeed take place. In his various letters, Paul demonstrated that the Gospel should be worked out in each specific community. This working out, however, must be conducted with great care (fear and trembling.)

Many of the evangelists with whom I've spoken have discovered that trying to get new believers into a Bible study is just as likely to fail as trying to get Muslims to read their Qur'an. It doesn't usually happen. I'm not sure about other cultures, but Muslims in general are not a reading society. While the Qur'an is there to provide doctrinal beliefs and regulations, most Muslims rely on the *umma* (decisions of the community elders) for their guidance.

In such a situation the discipler may need to help new believers find community-type situations and methods for understanding and guidance. (This is addressed in the third section of this book, *The Community*.) At the same time he still needs to emphasize the need and blessing of personal time spent in communion with God through prayerfully reading the Word on his own.

A Place of Refuge

When we think of reading the Scriptures, we usually think of finding a place alone in our house where we can read. When a Muslim thinks of reading the Qur'an, he often thinks of going to the mosque to read, meditate, and listen to others.

It is important for every discipler to visit the local mosque or temple to note what is happening throughout the day. There is more to the mosque than prayer and preaching times. Mosques and temples are usually open, day and night, and the faithful can always find a place to read and meditate. Some have study rooms or schools attached. Friends often meet outside and if one is traveling and has no place to sleep, the Muslim can always sleep at the mosque.

When he accepts Christ, the new believer is isolated from the mosque or temple. As a result, he needs a place where he can read, meditate, and quietly visit with fellow believers. Unfortunately, churches are often merely meeting halls which are normally locked between meetings and thus do not provide an alternative to the mosque.

The disciple maker's home may be the only place of refuge with a Christian spiritual atmosphere that he knows. As a result, it is very common for a new believer to want to come to the home of his teacher to read, meditate, and participate in discussion with others. As more and more come to Christ, a place of corporate refuge should be established.

On one occasion two Christian young men I knew led a Muslim man to Christ. The day after his conversion, Muhammad showed up at their house. He stayed for hours. He came back the next day and then every day the next week. Worried, the two boys spoke to me. I encouraged them to let him come because he needed a place to go. "You don't need to entertain him. You need to give him a place where he can read and meditate. He may just enjoy being around you guys in a place where there isn't foul language and continual discussion about women and money."

At first they felt awkward as Muhammad would come regularly to their house, often for hours at a time. He would frequently spend an hour or two reading, asking questions, and then would read again. He enjoyed the visits that others made to the house as well. Weeks went by, and these two young men gave him as much attention as they could, all the while allowing him space in their home.

A few weeks later, Muhammad brought his first convert to the boys. He didn't want the boys to do anything, except allow the young man to read, meditate and ask questions when he had them. In the weeks that followed, Muhammad brought more and more of his friends and acquaintances to Christ, and ultimately to the quiet solitude of these boys' home.

Personal Study

Anyone who comes to Christ needs to discover a personal way of prayer and praise that is not foreign to him along with a way and a place to meet with God through the Word. Here are some activities which might be useful:

· After reading a series of verses, ask him if he can identify a proverb or saying that expresses the same thought. If he cannot read, you may have to read it for him, slowly, several times.

· Ask him to memorize one key verse in each visit.

· After a while he can be asked to memorize and tell Bible stories.

· Ask him to construct a prayer based on the lesson. It may only be a sentence or two from each section, but it means he has something to offer to God, as well as serving as a reminder of what he has learned.

· The new believer also needs a place to fellowship where he may be encouraged, a place to find and understand God's will, and a way to relate his new faith with his community in such a way that he will eventually be free to be himself, both in his walk with Jesus and in his community.

Questions for Reflection or Discussion

1. Are new believers put into a place of tension in your community? Do you know people who have done the following? abandoned their new faith, became like foreign Christians, became secret believers, lived an unstable life swinging back and forth?

2. Is it important to counsel new believers in order to keeping them alive during their first few weeks after conversion? What would you say to them?

3. Have you recognized the "two faced syndrome" among new believers in your cultural setting? What do you think of this?

4. Think of a new believer you would like to help. In what ways could you work towards understanding how this new believer has related to his family group in the past?

5. Who do you think might oppose the new believer?

6. Are there specific sins or behavior that the new believer will have to address? How much of this was learned from his culture, family, group, or old religion?

7. What can you do to help unite the two faces of the new believer?

8. Do you have a plan for helping the new believer grow spiritually? What topics, or what material do you plan on using?

9. Do you have a good place to meet throughout the week so that two or three of you can study the scriptures together? Where is this?

10. How often do you plan on meeting? Is this adequate time? Is there some way you can meet more often?

11. Do the new believers have places of refuge that they can go to if they want to study the Bible, listen to recorded messages, and spend time with God or in fellowship with others? How accessible is it to them?

12. Read Acts 12:8-14. Did Peter have a place to go when he was released from prison? Whose house was it? What time did he arrive? Was this a place of refugee?

Chapter Ten
The Continuing Struggle

Every year, more and more Christian workers arrive in Muslim, Buddhist, and Hindu lands, having embarked on their careers as evangelists and church planters. Sadly, records show that few will stay long enough on the field to become proficient in language and ministry. The attrition rate among evangelists, especially in Muslim lands, is astounding.

Along with this, a more subtle on-field attrition rate also takes its toll. Many who started out with a dream of winning the lost to Christ and planting churches among them, eventually decide that they should be involved in some other type of ministry, even though they don't quit and go home. In the end, there are very few who stick to their original vision of evangelism and church planting. There are many reasons why people quit or change ministries. Not all of them are negative, but the high rate of attrition should alert us to the fact that many would-be messengers of the Gospel struggle with this difficult calling.

At a conference of evangelists and church workers in the Middle East, God spoke words of hope to us. We were looking at Acts 15 where it is recorded that the Jewish church had problems accepting the influx of Gentile believers. We then began comparing this situation with the struggle that the Middle Eastern evangelical churches are having in accepting Muslims into their congregations. Then the Lord spoke to us. He showed us that the Jewish problem soon disappeared. The church lost its Jewishness because the sheer number of converts from a Gentile background overwhelmed the church, making it a Gentile church, not a Jewish church.

The writing is on the wall. The number of converts from religions like Islam, Hinduism and Buddhism is growing. In a few Middle Eastern countries they already equal - or outnumber - evangelical Christians from Catholic or Orthodox backgrounds. The ranks of Christians in India continue to swell. Soon the sheer numbers of these new believers will change the face of the church forever.

God is calling out a new army of laborers who will have the joy and privilege of working with this harvest. Truly the harvest is ripe. The trouble is not a lack of finances nor is it a lack of tools. As always, the challenge is the need for laborers to be thrust out into the harvest field; laborers who are trained and equipped to do the job of harvesting. Today there are a wealth of strategies and many available tools for the evangelist to use. Today there are successful evangelists and church planters who have pioneered the way, who can help those just starting out. It is my dream that the next generation of church planters arriving on the field will be the ones who will see the breakthroughs in the Muslim, Hindu and Buddhist worlds.

Truly it is a privilege to be a messenger of the Gospel. It is an awesome responsibility and an exciting task to be the first follower of Christ to enter a new region or neighborhood in recent history. But being a messenger is not enough. If we are cross-cultural messengers of the Gospel, we will have to carefully consider all the elements of our message in order to make sure that it is understood by our listeners. How the message is expressed is equally important as the credibility of the messenger. Each must be credible to the observer so that he can grasp the message of the Gospel as it is applied to this own culture and situation. This brings us to section two: *The Message*.

Questions for Reflection or Discussion

1. Summarize in a couple of sentences what you learned in "The Messenger" section of this book.

2. Are there any new skills you would like to practice?

3. Which of your core beliefs have been challenged or strengthened through this section?

4. What do you want to change or address in your life or ministry?

5. What fears do you have?

6. What is one main goal you want to work on after reading this chapter?

7. Are there issues your team should address? Which ones?

8. How will you go about working on this as a team?

THE MESSAGE

Introduction to The Message

Every individual is different. He or she is a unique mixture of person, personality, religion, culture, and background. I strongly believe that there is no such thing as a generic key that will unlock the spiritual door to every person's life. Any missionary who dreams of saying the magic words that will suddenly open the eyes of an individual to the truth of the Gospel, is merely dreaming of a way to avoid the hard work of understanding, empathizing and effectively communicating the Gospel.

There are, however, special keys that we must hold and exercise if we are to do this work of understanding, empathizing and communicating to people in different cultures. Over the years missiologists have offered us a variety of these keys such as "redemptive analogies" and "chronological teaching." It is my belief that understanding "common-ancestor worldviews" is one of these important keys. Since the first publication of the book: *Honor and Shame, Unlocking the Door*, positive responses have poured in from all corners of the globe. Most of that material is included in this next section.

Explaining the Gospel to people who hold another worldview is never easy. If we are to be true cross-cultural communicators, we must endeavor to understand how the Gospel is applicable to other cultures.

In the first part of this book (The Messenger) we examined some of the qualities and philosophies that an evangelist/church planter must have if he is to be accepted by his target audience as a valid messenger. However, having gained a hearing, the evangelist or church-planter must be equipped to share a message that is culturally appropriate. This next section examines three common-ancestor worldviews and challenges the church planter to approach his audience in a culturally appropriate manner. I would encourage you to read through this section of the book even if you are familiar with the terms "worldview" and "culture." At the time of this writing, the materials and message found here are not presented in any other Christian book that I am aware of.

May God bless you as you read through these pages and may He give you the wisdom you need to discover what is relevant to the people God has placed in your path.

Chapter Eleven
Worldview

Being seen as a messenger is only the first step in sharing the Gospel and planting churches. Once having gained a hearing, it is important that we are able to share a message that is understandable and relevant to our listeners. If we are to be effective cross-cultural communicators, we must understand the worldview of our audience and be able to communicate effectively within that worldview.

In the last decade, the subject of worldview has become a standard topic of study in most Christian institutions. It has become a handy tool to explain why we Christians think and act differently from other people. Hundreds of popular books have come out on the subject, and Christians in North America and England have started to adopt the term "worldview" as if it were a biblical term. However, there are many models of worldview in existence and not everyone agrees what makes up a worldview.

Definition

A worldview is simply a model of how a group of people live, think, and relate. Charles Kraft puts it this way, "The worldview is the central systemization of conceptions of reality to which the members of the culture assent (largely unconsciously) and from which stems their value systems. The worldview lies at the very heart of culture, touching, interacting with, and strongly influencing every other aspect of the culture." (*Christianity in Culture*, Maryknoll Orbis Books, 1979, Pg. 53)

"Worldview, the deep level of culture, is the culturally structured set of assumptions (including values and commitments/allegiances) underlying how a people perceive and respond to reality. Worldview is not separate from culture. It is included in culture as the deepest level presuppositions upon which people base their lives." (Kraft, Pg. 385)

Barney's Four-Layer Explanation

G. Linwood Barney (1937) introduced the concept of four layers of understanding as one moves into the heart of analyzing another culture. When we first consider a culture we are initially impacted with people's behavior. Once we work through this, we are faced with their values and next the underlying beliefs that underlie these values. At the very heart of Barney's four layer model is worldview. However, it is at this level, the very heart of worldview, that sociologists have struggled to explain what worldview is. As a result a number of different scholars have presented various suggestions.

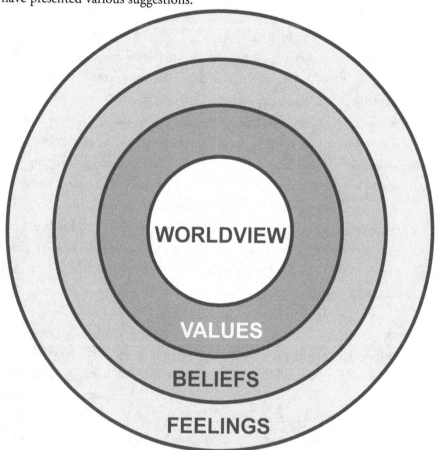

Four-Layer Model, G Linwood Barney (1937)

Origin of the term "worldview"

The German philosopher Immanuel Kant (1724 - 1804) most likely coined the term "worldview". He was one of the foremost thinkers of the Enlightenment and is considered one of the greatest Western philosophers of all time. He introduced a number of concepts, among them the word *weltanschauung*, literally meaning "one's look onto the world". This term implied all encompassing, unifying and underlying principles that define an approach to all aspects of life. Richard Kroner wrote a book about this term titled *Kant's Weltanschauung*. It was published in German in 1914 and in English in 1956. It was through this book, that the term "worldview" first came into more common usage in the English speaking world.

Kant however, did not really believe that everyone possessed a worldview, but rather that everyone was seeking a worldview.

Sigmund Freud summed it up this way: "'*Weltanschauung*' is, I am afraid, a specifically German notion, which it would be difficult to translate into a foreign language. If I attempt to give you a definition of the word, it can hardly fail to strike you as inept. By Weltanschauung, then, I mean an intellectual construction which gives a unified solution of all the problems of our existence in virtue of a comprehensive hypothesis, a construction, therefore, in which no question is left open and in which everything in which we are interested finds a place. It is easy to see that the possession of such a Weltanschauung is one of the ideal wishes of mankind. When one believes in such a thing, one feels secure in life, one knows what one ought to strive after, and how one ought to organize one's emotions and interests to the best purpose." (Lecture XXXV, *A Philosophy of Life*, 1932)

When Richard Kroner published *Kant's Weltanschauung* in English he brought the concept of worldview to the attention of philosophers, anthropologists, and missiologists all around the world.

Various types of worldview models

Here is where the confusion over worldview lies. No one has come up with a uniformly accepted set of criteria that must be dealt with when attempting to map what lies at the heart of worldview. Most Christian missiologists have simply defined worldview as a person's view of reality. Paul Hiebert puts it this way:

"Worldviews are the most fundamental and encompassing views of reality shared by a people in a culture. The worldview incorporates assumptions about the nature of things – about the "givens" of reality." (*Anthropological Reflections on Missiological Issues*, Baker Books, 1994 p 38)

However, if worldview is simply tied to a single person's view of reality, then everyone's worldview would be different. It would fail to explain cultural adhesion similarities found in radically different groups, such as Middle Easterners and North American native tribes.

Secondly, if worldview was simply attached to the basic assumptions that people make about the givens of reality, it would fail to explain how evangelical Christians in Africa, Asia and America have such radically different worldviews despite a similarity in theology.

As a result, a number of different models have been developed to illustrate how worldview works.

Nevertheless, it has been difficult for researchers to decide what factors should be considered when making up a list of issues for defining worldview. The problem is that different issues are important to different researchers, depending on the purpose of their model.

Another factor is the worldview of the researcher himself. Since the researcher is working from within the framework of his own worldview, that researcher defines what the important criteria are, based on his or her perception of what is important to worldview. For instance, someone with strong Marxist beliefs would include such things as class and class-struggle. Someone with strong evangelical beliefs would include issues like perception of God, sin, and salvation.

In actuality, these issues may have nothing to do with the actual worldview being analyzed. Thus researchers have produced many different models of worldview. Below are of some of these models.

The German Philosophic Model

This model was originally developed by Immanuel Kant and is taught in many universities. Webster's New World Dictionary (Third College Edition) defines worldview as "a comprehensive philosophy ultimately founded upon four institutions (i.e., established ideas or conceptions)." These four "institutions" (politics, economics, science, and religion) are supposedly the elements of all rational, intelligent thought. Thus, an individual's worldview is based entirely upon his inclusive perception of these four elements and upon his personal understanding of how society is best served by this perception. There are thousands of books and papers written on worldview using Kant's model.

Evangelical Models

In the 1970s Christian thinkers began adopting worldview vocabulary and thought. Over the following twenty years new ideas and concepts began to emerge as Christians wrestled with the question of what issues make up the heart of worldview.

1. Sire's Model (*The Universe Next Door*, 1976)

Sire defines worldview as "a set of pre-suppositions (or assumptions) which we hold (consciously or subconsciously) about the basic makeup of our world." He begins by saying that our first assumption is to think that something even exists. We all assume that something is there, but we often disagree from here on in and don't necessarily agree what that something is. Some people assume that the only basic substance that exists is matter. Others suggest that there are two things: matter and non-matter (a spiritual realm).

Sire goes on to establish five questions as his criteria for examining someone's worldview. What is real? Who is man? What happens to man at death? What is the basis of morality? What is the meaning of human history?

He then divides the world up into a number of worldviews such as Christian Theism, Deism, Naturalism, Nihilism, Existentialism, Eastern Pantheistic Monism, and The New Consciousness.

Sire admits that his seven worldviews are not comprehensive. In essence, his worldviews are a very Western interpretation of what worldviews look like. On page 15 of the introduction to his book he admits, "I have found it especially difficult to know what to include and what to leave out."

2. Geisler's Model (*Perspectives, Understanding and Evaluating Today's World Views*, 1984)

Norman L. Geisler and William D. Watkins define worldview according to how one sees the world in relation to God. Based on this one element, they deduce that the world can be divided into six great mega blocks of worldview: Theism (a world plus an infinite God), Atheism (a world without God), Pantheism (a world that is God), Pan-en-theism (a world in God), Deism (a world on its own made by God), and Finite Godism (a world with many Gods).

3. Olthuis' Model ("*On Worldviews*." Christian Scholars Review 14, 1985)

James Olthuis, a professor at the Toronto Institute for Christian Studies defines worldview this way: "A worldview (or vision of life) is a framework or set of fundamental beliefs through which we view the world, our calling, and future in it." He comments: "The vision may be so internalized that it goes largely unquestioned; it may be greatly refined through cultural-historical development; it may not be explicitly developed into a systematic conception of life; it may not be theoretically deepened into a philosophy; it may not even be codified into credal form. Nevertheless, this vision is a channel for the ultimate beliefs which give direction and meaning to life. It is the integrative and interpretive framework by which order and disorder are judged, the standard by which reality is managed and pursued. It is the set of hinges on which all our everyday thinking and doing turns. Although a [worldview] is held only by individuals, it is communal in scope and structure. Since a worldview gives the terms of reference by which the world and our place in it can be structured and illumined, a worldview binds it adherents together into a community."

4. Nash's Model (*Worldviews in Conflict, Choosing Christianity in a world of ideas,* 1992)

Nash tells us that the major elements in defining a worldview are: God, ultimate reality, knowledge, ethics, humankind, and additional factors, which he declines to define.

As can be seen by these models, and others that Dr. David Naugle of Dallas Baptist University points out in his book: *Worldview: The History of a Concept* (2002), there is no universal agreement as to what constitutes the essential elements of worldview.

Do these evangelical models work?

Sire's worldview model (or derivatives) is taught in many different Christian colleges and seminaries in North America and England. Let's consider how a Muslim would answer Sire's five questions.

Sire's Worldview - A Muslim Answer

What is real? - There is both spirit and matter.

Who is man? - A creature created by God.

What happens to man at death? - He faces judgment and then hell or rewards.

What is the basis of morality? - God's revealed message.

What is the meaning of human history? - A record of God's dealing with mankind.

According to Sire's model, Muslims and Christians should have quite similar worldviews. However, if we were to compare the worldview of a Middle Eastern Muslim and a Western Christian, we would find them almost diametrically opposed, even though they both agree in an all present, all powerful creator God who created the world and mankind, and has revealed himself through the prophets from Adam onwards. Even when they both agree that man will face God in judgment and that hell awaits the unbeliever, the two worldviews are actually in total opposition. On the surface their worldviews seem very similar. But when a Muslim and an evangelical are given time to talk, they seldom even begin to understand one another.

Thus it is my conclusion that worldview models based on religious criteria alone (such as God, man, and salvation) are models based on elements important to the worldview of the evangelicals developing the model and are not universal to everyone everywhere. Thus Sire's, Geisler's, Olthuis' and Nash's worldviews are useful in helping evangelicals understand others in comparison to their own religion, but they fall short of helping Muslims understand their own worldview. When Muslims are presented with the worldview models developed by evangelicals in the west they are often puzzled. Muslims have complained to me that these models do not really address the heart issues that divide us. In saying all of this, I am not saying that the worldviews developed by Sire and others are wrong. No, these worldview models are useful in themselves, as they help evangelicals understand why they are different from others. However, all these writers fall short of providing a model that people all around the world can identify themselves with.

Biblical Worldview

Discussing Biblical worldview has become popular in North America, and many books have been published on the topic. Missiologists such as Paul Hiebert (*Anthropological Reflections on Missiological Issues*, Baker Books, 1994) have tried to define Biblical worldview when he states that Biblical worldview defines for us the essential reality and history of the cosmos. This includes God's superintendence of history, God's creation of perfect humans and their fall through sin, God's work of salvation within those who believe in Christ – God himself among us and Christ's return to establish his kingdom of righteousness throughout the created universe" (pg 11)

The problem with this definition is that there are millions of evangelicals around the world, some Americans, some Asians, some Middle Easterners and so forth who posses radically different worldviews despite holding to the same tenants of evangelical faith. As I see it, each of these have a worldview that has been affected by the Bible, but is not in itself a "biblical worldview.' That is why American preachers must spend so much time researching and exploring the historical setting that the Bible was written in so that Americans can understand it. On the other hand, many Arabs claim that they have a biblical worldview because their worldview seems closer to that of the New Testament. For instance, they actually have seats of honor in their living rooms and understand Jesus' teaching about not taking the seat of honor unless invited to. Most Americans do not relate to biblical passages like this, yet some still claim to have a biblical worldview. In much the same way, there are people who claim that there is a Muslim worldview. However, in my years of ministry to Muslims in many different settings, I have to conclude that while Islam affects people's worldview, the issue of worldview is much deeper than Islam or any religious system. It is my belief that there are several fundamental common-ancestor worldviews that must be understood. Charles Kraft refers to these in his book *Christianity in Culture*, (Maryknoll, Orbis Books, 1979.) Kraft admits that he does not clearly understand common-ancestral worldviews, their origins or how they developed.

"The worldview of any given culture presumably originated in a series of agreements by the members of the original group conceding their perception of reality, and how they should regard and react towards that reality. This like all other aspects of culture, has undergone constant change so that it now differs to a greater of lesser extent from the original worldview and from other extant worldviews that have developed (in related cultures) from that common-ancestor worldview." (pg. 53)

As a historian I am not aware of any time in history when a group of people sat down and made conscious decisions about their perception of reality. As an evangelical Christian I believe that the common-ancestor worldviews Kraft seeks for are found in the Book of Genesis. Unfortunately, Kraft goes on in his book to wrestle with worldview and cultural issues without first giving us a clear definition of how worldviews began and how they developed into the worldviews we have today.

The common-ancestor worldview model introduced in the following chapters is an attempt at understanding worldview from a Biblical perspective.

Dodd's Model, Dynamics of Intercultural Communication

Dr. Carley H. Dodd, professor of communications at Abilene Christian

University, takes another track when developing his list of criteria that make up worldview (the center circle in Barney's diagram.) Dr. Dodd uses continuums between two opposite extremes. Some of his criteria are:

basically good ..... basically bad

shame based ..... guilt based

task oriented ..... people oriented

secular oriented ..... spiritual oriented

doing based ..... being based

no relationship ..... strong relationship

controlling nature ..... subject to nature

linear ..... cyclical

much control ..... less control

Dodd's model has found much wider acceptance, especially in Europe, because his criteria are more globally applicable. I believe that Dodd's model is much closer to the truth of what we find in cultures all around the world. However, the question that must be asked when using Dodd's model is: Which of these criteria are more important within different worldviews? In other words, it is not merely the point along the horizontal continuums that must be considered, but also the vertical order of the continuums themselves. This radically varies from worldview to worldview.

Missiology

Evangelical missiologists all have different explanations of what is at the core of worldview. Kraft tells us that "Worldview, the deep level of culture, is the culturally structured set of assumptions." (*Perspectives on the World Christian Movement*, 1998, p 385,) Paul Hiebert however claims that "At the core of our worldview are our values" (*Anthropological Reflections on Missiological Issues*, p 138) Barney, however claims that behaviors, values and beliefs are all based on worldview. Sire tells us that worldview begins with our concept of what is real. Geisler claims worldview is founded on man's view of God. And so the list goes on, each person talking about worldview, but defining it in different ways. This illustrates the problems that missiologists have faced in defining worldview without first understanding what the common-ancestral worldviews were and how they developed.

It is interesting to note that modern missiologists such as Hiebert, Kraft, and

Lingenfelter generally all use illustrations drawn from groups of people that have religious views far different from evangelicals. These authors all prefer such examples because the attention of the reader is captivated naturally by the radical differences. However, it would be more helpful to draw illustrations from religions that are similar to Christianity or even from evangelicals who hold different worldviews themselves. As we will see, this comparison will help us isolate and identify the real differences between various worldviews.

Conclusion

While the term worldview has become popular in the last few years, few writers seem to agree on what criteria should be used when constructing a universal worldview model. When I first ventured out to the mission field several experienced missionaries told me not to figure out Middle Easterner's thought patterns, as it was obvious that they didn't think logically. Such statements irritated me, and motivated me to search for ways of understanding other people's thinking. Twenty years later as the pieces started falling into place I began sharing my findings with others. They were first published in *Honor and Shame, Unlocking the Door* (2000). Much of that same material is re-printed in the chapters that follow.

Questions for Reflection or Discussion

1. Have you studied worldview in another setting? Was it a secular or religious setting? Did the model you studied help you in understanding the world around you?
2. Have you been exposed to other worldviews before this? What worldviews have you interacted with? Do you still think in terms of the worldview you grew up with, or do you think that you have begun to understand and think according to other worldviews?
3. Sire's five questions have become very well known in some circles. (What is real? Who is man? What happens to man at death? What is the basis of morality? What is the meaning of human history?) How well would they help you in understanding the worldview of the people you minister among?
4. Discuss your target culture in relation to Dodd's continuums.

Chapter Twelve
The Eden Effect

In the beginning there was only one language and one worldview. Everything in the Garden of Eden was in harmony. Communication was clear between mankind, and also between mankind and God. If I were to ask, "Where did all the languages of the world originate?" most Bible believing Christians would point to the Tower of Babel as the source of the original language groups. These "common-ancestral languages" have fragmented down through history and continue to fragment and change even in our own time. But if I were to ask, "Where did all the worldviews and cultures originate?", most Bible believing Christians would likely be puzzled. Since the word worldview does not appear in Scripture, most Christians fail to think in terms of the biblical basis of worldview. We struggle to both define and model worldview in a way which can be universally applied.

One of the challenges I faced during my missionary career was developing just such a model that could be universally applied I trust that what is presented below will be helpful to you.

The Biblical Bases for Worldview

There are three very basic worldviews presented in Scripture. The first two chapters of the Bible describe a worldview that is untainted by sin. While some writers have tried to imagine what it was like to live in the Garden of Eden and hold an *Edenic Worldview*, few of us can begin to imagine what this type of worldview was like.

In the same way, the last two chapters of the Bible describe a coming world without sin. Someday, the followers of the Lord Jesus will enter into this state. They will have known and experienced sin in the present world, but will live in a world without sin. This is what I call a *Heavenly Worldview*.

Between the first two and the last two chapters of the Bible we have what I call *Sin-Based Worldviews*. All of us are living under the influence of sin.

Edenic Worldview   ....   Sin-Based Worldviews   ....   Heavenly Worldview

It is important to grasp this larger picture in order to understand our own perspective on worldview. Every person on the face of this world is tainted by sin. Every one of us is affected by sin, and every one of us struggles to live in a world saturated with sin and the effects of sin. These are our first clues in identifying the common-ancestral worldviews found in the Bible.

A Missionary's View of Sin

The only reason that the Christian missionary enterprise exists today is because sin exists. Sin began in the Garden of Eden and has affected mankind ever since. The missionary enterprise of the church exists simply for the purpose of addressing sin and the results of sin among the peoples of the earth: communicating to people everywhere the Gospel of God's grace provided through the cross of Christ.

In much the same way, if there was no such thing as disease and everyone was healthy, then there would be no need for the health care industry. Doctors, nurses, medical technicians, pharmacists, administrators, and even the medical insurance industry would all be unnecessary. Just as disease is the very reason the medical industry exists, sin is the very reason the missionary enterprise exists.

It is interesting to note that the medical industry treats disease very differently from the way the missionary enterprise treats sin. Medical researchers spend countless hours and billions of dollars studying disease and its effects so that they can discover adequate cures. However, in the missionary world, we already know that the cure for sin is found in Jesus Christ. As a result, few of us spend much time studying sin or the effects of sin. In neglecting the study of sin we have neglected a critical element that is needed to clearly understand man, his worldview, and his spiritual condition.

Harmartiology

Since the missionary effort is so closely attached to sin, I believe it is important for us to have a clear understanding of how sin entered the world and the impact that this sin had on the human race. Unfortunately, most Christians know very little about sin, other than their struggle to overcome it. The study of sin is known as "harmartiology," but very few theological institutes offer courses by this name. As I embarked on my study I came to realize how little I knew about sin and how it manifests itself in our lives. With that realization I began to study sin and its effects on mankind.

As mankind multiplied on the face of the earth, sin multiplied until today we have a world full of people, and thus a world full of sin and the results of sin. If we can understand the significance of what took place in the Garden of Eden, I believe we can also begin to understand the peoples of the world today in their various worldviews as they try to cope with sin and its influences, as sin is expressed differently through different worldviews.

I believe that whenever we set out to understand the mindset of a certain culture or worldview, we need to start in the Bible, with the Garden of Eden. It is my belief that if we can understand man in the Garden of Eden, then we can begin to understand how man's thinking has developed in different directions since then.

The Results of Sin

When I ask most people what the results of sin are, they usually list things like, separation from God, pain, death, sickness, frustrating work, etc. While these are real, they aren't really the results of sin. Rather, they are the results of God's punishment on sin. To find the results of sin on mankind you need to examine Genesis chapter three and discover what happened to Adam and Eve during the time between their sin and God's sun subsequent judgment. That is the key to understanding what sin does to mankind. Once you understand what sin does to mankind, you can begin to understand how mankind responds and deals with the effects of sin. This response is fundamental to understanding common-ancestral worldviews.

Guilt

In the Bible we find three specific ways that sin affected Adam and Eve in the garden. These three are found in Genesis chapter three. In verse seven, the scriptures tells us that Adam and Eve "knew" that they had sinned. This knowledge of sin is nothing other than our conscience speaking or the feeling of guilt. When Adam and Eve sinned, they felt the sting of a guilty conscience. For the first time they experienced knowing right from wrong through their conscience. This knowledge of good and evil is common to us today. While Adam and Eve were in a perfect state, they never felt their consciences condemning them.

The problem with the conscience is that with repetition of sin the conscience can be progressively silenced. However, even if this is the case and conscience is no longer operating, this does not mean that a sinner is not guilty. When Adam sinned he was guilty of eating forbidden fruit. In that one act guilt passed through Adam upon all of mankind, forever.

All of this, of course, is familiar territory for most Western evangelical Christians. Every Western book on Christian theology examines man's guilt, which originated in the Garden of Eden. Guilt is then traced through the Bible, as God addresses guilt in the Old and New Testaments. Theologians are quick to explain things like the meaning of the scapegoat in Leviticus, the guilt offerings, and so forth.

This is all sound theology, but unfortunately some Christians and some Christian theologies stop at guilt, or rather, get so wrapped up with 'guilt-based theology' that they fail to notice the other results of sin.

The Western attraction to the guilt aspect of the fall and, consequently, the guilt aspect of salvation is due in part to Western preoccupation with guilt within the Western worldview. Much of the English speaking world, and parts of Europe, possess worldviews that focus on this aspect of man's guilt, and/or his freedom from guilt. This is what I will call "guilt-based ancestral worldview." In chapters thirteen and fourteen we will examine the guilt-based ancestral worldview, how it came into being, and the impact it has had on Western Christian theology.

Shame

Guilt was not the only influence of sin in the Garden of Eden. When Adam and Eve realized they had sinned, they immediately hid themselves (v. 8). Adam and Eve were ashamed. Shame had come upon Adam and Eve, but their shame was not for them alone. Shame, like guilt, passed upon mankind from that point on. As a result, man is not only guilty from this point on, but man is also in a position of shame before God.

It is interesting to note that the subject of shame is addressed in both the Old and New Testaments. You can find references to it in the imagery of the temple, in the messages of the prophets, and, more importantly, in the death of Christ on the cross. Shame is repeatedly mentioned in the New Testament, especially in the teachings of Christ in the Gospels.

Anthropologists and sociologists have pointed out to us that many cultures round the world place shame and honor at the center of their value system rather han right and wrong. Shame and honor are paramount to understanding their vorldviews. The shame-based cultures of the world span an area from Morocco o Korea and cover much of what is known today in mission circles as the 10-40 Window. They also include some of the aboriginal natives of Australia and North America.

In this book we will look at shame-based ancestral worldviews in some detail nd consider examples from both Islamic and North American First Nations aboriginal) cultures.

Fear

There was a third result of man's sin. When God came to speak to Adam and Eve in the garden, Adam told God that they had hidden themselves because they were afraid (v. 10). The third result of sin was fear; and fear came upon Adam and Eve as well as upon the whole human race. Before this, man enjoyed the presence of God. Now he cowered in fear, and fear passed upon all mankind. Many works of Christian theology omit this facet of sin even though missionaries have long talked about "fear-based cultures" that exist among animistic people.

From Genesis three we see that man is not only in a position of guilt and shame, but also in a position of fear before God. Moreover, it is interesting to note that the subject of fear is also addressed in the Old and New Testaments. You can find it in the imagery of the temple, in the messages of the prophets, and also in the Garden of Gethsemane and the death of Christ. The New Testament further addresses the issue of fear with such comments as, "You did not receive a spirit of slavery to fall back into fear, but you have received the Spirit of adoption as sons." Romans 8:15 (ESV) and "There is no fear in love, but perfect love casts out fear." 1 John 4:18(ESV)

Anthropologists and sociologists tell us that many cultures in our world can be grouped together into what are known as fear-based worldviews. The focus of these cultures is often centered around fear of spirits and the supernatural world. The importance of fear is paramount to understanding their worldview. Fear-based cultures are found in Africa, Central and South America, and some islands in the Far East. We will look at the fear-based ancestral worldviews in chapter fifteen of this section.

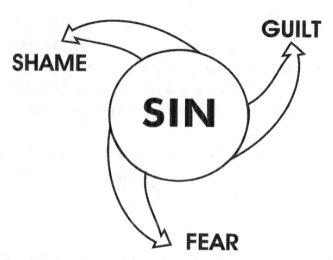

Confusing Terms

In Western evangelical theology, Christians often confuse guilt and sin, freely interchanging them as if they had the same meaning. I would like to carefully distinguish between the two. Sin is an act of rebellion against God. It can be a willful act, or something we fail to do. Guilt, shame, and fear, on the other hand, are the results of sin, as illustrated in the drawing above.

We will discover as we work our way through these topic that when the Gospel message deals with sin, it effectively deals with the guilt, shame and fear attached to that sin, but more on that later.

Common Ancestral Worldviews

In the Garden of Eden, Adam and Eve experienced guilt, shame, and fear. I believe that these three responses to sin make up the basic building blocks that created mankind's common-ancestral worldviews. This situation is similar to the three basic colors that an artist mixes to make all the colors of the universe. On my computer, I can mix the three primary colors to make up 64 million other colors. That's the way it is with worldview. There are many different kinds of worldview, but when carefully examined, they can all be understood in the light of man's response to guilt, shame and fear.

In the Garden of Eden, man had one language, one worldview, and one culture. The Bible tells us that the languages of the world originated at the Tower of Babel, but where did all the worldviews and cultures of the world come from? I believe that worldviews are the natural outworking of wrestling with the three results of sin. Some, like Cain in Genesis 4:14 experienced events that filled their existence from that time onward with fear. Others, like Ham, the son of Noah (Genesis 9:21-25) lived under the stigma of shame. As people spread out over the earth, some of the cultures that emerged were more sensitive to guilt or shame or fear than others. And so today it is possible to classify many worldviews according to their common-ancestral worldviews.

C. H. Dodd list of critical elements that make up worldview (page 144) include continuums of guilt and innocence as well as shame and honor. I believe that the Bible clearly presents us with a third continuum, that of fear and power. Sociologists have used terms like guilt-based cultures and shame-based cultures for years. These are not new concepts. The Bible also talks about guilt, shame, and fear. They are also not new concepts to most of us.

What is new for most of us, however, is understanding how to share the Gospel with people whose common-ancestral worldviews are made radically different from our own. If we come from a guilt-based worldview, our explanation of the gospel may have little relevance to their shame or fear based worldview.

If the Bible is what it says it is, (i.e. God's communication to mankind in every situation) then the Gospel should address each of these common-ancestral worldviews and speak specifically to them.

We must be careful, however, not to try and fit each culture into one specific category. As I stated, these common-ancestral worldviews are similar to the thousands of variations that can be created from three primary colors. How much of each primary color determines what the final color will be. In the same way, all three common-ancestral worldviews are present in all cultures and worldviews, but the amount of each one present determines the actual type of worldview that emerges.

Having recognized the particular mixture, one must then consider how members of a particular culture react to various issues. As an example, when Arabs are shamed, they often react by taking revenge on those who cause the shame, but when Japanese are badly shamed, they may react by committing suicide. So when we observe an action taking place in a culture that we do not understand, we must consider how these three common-ancestral worldviews influence that culture and thus bring about the specific. While observing worldviews and their subsequent cultures around the world I have come to the conclusion that it is possible to speak of three great mega-blocks of the world possessing similar worldviews. While this is a simplistic approach, it may help us see how guilt, shame and fear are major influences in our world today.

Where are the major blocks? Many Western nations (Northern Europe, North America, Australia, and New Zealand) possess worldviews that have dominant (but not exclusive) guilt-based characteristics. On the other hand, much of the 10-40 Window (largely Islamic, Hindu and Buddhist) is made up of shame-based cultures. Most of the primal religions of the world (such as those who have emerged from tribes in the jungles of Africa, Asia, and South America) have dominant but not exclusive fear-based characteristics.

We face a problem when we want to simply label cultures under one of these three basic classifications. They do not all easily fit, because while they may exhibit dominant characteristics, in reality all cultures are made up of blends of all three.

When analyzing a worldview, one must look for both the primary and secondary characteristics. For example, many North American First Nation (native) cultures consist of elements drawn from both shame-based and fear-based worldviews. When surveying individuals from North American First Nation peoples I discovered than some of them have adopted elements of guilt-based thinking, especially those influenced by Western Christianity. On the other hand, much of mainstream North American worldview has been made up of primarily guilt-based principles, although this has been changing in the last two decades.

In the material that follows I will use the terms guilt-based, shame-based and fear-based when describing worldview. By using these terms I simply intend that shame, guilt or fear, is the dominant characteristic. I am not attempting to make a statement of exclusivity, nor am I trying to downplay other criteria that are used when describing worldview or constructing ethnographic surveys. I am simply pointing out the importance of classifying worldview emphasizing guilt, shame and fear before moving on to other factors.

Missionary Efforts in the Past

Since its inception, the church has related well to guilt-based worldviews. The modern missionary movement has done well among some cultures but has related poorly to others. In the last two hundred years, the majority of missionaries have been sent out from guilt-based cultures into areas of the world that had worldviews focused on fear. In many cases they did reasonably well, as there was also an understanding of guilt in most of these cultures.

In the shame-based worldviews of the 10-40 Window, however, we have not done as well. Where there has been a blend of shame and guilt-based worldviews, the church has advanced, but in the various Muslim cultures which are primarily shame-based, the evangelical church has struggled to communicate the Gospel in an effective manner.

Since publishing the book *Honor and Shame, Unlocking the Door*, I have been greatly encouraged by the response of readers from all around the world. Missionaries working throughout the 10-40 Window, as well as those working among the First Nations of the Western world, have all reported that the principles outlined in the book have helped them in effectively communicating the Gospel.

In the Middle East I have also observed missionaries using the principles outlined in the book. Such principles have helped unlock the riches of God's grace for those possessing a shame-based worldview.

Conclusion

When man sinned, three great conditions came upon mankind. By sinning man broke God's law and consequently was in a position of guilt. By sinning man also broke God's relationship and consequently was in a position of shame. Finally, when man sinned he broke God's trust and was from that point, in a position of fear.

Over the millennia that followed many different worldviews developed, all of them built around sin's effect on mankind. The worldviews that we experience today are all trying in some way to negate these effects. Thus it is unwise for missionaries to champion one worldview over others. As cultures and worldviews developed over the millennia, many gravitated towards one of the three perspectives of guilt, shame or fear. This polarization has created three mega-trends in worldview. While the majority of worldviews generally fit into these three classifications, there are many worldviews which draw equally from two or all three common-ancestral worldviews.

This mixing of worldviews is especially noticeable in South America where jungle tribes with fear-based worldviews have come into contact with both shame-based worldviews originating out of southern Spain and Portugal, and guilt-based worldviews brought by Western missionaries and Western business.

My goal in writing what follows is simply to introduce the guilt, shame and fear-based common-ancestral worldviews, and then to examine how the Gospel message might be best communicated in these contexts.

In order for us to examine these three worldviews, I start with a quick look at the Western guilt-based worldview. This is the basis for the culture that I was born in and one that claims me as its own. My study of this worldview has helped me understand my own culture and so we will start with guilt-based worldviews in the next chapter.

Questions for Reflection or Discussion

1. Describe some ways that the Edenic Worldview (Genesis 1 & 2) differs from the Heavenly Worldview (Revelation 21 & 22)

2. How do these differ from the sin-based worldviews that we now possess?

3. Have you studied sin as part of your theological training? How did it impact your life and understanding of the Bible? Is dealing with sin a central part of your Gospel message?

4. Do you find yourself championing one worldview while marginalizing others? Why do you think this is?

5. What do you think is the difference between worldview and culture? Are some cultures or worldviews evil? How so?

6. Which of your core beliefs have been challenged or strengthened through reading this chapter?

Chapter Thirteen
Guilt-Based Worldviews

Few of us live with exactly the same worldview. Worldview can vary from town to town, family to family and sometimes even from individual to individual. All of us are different. We come from different backgrounds and are changed by the different experiences that come into our lives on a day to day basis. Even those who try to define the wider concept of worldview struggle to know what makes up any particular worldview. 'American' or 'Canadian' worldview can only be addressed in vague generalizations. Americans come from all kinds of ethnic backgrounds and have all kinds of values. Some live in middle class housing, some in cardboard boxes on the street, and some in large impressive mansions. It's hard to place categorizations and descriptions on people who are so diverse.

Despite this, there are some general characteristics or mega-traits that fit the majority of people in the Western world. Certain basic fundamental beliefs have molded Western civilization. These beliefs have laid the foundations upon which Western nations are built, and from which the fabric of their society has been formed.

One of these basic foundations is the belief in right versus wrong. The importance of right and wrong are so deeply ingrained in Western culture that most Westerners analyze everything from this perspective. There is a right way to do things. Other ways are not right, unless it can be proved that they are more efficient or beneficial. Most Western forms of entertainment are built upon "the good guys versus the bad guys." This thinking is so familiar to Westerners that few question its validity. It is such an integral part of religion and society that Westerners often cannot imagine a world where 'right versus wrong' isn't the accepted basic underlying principle.

"Right versus wrong" is the yardstick used in Western worldview to measure most everything. Westerners talk about the rightness and wrongness of someone else's actions. Westerners talk about things being "right for me." They are obsessed with knowing their rights and exercising them. Many Western societies spend countless hours and billions of dollars debating the rights and wrongs of society. Is homosexuality right or wrong? Is spending billions on the military right or wrong? Is possession of drugs like marijuana right or wrong? How about possession of nuclear bombs or weapons of mass destruction?

Almost every major issue the West struggles with, involves an aspect of deciding whether something is right or wrong. Westerners arrive at this basic tension because almost everything in Western culture is plotted on a guilt-innocence continuum (innocence being something defined as being right or righteousness).

guilt .... innocence

The pulls and demands of these two diametrically opposed forces dictate much of Western human behavior. Guilt can plague and haunt people, bringing fear and condemnation upon them. Many Westerners do everything they can to avoid being or feeling guilty. Psychologists spend a great deal of their time helping people deal with all sorts of guilt complexes.

Western evangelicals in particular, often live in circles that are governed by guilt principles based on the authority of the Bible. Outside of these circles, guilt is defined in other ways. It can be a sense of public disapproval, being in trouble with the authorities, or not being politically correct. However guilt is defined, and to what extent it influences a culture varies widely from location to location. No matter how it is obtained or experienced, the understanding of right and wrong has been instrumental in forming much of Western society.

On the other end of the guilt spectrum is righteousness, or innocence. This is the unspoken goal of much of Western society. "I'm OK. You're OK" is the comfortable ideal that people seek. Many Westerners express their innocence with the statement that "they are as good as the next person." If this is true, then they can get on with the business of pursuing happiness and pleasure within the bounds of being OK and not feeling guilty.

Most Westerners do what they can to avoid feeling guilty and at the same time exercise their rights. This guilt-innocence thinking is so ingrained in Western society that most people have immediate reflexes to events that catch them off-guard.

Have you ever noticed what happens in the swimming pool when the lifeguard blows his whistle? Almost all Westerners will stop swimming to see who is guilty, and when they realize they are innocent will resume swimming. This is a normal scenario in the Western world, but it is not true in much of the Eastern world where whistle blowing does not produce pangs of guilt. When those in the Western world do something wrong, like unintentionally running a red light, they may feel guilty. This is also not necessarily true in the Eastern world. In the Western world, something as simple as beeping your car horn sends messages of guilt to others. In the Eastern world, guilt is seldom attached to the beeping of car horns.

Or how about this scenario? Imagine a classroom full of grade school kids. Suddenly, the intercom interrupts their class. Johnny is being called to the principal's office. What is the immediate reaction of the other children? In the West the immediate reaction would almost always be, "What did you do wrong?" By the time they are ready for school, most Western children will have adopted a worldview where they immediately assume guilt. In my seminars I have noticed that many Easterners respond in another way. They realize that the school principal would never publicly shame an individual, so their conclusion is that the principle was handing out rewards. Given the same situation, people from different cultures respond differently. Much of Western society conditions people to expect the worst, and they feel pangs of guilt.

When Westerners try to share the Gospel with people from their Western culture, they usually start from the premise of guilt as taught in Romans 3. All are guilty of breaking God's law. I've often noticed that Western people respond with statements such as: "Well, I think I'm as good as the next person" or "I'll take my chances." Even people on the street immediately associate the Christian religion with guilt. A mosque in Canada once displayed a sign, "We accept everyone, and tell no one that he is a sinner."

So much of Western thinking is wrapped up in guilt. Wars are justified on the basis of establishing guilt. During the opening days of the Gulf War, the American government spent many hours and millions of dollars determining if Saddam Hussein was guilty. Once they thought they had established that he was guilty of having weapons of mass-destruction and committing atrocities, they then had the right to take military action against him. Throughout the war, they continued to make statements about Mr. Hussein's supposed deranged mental state and irrational actions. All of this helped to justify the war. In fact, all during the history of Western civilizations, wars have had to be justified, and each side identifies the other as being the 'bad guys.' Wars have many triggers, but in the Western world in almost every case right and wrong are invoked in order to justify action. This is not the case in the east, where loss of shame and restoration of honor are often invoked in order to justify action. We will address this topic more fully in a later chapter.

Westerners struggle with their obsession to plot everything on a guilt-innocence continuum. Some things however, are not easy to chart between right and wrong. Is a starving child who steals food guilty? Should he be punished for his hunger? These questions disturb Westerners because they feel that everything in life must fit somewhere between guilt and innocence.

In fact, Western association with guilt has gone so far as to provide an avenue for people to develop guilt complexes. They feel guilty for what they have done and also guilty for what they have not done. They even feel guilty for what others have done. People who struggle with a guilt complex can be overcome with embarrassment and feelings of guilt from the actions of others.

The flip side of guilt is innocence, righteousness, and exercising rights. As I mentioned, "I'm OK, You're OK" is an important philosophy in Western culture especially among young. In order not to point a finger at others Western youth continue to expand the limits of what is acceptable activity. By making everything acceptable, guilt is denied and suppressed. In effect many western young people are accepting hedonism as acceptable as long as it doesn't hurt anyone. For instance, homosexuality is more acceptable because this helps thousands of people avoid feeling guilty. This alone is enough to convince many people in Western society that it's OK for people to participate in homosexuality. In fact, almost anything is tolerated as long as it doesn't hurt another person.

I have also been surprised to discover that many people in the Western world believe that our fixation with right and wrong is not only normal, but it is the only correct way to think. They assume that anyone who does not think in these terms does not think rationally or logically.

Furthermore, there are many Christians who believe that a worldview that is based on right and wrong is based on Judeo-Christian principles and therefore is correct. I've noticed that this objection is later withdrawn as people look into the origins of guilt-based worldview where they can honestly ask themselves if this is the only valid pattern set down in the Scriptures.

In order to understand guilt-based worldview we must go back to Greek and

Roman times, examine the origin of this pattern of thinking, and discover how this has had an impact on the Western church and on their understanding of the Scriptures.

Questions for Reflection or Discussion

1. What are some of the ways that the guilt-based worldview is evident in Western culture? Can you think of current issues that Western society is struggling with? What other expressions of guilt-innocence can you think of?

2. What are some of the things we do in order to not be guilty or to appear as not being guilty? What special precautions do people take?

3. Can you think of issues that Western society is grappling with, that are not easily plotted on a right – wrong scale? How does society around you deal with these ethics issues?

4. Are there things or instances where you may feel guilty and you should not? How is guilt transferred to you?

5. Can you imagine a world were right and wrong were not the basis on which decisions were made? How easily could you fit into such a world?

6. Read Joshua 2:4-6, Hebrews 11:31, & James 2:23-25 What do these passages tell us about lying? How do people deal with these verses in a guilt-based culture? Do you think that there might be other interpretations in other cultures? What might these be?

Chapter Fourteen
The Roman Connection

The Roman Empire has come and gone, leaving us with a few ruined cities and a wealth of stories about conquest and heroism. While most of what the Romans accomplished has disappeared, there is one facet of Roman life that has impacted the West right down to the present. It is Roman law, or the *'pax romana'* (Roman peace), which was brought about by everyone obeying the Roman law.

Roman law introduced the concept that the law was above everyone, even the lawmakers. This idea was not totally new as Greek politicians had developed a similar concept with their city states much earlier. The Romans, however, perfected the system, and put it into widespread use. They developed a type of democracy known as the republic. They put in place a complex legal system that required lawmakers, lawyers, and judges. This Roman system of law left a tremendous impact on Western society. Even to this day, much of the Western legal system is still built around the basic Roman code of law.

Western civilization today is filled with references to the Roman Empire. Coins, architecture, and language have Roman roots. Legal and economic theories are so filled with Romanisms that Westerners no longer see them for what they are. They have become so much a part of Western mental furniture that few Westerners question them. As an example, Roman law during the Roman Empire assumed that the individual's rights were granted by the state (by government) and that lawmakers had the right to make up laws. Under Roman law, the state was supreme, and rights were granted or revoked whenever lawmakers decided. This philosophy is sometimes called *'statism.'* Its basic premise is that there is no law higher than the government's law.

Roman politicians were not the first to invent statism, but they did such an effective job of applying it that the Roman Empire has become the guiding star for politicians in the West. Statists see the "pax romana," the period in which Rome dominated the Mediterranean world, as the golden days of statism. The Western world was "unified" and controlled by one large government. This unification was symbolized in Roman times by something known as the fasces. This was a bundle of wooden rods bound together by red-colored bands. In ancient Rome the fasces was fixed to a wooden pole, with an ax at the top or side. This symbolized the unification of the people under a single government. The ax suggested what would happen to anyone who didn't obey the government. The Roman fasces became the origin of the word fascism.

During Roman times, pax romana (the Roman peace) meant, "Do as you are told. Don't make waves, or you will be hauled away in chains." Roman law was supreme. At the same time, there was freedom to act as you wished within the bounds of the law, giving people more freedom than living under the whims of a despot.

Life under a despot, whether king, tribal leader, or dictator was difficult. The word of the ruler was always law; but that law might change. The Babylonians tried to deal with this problem by writing down a code of laws, but in the end, the particular ruler at the time still had power to make and create laws. With the Republic, the Romans elevated the law so that it was above the ruler. Now everyone, even the emperor of Rome, had to obey the law. The law, not the ruler, determined if people were innocent or guilty.

It is interesting to note that as the early church developed and grew, Roman law also had an impact on Christian theology. Since Roman law interpreted everything in terms of right versus wrong, early Christians were deeply influenced by this thinking.

Early Church Theologians

Tertullian, the early church father who first developed systematic theology, was a lawyer steeped in Roman law. Using his understanding of law and the need for justice, guilt, and redemption, he laid the basis for Christian systematic theology as it would develop in the West.

Tertullian was born shortly before 160 AD into the home of a Roman centurion on duty in Carthage. He was trained in both Greek and Latin, and was very much at home in the classics. He became a proficient Roman lawyer, taught public speaking, and practiced law in Rome where he was converted to Christianity. In the years that followed, he became the outstanding apologist of the Western church and the first known author of Christian systematic theology.

Basil the Great was born in 329 AD, and after completing his education in

Athens he went on to practice law and teach rhetoric (the science of arguing the law). In 370 AD, Basil the lawyer became Basil the Bishop when he was elected Bishop of Caesarea. During his time as Bishop he wrote many books in defense of the deity of Christ and of the Holy Spirit. Basil's training in law and rhetoric gave him the tools he needed to speak out in defense of the church.

Next came Augustine who was born in 354 AD into the home of a Roman official in the North African town of Tagaste. He received his early education in the local school where he learned Latin to the accompaniment of many beatings. He hated studying the Greek language so much that he never learned to use it proficiently. He was sent to school in nearby Madaura and from there went to Carthage to study rhetoric, or the art of arguing a legal case. He then taught legal rhetoric in his hometown and Carthage until he went to Milan in 384 AD. He was converted in 386 and became a priest in 391. He returned to Africa and became a prolific writer and bishop. No other Christian after Paul has had such a wide and deep impact on the Christian world through his writings as Augustine has.

Ambrose was born around 340 AD in Gaul. When his father, the prefect of Gaul, died, the family moved to Rome where Ambrose was educated for the legal profession. Later, he was appointed civil governor over a large territory, being headquartered in Milan. Upon the death of the Bishop of Milan in 374, the people unanimously wanted him to take that position. Believing this to be the call of God, he gave up his high political position, distributed his money to the poor, and became a bishop. In 374, Ambrose demonstrated his ability in the fields of church administration, preaching, and theology. But as always, his training in Roman law enforced his views of guilt and righteousness.

Have you noticed the impact that law and lawyers had on the development of the early church as they contextualized the gospel from its original Jewish setting into a Roman one? This legal trend did not stop with the early church.

Reformation Theologians

John Calvin was born in 1505 in north Eastern France where his father was a respected citizen. He studied Humanistic Studies at the University of Paris, and then law at the University of Orleans, and finally at the University of Bourges. Sometime between 1532 and 1533 he converted and adopted the ideas of the Reformation. The writings of John Calvin, lawyer and theologian, have had a tremendous impact on our society.

Calvin was not alone. Arnauld Antoine, the French theologian (1612-1694), studied at Calvi and Lisieux; first law, then theology. He was made a priest and doctor in 1634. Arnauld spoke out against the Jesuits, and his writings added to the impact of the reformation.

There are many more examples of theologians who were also lawyers, or who studied law (such as Martin Luther), but those listed here will have to suffice to point out that legal thought and expression had much to do with the development of the theology of the early Western Church and the Reformation. Each of these church leaders continued to develop the relationship between Christianity, as it was understood in the West, and the legal understanding of guilt, justice, and righteousness. These lawyers were concerned with establishing guilt or innocence, and they brought this emphasis with them into their theology.

In the ensuing years, new nations in the New World would be founded on the theological basis developed by these church leaders. The United States of America was founded on these principles. The American founders attempted to establish a nation built on the Roman principle of a republic, and on the early church's understanding of right and wrong.

Today, it is interesting to notice that there are many non-Western sources who also link guilt-based culture with Christianity. In October 1999, Isaiah Kalinowski, the Opinion Editor for the Jordan Times, wrote an article entitled "*The Shame Culture that is Wabash.*" In this article he pointed out: "... guilt culture is due largely to Christianity. A shame culture is one in which individuals are kept from transgressing the social order by fear of public disgrace. On the other hand, in a guilt culture, one's own moral attitudes and fear of retribution in the distant future are what enforce the ethical behavior of a member of that society."

From Kalinowski's perspective, guilt-based cultures are linked to Christian theology. This is an unfortunate misrepresentation, as the Bible speaks to all cultures and worldviews (as we will see later.) On the other hand, we as Christians must recognize the incredible impact that guilt-based worldview has had on our understanding and interpretation of the Bible in the Christian West.

The Eastern Church

Christianity in the east, however, developed differently. Eastern theologians did not use Roman law as a vehicle for interpreting the Gospel. Rather, the Eastern world was caught up in the shame-honor relationship that was prevalent in societies scattered from the Middle East to the Far East. Eastern Orthodox theology didn't deal directly with sin, guilt, and redemption. They dealt more with the issue of us being able to stand in the presence of God or not, and in our relationship with God and with others around us.

Irenaeus, born around 130 AD, lived during a time of expansion and inner tensions in the church. He mediated between various contending factions that were arising between the Eastern and Western arms of the church. He also spoke out against the Gnostic movement that espoused dualism. In many ways Irenaeus was the first great catholic theologian, the champion of orthodoxy against Gnostic heresy, and a mediating link between Eastern and Western churches. Although he was born in Asia Minor, he spent a great deal of his life as a missionary among the Gauls in Lyons, providing him with a background in both the Western and Eastern parts of the church. In his writings, Irenaeus never speaks about the Gospel in legal terms.

Origen, born around 165 AD, lived during many of the Roman persecutions. He spoke out against the Gnostics, and wrote several works, where he emphasized that man was continually moving forward, drawn by God's love. Salvation to Origen was more than attaining heaven, it was the restoration of all under God.

Athanasius, was born in Alexandria in 297 AD. As the bishop of Alexandria he spoke out against the Arians at the Council of Nicene. Besides his defense of the deity of Christ, he is known for preaching that the main vindication of the faith is seen in its practical results, not just a declaration of faith.

Ephraim of Syria was born in 306 AD in Syria, and is considered as the Prophet of the Syrians by the Syriac Church today. His preaching on judgment helped to evangelize Syria but his writings and homilies emphasized God's mercy and desire to raise his people up.

Chrysostom, the early church theologian for the Eastern Church, was born about 345 AD into a wealthy aristocratic family in Antioch. He was a student of the sophist Libanius who had been a friend of the Emperor Julian. This man gave him a good training in the Greek classics and rhetoric that laid the foundation for his excellent speaking ability. After his baptism in 368, he became a monk in the Eastern churches. Chrysostom rose to being an outstanding preacher, even winning the acclaim of the emperor. Today we have a record of around 680 of Chrystostom's sermons and homilies, and I am told that he never once preached on justification. In the end, he was banished because he spoke out sharply against the views of the Western theologians.

John Wesley was born in England in 1703, and became an Anglican priest in 1728. His contact with Moravian missionaries started him searching for truth outside of the Church of England. He read many of the Eastern Fathers, including Irenaeus, Cyprian, Clement, Macarius of Egypt, Origen, Athanasius, and Ephraim of Syria. These Eastern writers influenced Wesley's theology and preaching, causing him to express his faith in terms wider than the legalistic terms used in the West. In many ways he attempted to harmonize Western and Eastern thought into a synthesis of Christian thought.

Islam

Islam, which rose to prominence around 700 AD, was founded and developed within the shame-based Bedouin worldview of the Arabian desert. Muhammad's message to the Arabs was saturated with concepts drawn from a shame-honor based society. Principle to this was the teaching that God remains over all, and that law is in His hands, not the hands of lawmakers.

The Qur'an demonstrates this principle with the story of Pharaoh and how he was shown Allah's "mightiest miracle" which he denied and thus rebelled. Pharaoh quickly went away and summoned all his men and made to them a proclamation. "I am your supreme Lord." The Qur'an then tells us that Allah 'Smote him' and goes on to warn: 'Surely in this there is a lesson for the God-fearing.'

Therefore it would be unthinkable to a Muslim that a lawmaker could make a law that is over all. This is why Islam presents both a religious and a cultural pattern for people to live by. For Muslims, God dictates both moral and civil laws.

It is interesting to notice that both Islam and Christianity have roots in Middle Eastern shame-based worldviews. Islam, however, struggles to relate to the guilt-based cultures of the world, whereas evangelical Christianity has eventually become almost solely identified with guilt-based cultures. We will examine Islam in much greater detail in future chapters.

Biblical Perspective

It is important to realize that as Christians we must carefully examine our biblical perspectives. Certain passages of Scripture are very meaningful to us because they speak to our own worldview, but they may not be as meaningful to people from other worldviews. Sometimes we assume that because we are Christians, we have a "Christian worldview" rather than realizing that the Bible is speaking to us in whatever worldview we have. It is possible to be an American, hold an American worldview and be a Christian. It is also possible to be an Arab, hold an Arab worldview, and also be a Christian.

When we read our Bibles we should realize that certain parts of the Bible speak to different people because they hold a different worldview. Western Christians often quote John 3:16 as the verse that sums up the Bible, but this is quite a modern trend when considering the writings of the church fathers. Likewise, the problem of suffering (if God is a God of love...) was hardly discussed by anyone two hundred years ago. Similarly, when explaining the Gospel, Westerners often find Paul's letter to the Romans most useful. However, we must think carefully about Paul's intended recipients of the letter. Paul was writing to people living in Rome under Roman law. If Paul contextualized his message to the Greeks at Mars Hill as recorded in Acts 17:16-34, there is no reason to think that he is not contextualizing his message to the Romans who lived under Roman law.

Living in a culture that has been greatly influenced by a guilt-based worldview, Westerners usually find the best biblical explanation of the Gospel in Paul's letter to the Romans. Perhaps this is because the book appeals to our guilt-based mind set. If you read Romans with a shame-honor mind set, you might understand it differently. There is nothing wrong with this. Westerners live under governments patterned after the Roman form of government, so their thinking and theology is very Roman in nature, and it is only natural that they will be drawn to Paul's letter to the Romans to find an explanation of the Gospel that is meaningful to them.

Once when presenting this material, I was asked by an American if I was saying that evangelical theology was wrong. I had to smile at this, as I realized that my listener was trying to fit the material I was presenting on a continuum between right and wrong. It sounded like I was criticizing my own Western Christian heritage and interpretation of the Bible, and thus saying that evangelical theology in the West was wrong. This is not the case. I am merely pointing out that the Bible verses Westerners find meaningful are influenced by their history and worldview.

The danger comes when we Westerners take their Roman understanding of the Gospel and attempt to apply it to those who do not have a Roman-based culture. They fruitlessly spend untold hours and incalculable amounts of energy explaining to someone that he is guilty of sin, and needs to be justified before God. The poor person, on the other hand, may not even have a proper word for sin in his language, and he may even be struggling with the concept of what sin is. He may also struggle to understand guilt and wonder why a person needs justification. This is not simply a blind-spot that people from another culture might have. It is a completely different way of looking at things. If a person regards guilt as something that happens when you are found out, and something that brings shame on his people, then he may happily say he is not guilty. So far he has not been found out, and his family name is still honorable. He may also regard declaring one's guilt as unthinkable, because it affects the honor of others.

When their listeners don't respond appropriately, the Westerner may label them as resistant. He might even feel good about having presented the Gospel, because he is analyzing his efforts by the measuring stick of right and wrong. If he does all the right things in witnessing, and the people listening do not respond, then the listener must be at fault and therefore resistant.

The answer to this dilemma is quite simple. Either we must change our listener's worldview to be more like our own, or we must find a way to communicate the Gospel so that it speaks to the listener's worldview. There are a good number of Western Christian organizations that encourage their missionaries to spend hundreds of hours teaching their listeners so that they can comprehend the Westerner and his worldview and then correctly understand the Gospel as the Westerner understands it. This works fine if the listeners are prepared to sit for long lengths of time under Western teaching. This usually happens in situations where the people consider Western culture to be superior to their own. It seldom happens in situations where the listeners consider their culture to be better than the missionaries.

In the Muslim world, missionaries are fortunate to get a couple of hours with a listener. As a result, we desire to share the Gospel in ways that are immediately relevant to our listeners. In this case, Westerners must put their Roman, guilt-based understanding of the Gospel aside and strive to understand other worldviews and ways of thinking. They need to return to the Bible and discover ways of communicating the Gospel to a mind-set that is not pre-occupied with right and wrong or guilt and innocence. God's grace is equally applicable to every society and every worldview. It is the duty of the cross-cultural communicator to discover exactly how he or she can best communicate the Gospel. We do this so that others can understand God's grace offered to mankind in their own culture and worldview.

The Legal Model of Salvation

Western Christians have perfected the legal view of salvation. In saying this, I am not saying that they have entered into legalism, but rather that they usually express the Gospel message in legal thought and terminology. They talk about guilt and the need for redemption. They talk about breaking God's laws and being under condemnation. These are all legal (and biblical) concepts.

Expressing salvation in legal terminology is okay. It is perfectly acceptable to draw out of Scripture the legal references to salvation and to express God's plan of salvation through them. Not only is it acceptable, it is probably preferred for those who live in a world that functions within legal paradigms.

Western church historians, from Tertullian to today, have worked hard at expressing theological concepts in a way that relates to Western culture. This is important, but the legal view of salvation isn't the only view of salvation.

In the West we have developed a number of popular methods of sharing the Gospel with people from guilt-based cultures. However, since they draw almost exclusively on legal concepts, they are difficult, if not impossible, for those living in a completely shame-based culture to understand.

One of these methods is called The Romans Road. It is based solely on the book of Romans and takes the audience through three short steps, showing them that they are guilty sinners, that God's penalty for sin is death, and that a person can escape God's wrath by saying a simple prayer and believing in his heart.

One of the limitations of this method is that it requires the hearer to have an understanding of the concept of sin and guilt and secondly, that it stops at the cross. There is little in The Romans Road to address the issues and problems that the believer will have after he confesses and believes.

A second popular method is known as The Four Spiritual Laws. Once again, this method of sharing the Gospel is based on a legal interpretation of the Gospel message and works well with people who have an understanding of guilt and innocence. I believe that this plan, like The Romans Road, has severe limitations for hearers in a shame-based culture. It requires an understanding of the concept of sin and guilt, and it fails to address the life of the believer after he confesses and believes.

These explanations of the Gospel seem to work in the West because most people understand that there are higher laws and something called sin. Secondly, most people in Western society live with a certain understanding of guilt, and so these two methods of expressing the Gospel help people deal with their felt sense of guilt.

The Western church has augmented these methods of sharing the Gospel with other avenues of teaching. Because of their simplistic explanation of the Gospel message, they expect that new believers will take discipleship lessons so they can grow spiritually and come into a fuller understanding of what the Gospel is all about and what their simple prayer of accepting Jesus really meant.

Is it any wonder that many Western believers, when following the legal model of salvation, become content with having salvation, and seldom move onto deeper spiritual things? Once they have invested something in the "life-insurance" aspect of salvation, they are content to live their lives in comfort, as their view of salvation demands little else beyond confession of sin and acceptance of a Savior. Those who want more are often disillusioned with such a simplistic view of the Gospel.

Legal Issues

It is interesting to notice that the legal view of salvation spawns legal problems. Many of the issues that Western Christians face today stem from their legal perspective of the Gospel. These issues are then studied and debated in what amounts to "religious courts." These debates require the services of spiritual lawyers and judges to argue the different sides. We often call these spiritual lawyers theologians, and in reality many of them function as lawyers who carefully debate the legal problems that arise from the legal model of salvation.

For instance, if a judge has pardoned you, are you pardoned for the past only or also for the present or even for the future? This legal question, often classified as eternal security, is primarily a legal question that besets those who follow the legal model of salvation. Another question that is asked is: Is it possible to reach a place where you do not continue to break God's law and where you become a "law abiding citizen" in the kingdom of God (sanctification)? This question requires that spiritual lawyers define sin and what it means to digress from God's law. Even the keeping of the Jewish law comes into question. Were the laws in the Old Testament God's eternal laws? If they are God's laws, why don't we follow them today? Did Jesus fulfill all the laws, including the health laws about eating pork meat? Did God's law change?

This is just a sampling of the legal issues that spiritual lawyers spend countless hours and finances on. This action is not necessarily wrong; it is simply the natural outcome of a legal understanding of salvation.

My hope, however, is that Western theologians will also wrestle with the best way to communicate the Gospel to different peoples in different cultures. Some of this is starting to happen as African and Asian theologians are beginning to develop their own expressions of Christian theology. Shame-based cultures and fear-based cultures need other models for understanding salvation than the legal ones we have developed in the west, but we must work together to help balance and check one another, so that extremes can be avoided.

Conclusion

Just as an artist mixes colors of paints, basic worldviews are made up of a mixture of elements. Very few worldviews are made up of purely guilt-based thinking, and many of the classic guilt-based worldviews in existence today are moving away from the influences of guilt and innocence. Some sociologists describe these Western worldviews as being post-guilt or post-modern.

In the next chapter we want to explore the second primary common-ancestral worldview, that of fear. Once again there are few purely fear-based cultures in existence today. As the world becomes more global, the purely fear-based cultures are giving way to a more mixed variety. Nevertheless, by looking briefly at fear-based worldviews, we can begin to recognize them when they are mixed in with guilt or shame.

Questions for Reflection or Discussion

1. What did you learn from this chapter about the impact of Roman thought on our modern world?

2. Before reading this chapter, had you ever considered the impact that worldview had on the writers of early church theology?

3. Do you think that worldview also had an impact on the writers of scripture?

4. How many different worldview/cultures can you think of that affected the writers of scripture?

5. Have you been influenced more by Western or Eastern theologians (or African or Asian. etc.)?

6. Do you think that guilt-based cultures have come into being because of Christianity, or has Christianity penetrated guilt-based cultures?

7. What do you think about references to a Christian or Biblical worldview? What is meant by these terms? What is a Christian or a Biblical worldview? How is it different from the worldview held by others? Is it possible to hold an Asian or African worldview and be a follower of Jesus?

8. What do you think is the meaning of the term "resistant people?" How might they be resistant? What would cause this resistance?

9. Think through a simple gospel presentation as is typically given in the west. What terms and concepts do Western missionaries use that may not be clearly found in scripture? Is there a better way to express salvation?

10. What is the difference between sin and guilt? Can you express a salvation message without using the terms guilt, redemption and justification? These are all legal terms that may not be understood by your target people. How might you express the gospel in other ways?

11. For further study: check out some missiological journals to learn more about African Theology, Asian Theology and South American Theologies. What are these people trying to express that they feel is lacking in our North American theology?

Chapter Fifteen
Fear-Based Worldviews

As the missionaries drew near to the village, the sound of drums could be heard. Drawing closer, they could see a large group of painted people dancing and writhing. A man approached the missionaries and explained that they could not go further. The village was doing a sacred rite to improve the economy and bring more trade to the area. The missionaries were escorted away and not given an opportunity to share their Gospel presentation. Later the missionaries heard that a human sacrifice had been offered to the spirits that day.

In another situation missionaries arrived in a village when a rain-making ceremony was about to begin. They were invited to watch. A black bull was led to the edge of the village where it faced the direction from where the rain would come. The animal's throat was cut and it fell over on its left side, to the delight of all. This indicated that the sacrifice was acceptable. The men then cut up the meat and cooked it. As the meat was cooking, an old man began to shout out a prayer to the spirits for rain. Soon everyone joined in. After the meat was eaten, the shouting turned into dancing. The villagers danced all afternoon until the rain came. It rained so heavily that everyone had to run for shelter. Did the rituals bring the rain? To the natives, this was the obvious conclusion, and there was no way that the missionaries could convince them otherwise.

As these two stories illustrate, there are many people in the world today whose lives revolve around interaction with the spirit world. They believe that gods and spirits exist in the universe, and they must live in peace with these unseen powers either by living quietly, or by appeasing these powers.

Much of the missionary effort during this last century has been directed at reaching people who lived in areas of the world where elements of fear-based worldviews were strong. As missionaries entered the jungles of Africa, South America, and other places such as Borneo they were faced with people whose worldview had strong elements of fear. While beliefs varied from place to place and culture to culture, the underlying principles were the same, the universe was filled with things that brought fear, and one of man's chief goals was to find sources and methods of power to overcome or appease the object of fear.

Based on their worldview, these people viewed the universe as a place filled with gods, demons, spirits, ghosts, and ancestors. Since man needs to live at peace with the powers around him, he often lives in fear of disrupting that peace and bringing the wrath of some power against him.

This fear could be based on a number of different things. Foremost it may be man's fear of man. In the jungle, tribal wars are endemic, with captives becoming slaves or, sometimes, a meal for cannibals. Whenever these tribes encountered people from outside of their own group, they approached them with suspicion and fear. This fear of man can also be found in what we consider more advanced societies. It may be based on fear of a dictator, or even the fear of a ruling class of people.

A second factor is often fear of the supernatural. All around us events are taking place that might be seen as the supernatural world interacting with ours. If crops fail, then specific gods, demons or other forces are seen as responsible. If sickness comes, then other gods, demons or other forces are responsible. If a tribe fails in battle, it is because of the activity of a god or demon. Sickness is often viewed as a god reaping revenge. Everything in life, even romance, is somehow attributed to the activities of gods, demons or other forces.

The very fact that we have a word such as 'supernatural' should alert us to the fact that we have a particular worldview based on the natural laws of nature. Since Newton's formulation of this theory, most Westerners have become so used to thinking in terms of natural cause and effect that we cannot imagine what it is like to live with a worldview that rules nothing out, and in which nothing is truly predictable. We bring this Newtonistic view into Christianity, and try and explain everything in life based on immutable laws. Thus we struggle to understand people who live in an open universe not controlled by comprehensible laws. For the animist, there is no clear distinction between the natural and supernatural. While we think in terms of science and psychology, the animist thinks in terms of the forces that affect their lives.

The struggle that these people face is simply one of needing power. Using their voodoo, charms, and other methods they seek to gain control over other people and over the controlling powers of the universe. The paradigm that these people live in is one of fear versus power. Everything is expressed in these terms, including moral issue which are expressed and enforced in terms of power.

fear .... power

At the end of the 19th century, E. B. Tylor attempted to understand the difference in thinking between Europeans and peoples living in Africa and South America. In his writings he coined the word 'animism' from the Latin word anima for 'soul.' He saw the animistic worldview as interpreting everything from a spiritual philosophy rather than a materialistic philosophy. Many sociologists of Tylor's era saw mankind moving from an ancient worldview based on the supernatural to a modern worldview based on science and reality.

Dave Burnett states in his book *Unearthly Powers*, that H. W. Turner later advocated the use of the term primal religion, meaning that "these religions both anteceded the great historic religions and continue to reveal many of the basic or primary features of religion." This is a commonly held theory in many academic settings, although from the Bible we know that monotheism predated primary religions (Romans 1:18-23, and Genesis 3-6). Almost everywhere you find animists or primal religions you find people living under the influence of a fear-power thought.

Burnett goes on to state, "Power can be understood in many ways: physical, political, economic, social, and religious. The secular worldview tends to regard all power as originating from within the material world ... in contrast, primal worldviews see such powers not only as being real within the empirical world but as having their primary origin outside the visible world."

In this way, those whose lives operate in the fear-power paradigm often see themselves living in a physical world that coexists and is influenced by unseen powers. These powers may be present in people or animals, or even in inanimate objects like trees or hills. In some cultures, powers may be perceived in personal terms such as we would use for living beings. These powers are often regarded as having their own particular character, feeling, and ability to relate to others, and often even have a will of their own. Like people, they may be angered, placated, or turned to in time of need.

Power is an important concept in fear-based cultures. In the Pacific Islands it is sometimes called *mana*, while the Iroquois of North America called it *orenda*, which particularly refers to the mystic power derived from a chant. The Inuit (Eskimos) have the notion of *sila*, a force watching and controlling everything. The Chinese have the concept of *fung shui* or the powers within the earth and sea. In folk Islam the term *baraka* (blessing) can embrace some of these concepts.

In most fear-power worldviews the main way of dealing with a power is to establish rules to protect the unwary from harm and procedures to appease those powers that are offended. These rules and procedures are generally referred to as taboos. Taboos have to do with special people, forbidden or unclean foods, sacred objects, special acts or rituals, and special names. Appeasements are usually made in the form of sacrifice or dedication to the invisible powers.

In order to deal with these powers, rituals are established which people believe will affect the powers around them. Rituals are performed on certain calendar dates, at certain times in someone's life (rites of passage), or in a time of crisis.

In order to appease the powers of the universe, systems of appeasement are worked out. They vary from place to place. Some civilizations offer incense while others offer a chicken or even their children as sacrifices. However it is done, a system of appeasement based on fear is the norm for their worldview.

Wherever this system of appeasement comes into being, religious persons come to the forefront to control these systems. They are known as priests, witch doctors, shamans, or gifted people. Whatever their title, their role is the same. They are the ones who hold power. Often they are the only ones who understand the needs of the gods or demons, and they are the ones through whom the demons or gods communicate.

In every fear-based worldview, the pattern is much the same. The witch doctor, priest, or shaman controls people through the use of fear. They are very effective in their roles, and as a result, whole cultures and people groups are held in their iron grip.

As missionaries have entered these areas, they have often found themselves involved in a power struggle. Shamans, priests, and witch doctors hold considerable spiritual power. It is real power, backed by the satanic world. Satan and his hosts are determined to keep fear-based cultures in their grip. In almost every case, a power struggle develops when missionaries confront fear-based worldviews.

In the past, many missionary have avoided power confrontations and have opted to preach a guilt-based Gospel message. In most of these worldviews there is some understanding of guilt, and so some people have responded to the Gospel. Often that response also includes an invitation to a better economic lifestyle, better education, or health care. In many African nations, there is only a small mix of guilt in people's worldview, and thus Christianity has impacted only a small part of the lives of those who follow Christ. One missionary described it this way: he said. "Christianity is very widespread, but only an inch deep." This is a typical situation that arises when people respond to only one aspect of the Gospel, in this case the guilt aspect of the Gospel.

Today Christian missionaries are learning to share the Gospel in ways that make sense to those living in a fear-power based worldview. Missionaries are sharing stories from the Bible and are bringing people to the conclusion that the power available through Christ is greater than the powers of darkness. Missionaries are sharing from God's Word, demonstrating God's power, and living out their Christian lives for all to see. As they have boldly preached and confronted the powers of the enemy, people in these cultures have begun turning from darkness to light.

As a result, today in Africa, South America, and East Asia there are large numbers of people who have come to Christ from fear-based worldview backgrounds. However, as many African worldviews have a strong mix of honor and shame, the Gospel is still not addressing all of the areas of people's lives.

Fear-based cultures are not limited to the animistic areas of the world. As I have presented seminars in many countries, a number of listeners have responded enthusiastically to this part of my presentation. They have admitted that even though they were raised in a Western culture, their coming to Christ had more to do with the fear-power paradigm than guilt and innocence. In our world today, many children grow up in an atmosphere of fear. A drunken father or an abusive parent causes them to live in great fear. One man told me that as a child he went to bed every night afraid for his life. His father used power and fear to control the home and would often come home drunk and beat his wife and kids. As a result, this man found that he did not so much relate to the guilt-innocence message of Christians but rather to Christ's work on the cross to deal with our fear. In this way, Christians have found that they can relate to those from abusive backgrounds or even those who have lived under the fear-power paradigm of communism.

Conclusion

From the Garden of Eden, we see that the influence of sin brought more than guilt upon mankind. It also brought fear. This fear is very real to many people in the world today. Some worldviews can be described as being almost totally fear-based.

Other worldviews mix aspects of a fear-based worldview with the other common-ancestral worldviews: guilt and shame. Some elements of fear-based worldview are even present in today's Western world where people live in an atmosphere of fear. It may be from an abusive parent or as a result of consulting psychics and dabbling in the occult. Many Westerners are very uncomfortable with breaking a mirror or observing a black cat crossing their path. To some people these are very serious events, while others laugh them off. While it may be unimportant to some, fear and power are fundamental to many people's worldview. They may live in fear of terrorists or local criminals. They may barricade themselves in their homes behind multiple locks, and keep guns or batons close at hand. While this may be necessary to live in their location, we as Christians have a duty to share the love and grace available through Christ in such a way that people in a fear based worldview can clearly understand them.

A missionary to Russia shared with me his concern for the Russian people. Back in history they lived with a strong mix of fear of the Tsar. This was replaced by a fear of the communists. Today they live with a fear of organized crime in Russia. While the exterior circumstances may change, their basic worldview remains the same. Wherever we serve, missionaries must be aware of the fear-power worldview and be prepared to share a gospel message that not only speaks of our guilt, but also addresses people's needs, as they live in a worldview with a strong mix of fear.

Questions for Reflection or Discussion

1. Most fear-based worldviews deal with gods, demons, spirits, ghosts, and ancestors. List some ways that a fear-based worldview has invaded Western society?
2. Is there an aspect of fear-based worldview among the people you are ministering to? How is it expressed in their culture and actions?
3. An aspect of fear-based worldviews is fear of other people. How is this demonstrated in the culture around you?
4. Fear-based worldviews often give way to fatalism or fanaticism. If something fails it is because the spirit world is against you, or it is because you did not work hard enough at pleasing them. Is this expressed in any way in your target culture?
5. What do people do to gain power over the things that bring fear into their lives? Is there a way that Christ answers or fulfills this?
6. What is the difference between the "fear of the Lord" and the fear in a fear-based worldview?

Chapter Sixteen
Shame-Based Worldviews

The missionary's taxi screeched to a halt. Lying in the middle of the street was a teen-age girl, dying. She had been shot in the head four times. Just then her brother walked across the street with two policemen and stated, "There she is. I killed her, because she was in an immoral situation with a man." Under the laws of the country, the young man was innocent. He had not committed murder but had preserved the honor of his family.

In another case, a girl ran away from home. Later her family learned she had married someone from another religion. They were furious. The police imprisoned the girl so that she would be protected from her family. Elderly grandmothers taunted the brother and father. "How long do we need to keep our heads to the ground in shame? Won't you do something to cleanse the shame from our tribe so we can raise our heads and live in honor once again?" The family finally agreed to pay the police a $50,000.00 guarantee that they would not hurt her and she was released into their custody. Within hours her father and brother shot her thirteen times. The entire family was pleased that honor had been restored.

When faced with such situations, many Western missionaries are exasperated. The people they are ministering to seem to have no sense of right and wrong. Murdering your own child seems incomprehensible to them. They fail to realize that ignoring the scandalous behavior of an immoral or defiant daughter is likewise incomprehensible to those in a shame-based worldview. The Western missionary may feel totally defeated if people don't feel they have broken God's law and thus do not feel any need for salvation or a savior. Christ's death on the cross seems futile and meaningless. The Western evangelist, locked into his legal model of salvation, seems powerless to explain adequately the Gospel so that people like this will respond.

For many years, I was one of those missionaries. The guilt-innocence perspective lictated much of my thinking and actions. However, I soon discovered that not everyone in the world operates within this paradigm. As I mentioned earlier, while living in the Middle East I noticed that when the lifeguard at a swimming pool blew his whistle, the Westerners all stopped to see who was guilty, but others kept right on swimming.

As I observed this and other phenomena, I began to realize that Middle Easterners and Middle Eastern society were operating in an entirely different dimension. Guilt did not have the same power and influence as it did in the West. While they were aware of guilt, it didn't have the same strong connotations for them as it had for me.

If a policeman pulled me over, I would immediately feel guilty, thinking that perhaps I had done something wrong. But when my Middle Eastern friends were pulled over, they didn't display any sign of guilt. They talked boldly to the policeman, and even argued loudly with him over the issues at hand.

It was only after many years of living in a Muslim culture that it started to dawn on me that people around me were not thinking in terms of guilt versus innocence. Nor were they operating in a fear versus power paradigm of which I had heard much from missionaries living in Africa. These concepts didn't seem to apply very much to the Arabs of the Levant (Jordan, Syria, Lebanon, Palestine). Rather, I discovered that these Arabs were living with a worldview where the dominant paradigm was shame versus honor.

shame .... honor

Once I recognized this, I began to explore this concept and tried to verify it on all social levels. I was amazed to discover what I found. When a young Christian lady who was very active in the church was asked why she was so dedicated, she said that she felt that God would shame her in front of people on the Judgment Day, so she worked hard in the church. I was appalled at first, until I recognized this same motivating factor at work in many situations.

When I would visit my friends, I would try to act correctly, and they would try to act honorably, not shamefully. I was busy trying to learn the rights and wrongs of their culture and explain these to new missionaries arriving on the field. But somehow my framework of right versus wrong didn't fit what was actually happening. The secret wasn't to act rightly or wrongly in their culture. It wasn't that there was a right way and a wrong way of doing things. The underlying principle was that there were honorable and dishonorable ways of doing things.

Every part of the Muslim culture I lived in was based on honor and shame. When I visited my friends I could honor them in the way I acted. They could honor me in the way they acted. Three cups of coffee bestowed honor on me. The first, called *salaam* (peace) was followed by *sadaqa* (friendship), and the third cup of coffee was called *issayf* (the sword). The meaning was clear in their culture. When I arrived I was offered a cup of coffee that represented peace between us. As we drank and talked, the cup of friendship was offered. The last cup, the sword, illustrated their willingness to protect me and stand by me. It didn't matter if I was right or wrong, they were bound by their honor to protect me.

Everywhere I moved in the Middle Eastern culture there were things that pointed to honor or shame. What chair I chose to sit in, who entered the door first, the way I expressed myself in Arabic, the very way I walked and held myself, all communicated to others around me 'my place' in the world. The cultures of the Middle East are filled with thousands of tiny nuances that communicate messages about shame and honor.

Shame is a popular topic today in Western society. Shame for us, however, is closely identified with a lack of self-esteem or feelings of guilt. For us, shame often stems from some form of abuse resulting in people, especially children who are violated, failing to learn trust.

This is quite different from the shame-based societies of the east where shame and fear of shame are used as controlling forces in people's lives (rather than right and wrong being used as a controlling factor.)

As parents, we teach our children to act rightly. If they don't, we teach them that feelings of guilt are the proper response. In a shame-based culture however, children are taught to act honorably, and if they don't, feelings of shame are the proper response. But it goes farther than just feelings. Shame and honor are positions in society, just as being right and justified is a position in our Western culture.

In the West, young people are free to act as spontaneously as they want, as long as they are within the framework of right and wrong. They can be loud, boisterous and happy as long as they don't break things or abuse others. The rule in the West is "As long as you don't hurt someone else or their property, you are generally OK."

Young people in a Muslim setting are different. Wherever they go, they represent their families and tribes. Young people are not free to act as they want. They must always act honorably so that the honor of their family and tribe is upheld. If they damage someone else's property, it is bad because it brings shame on their own people, not primarily because it offends the victim. If no one knows who did it, there is no shame, or feeling of guilt. They feel guilt for bringing shame on their own people, but not for offending a third party.

So when shameful acts are discovered the family or tribe will react. Shameful deeds are first covered up, then denied. If they can't be covered up, they are avenged. It is the unwritten rule of the desert. The whole concept of a shame controlling society can be traced back to the early pre-Islamic and Nabataean culture which existed in Arabia long before Islam arrived. (Nabaioth was the eldest son of Ishmael. See the Internet site: http://nabataea.net for more information on the Nabataean people.) This shame-based code of conduct, still much in existence today, affects not only the way individuals act, but also the actions of entire nations.

As I have visited with missionaries and nationals from non-Western countries, I have explored the concept of honor and shame in these other countries. It has helped me understand and communicate with people from Afghanistan, Pakistan, India, China, Japan, and Korea.

In fact, I have discovered that the concept of shame and honor makes a great discussion topic. I often ask people from shame-based cultures what things they consider to be honorable or shameful, and how does one tell if someone else is honorable. The discussion that follows is often highly stimulating, and usually reflects or contrasts similar attitudes right across the shame-based cultures of the world.

As an example, one Korean missionary mentioned that older Korean men were very quiet while their wives were the ones who usually talked. He explained to us that in Korea, men were taught to be quiet. I then entered the discussion and brought up the topic of acting honorably. The Korean man brightened considerably and began to explain how Korean men are taught to act honorably. One of the signs of honor is to hold off speaking until you have something wise to say.

He concluded that Korean women were freer to speak and thus they were the ones who spoke out, not their husbands. As a result, Korean women are the ones who usually learn foreign languages better. However, younger Korean men are usually less inhibited by the old honor code, and many are participating in open discussion much more freely.

A few weeks later I spoke with a medical doctor from Iraq and told her what I had learned from the Koreans. She immediately responded that in the older Iraqi culture this is true as well, especially among the older men. Honor is demonstrated by silence or by speaking only wise and careful things. Often the speech of wise people is full of proverbs and parables. The more proverbs a person knows, the wiser he appears in the eyes of others.

In some cases there are distinct differences between cultures. As I mentioned earlier, if someone is badly shamed in an Arab culture and the shame cannot be hidden or denied, then it is avenged, and the person responsible for the shaming is killed, or a payment of money is negotiated. In many Far-Eastern cultures, if a shame cannot be hidden or denied, the way out is suicide. While there are differences, there are also similarities. I have heard of a number of students in Jordan committing suicide because of their poor school marks, just as happens in Japan.

In order for shame-based cultures to work, shame and honor are usually attached to something greater than the individual. Honor is almost always centered around a group. This can be the immediate family, the extended tribe, or in some cases, as large as an entire nation, as was demonstrated in Japan during World War II.

In most Middle Eastern cultures, honor is wrapped up with one's tribe. Everyone grows up within a tribal concept. If someone is from the Beni Hassan tribe, he or she thinks, acts, and dresses as a Beni Hassan. Every action reflects on the honor of the Beni Hassan tribe. If tribal members act honorably, the Beni Hassan tribe is honored. If they act shamefully, the whole tribe is shamed. If the act is vile enough, such as rejecting their religion, or if a girl becomes pregnant out of wedlock, the Beni Hassan tribe will react and execute the offender, even though he or she is a member of their own tribe, and perhaps even their immediate family. Thus the shame is removed and the honor of the tribe is restored.

Many years ago an Arab soldier's gun accidentally discharged and killed his companion in the army. After serving seven years, he was released on condition that he leave his country as the dead soldiers family threatened him, wanting revenge for their son's death (the eye for an eye, tooth for a tooth, blood for blood principle). He lived for nearly twenty years in the West but one day decided to return to see his family. When it was learned that he had returned, several young people from the dead soldier's family, some of whom had not been born at the time of the killing, surrounded the house where he was and riddled his body with bullets. Their family honor was restored, and the shame removed.

If someone shames another tribe, tribal warfare could result, and often only the skillful intervention of a third party ends the strife. Arab lore is full of stories of how wise and skillful men have mediated in difficult situations. In fact, many national rulers gain their fame and reputation from their skills at ending tribal strife.

In the Middle East two methods are recognized. First, a skillful ruler, through diplomatic efforts and displays of great wisdom, can end disputes. Solomon's dealings with the two mothers who claimed the same baby displayed the kind of wisdom that Arabs appreciate and desire in their rulers. The second kind of ruler crushes all of the tribes and by force makes them submit to himself. Peace may then rule, but once the controlling power is removed, old animosities return. This was illustrated in the Balkans conflict where the domination of communism brought about a measure of peace. Once freedom returned, however, old conflicts and animosities flared again.

The storytellers who frequent the coffeehouses of the Middle East excel in telling stories of both kinds of rulers and heroes, especially heroes who can effectively deal with shame and restore honor. This is very different from the entertainment styles of the West where the hero determines who is guilty, punishes him, and right and goodness are restored. This is because in the Western worldview, people try to hang onto the concept that "in the midst of a crooked and perverse world, right still reigns and has the upper hand." Those from shame-based worldview, on the other hand, cling to the idea of maintaining honor in the midst of a shameful and alienated world.

For many Western people it is very hard, if not impossible, to try and comprehend a worldview that is based on shame, not right versus wrong. In the first section of this book, I gave a number of examples of how this affects the Muslim cultures of the Middle East. I would like to add the illustration of *telling the truth*.

In most Western cultures, telling the truth is right and telling lies is wrong. In the Middle East, people don't think of lies as being 'right' or 'wrong.' The question is, "Is what is being said honorable?" If a lie protects the honor of a tribe or nation, then it is fine. If a lie is told for purely selfish reasons, then it is shameful.

Thus, in the West we debate ethics by trying to determine if things are right or wrong. In the East, they debate ethics by trying to determine if things are honorable or shameful.

Shame in Western Culture

In the past, shame has played a role in Western culture. One has only to read Tolstoy's *Anna Karenina*, or any of Shakespeare's works to see the role that shame used to play. Shakespeare uses the word shame nine times as often as he does guilt.

In the Western evangelical world, old Christian songs mention Christ's death on the cross for our "sin and shame," while many songs written during the twentieth century mention only our "sin and guilt."

Why is this? I suspect that the popularity of Freud's teachings is one reason. Sociologists generally credit Freudian psychology for the removal of guilt from Western culture. Since his teachings have become popular, in many universities, the concept of guilt has become unpopular and guilt has been assigned to others, such as our parents. Other factors, like the lack of responsibility within modern politics, have influenced young people today. Nixon and Watergate and then Clinton and Lewinsky have illustrated to people today that "right versus wrong" is not the only way to think.

During the period of 1960 to 2000 Western civilization has begun a slow but steady shift away from the "right versus wrong" paradigm. Today, young people are very reluctant to label anything as right or wrong. Instead, things are assigned the label "cool." In the eyes of many high school students, being cool is equivalent to being honorable. Those who are not cool are assigned terms such as "loser" or "nerd." Being not cool is the equivalent of living in shame. Many young people choose their actions on the basis of honor and shame rather than on the basis of right versus wrong. I believe that this slow shift in worldview is responsible for many of the differences between Boosters, Boomers, Busters, and Generation X'rs, and is also at the root of post-modern thinking that is growing in the Western world.

Shaming in History

While the Romans developed a legal system and made it universally applicable throughout their empire, they were still sensitive to the feeling of shame.

In republican Rome, criminals had the doors to their houses burned as a public sign that a criminal was living there. Those who had been wronged could legally follow the criminal around, chanting and accusing him in public places.

The concept of public shaming carried on into the Middle Ages, and even into Victorian England where criminals were put into stocks. These stocks were located in public places so that the criminal would be known and shamed before all. Pillories were rife during the Victorian Age when those who were pilloried had to endure the shame of publicly having rotten vegetables thrown at them. Branding criminals was practiced in England until the eighteenth century. Brands were often placed on the hands or face so that the criminals would be publicly shamed wherever they went.

The major difference between East and West is not the presence of the shame concept. In Rome and Medieval Europe shame was used in the legal process as a way of punishment. This is not the same as having a shame-honor mind-set. In the East shame rests on a person's group rather than the individual. Since many Eastern societies function in a group setting, the whole group rather than an individual suffers. If the crime is bad enough, the group itself may oust or, for a severe offense, kill the offender.

In 1999 at least twenty-five women were killed to maintain the honor of their families in the country of Jordan. Many others were killed in countries like Egypt, Sudan, Syria, and Iran. On the positive side, prostitutes do not walk the streets of these countries, and most girls prefer to wait for marriage and restrict their sexual activities to within their marriage.

In many countries where shame-based culture is predominant, the names of criminals and those disowned by their families for shameful activities are publicly printed in the newspapers. In Western countries we tend to isolate criminals from their surroundings and then determine if they are guilty. Criminals are then locked away out of sight, rather than publicly shamed in stocks in the public square.

It's interesting to notice that in the Crow First Nations culture (North American Indian culture), mocking of someone else's inappropriate behavior relates to shaming. This is sometimes called "*buying-of-the-ways*". If you imitate someone else's inappropriate behavior, you are "*buying his ways.*" In some cases a person actually offers money to buy someone else's inappropriate behavior. This points out someone else's inappropriate behavior and brings shame upon them in an acceptable way to the rest of the tribe. In other words it is an accepted way of mocking shameful behavior.

In many shame-based cultures, rather than encourage, people criticize and question others. This is seen as positive, as it keeps them from becoming too proud.

Ken Guenther, in his paper *Pain in a Shame Culture, Help for the Filipino Pastor*, (a 1997 research paper for Dr. James Houston, Regent College) states, "Because the pastor may be perceived as distant, his motives may be questioned, which is the most painful form of shame for the Filipino. Once the leader is seen to be going too far in his exercise of authority or to be too ambitious or proud, he is put down through the moral mechanism of shaming. The widely recognized "crab mentality" of Filipino culture is an illustration of this mechanism.... In a shame culture, however, mere success is not sufficient (it is not enough, for example, to know in your own mind that you are the best); public acknowledgment of one's superiority is essential."

In the same way, Arabs are often quick to criticize leaders and pastors if they perceive that they are too ambitious or proud. They are sometimes publicly questioned or shamed, and often they leave the ministry. If we do not like a pastor in the West, we usually quibble with his theology, and say he is not quite sound or we attack scholarship, or morals. We use different tactics because we live with a different worldview which demands different justifications. In the Middle East, new language students often experience that their neighbors are quick to point out that someone else speaks better than they do, or they are asked why they speak so poorly after being there for "a whole four months"! This criticism is often meant to keep them from being proud of how well they have done. Arabs understand that the criticism may be a compliment, but the poor Westerner is often crushed.

Conclusion

While all worldviews have certain elements of shame, there are worldviews that are primarily built on the element of shame versus honor. Just as guilt, fear and shame came upon mankind in the Garden of Eden; guilt, shame, and fear exist in all worldviews today. What makes a shame-based worldview unique is that its people have a much greater mix of shame and honor in their worldview than guilt and righteousness or fear and power.

The question that we as Christians must ask then is: What does the Bible say about all of this? Does the Bible have a clear message of God's grace that can be expressed with shame and honor terminology rather than with legal terminology? I strongly believe it does, and this is what we will look into in the next chapter.

Questions for Reflection or Discussion

1 .Have you been raised to think that, "It doesn't matter what people think, it only matters if it is right or wrong?" If so, how has this chapter challenged you? If you were not raised this way, how would you answer someone who applies this rule to most everything?

2. How do you think a Western concept of shame differs from an Eastern concept of shame?

3. Do you think people in your target group are bound more by religion or by culture? Why?

4. What happens in your culture when someone is badly shamed? Perhaps they fail

146

a test, or perhaps they fail society. How do they and others respond?

5. If there is a measure of honor in your target culture, what does it center around? Eg. individuals, families, tribes, religion, nation, gender, politics?

6. In your target culture, if someone is in a place of dishonor, how can their shame be removed and honor restored? Give examples.

7. What sort of heroes are upheld by your target culture? Do they defend right, provide power, or restore honor? Give examples from famous stories and also modern entertainment.

8. Do people tell lies in your target culture? In what situations would lying be OK and in what situations is it frowned on?

9. Have you noticed honor and shame issues in the West? What are they and how are they expressed?

10. How are people publicly shamed for their bad behavior in your target culture? Are new Christians treated in a similar way? Why or why not?

Assessing Worldview

Use the following table of decision making issues to help determine worldview makeup. Remember that there are no right answers and no better answers. For each decision assess how much guilt, shame or fear thinking went into (or will go into) making the decision. The answers for each decision should add up to 10. For instance, a decision not to rob when money is need might be based on guilt/innocence - 7, shame/honor - 2, fear/power - 1. The total must equal 10.

Guilt-Innocence: Decision made on basis of right and wrong, or what felt right or seemed good. The decision may also be made on the basis of not wanting to do the wrong thing.

Shame-Honor: Decision made on the basis of building or protecting the honor of self, family or group, or avoiding shame to self, family or group. Decision was made with others in mind, and what they would think.

Fear-Power: Decision made on the basis of fear, or finding a way to overcome things you were afraid of. For example, perhaps you pursued a specific career because of fear of financial failure.

Add up the totals in each column. They should equal 100 when combined. The totals of each column represent the percentage of guilt, shame, and fear in the worldview being assessed.

Assessing Worldview

Major Life Decision	G/I	S/H	F/P
Which school to go to			
What subject to major in			
What career to pursue			
Decision not to rob when money is needed			
Person to marry			
What to spend on			
Where to live			
Car to drive			
How/where to educate kids			
What to do with elderly parents			

Totals

G/I - Individual decision of what is best for self (Eg. Choice pleases you not your parents)
H/S - Decision included others, what they think is best (Eg. Choice pleases parents not you)
F/P - Decision because of outside factors, not about wants. (Eg. Choice because of fear of economic factors)

The above assessment form is only an approximation and is not intended to be a professional tool for analyzing worldviews.

Chapter Seventeen
Honor and Shame in the Bible

Mohammed worked for the Ministry of Information at our local post office in Jordan. His job was to read mail that came in and out of the country. After a while, he discovered that the mail that came to my post box was rather interesting and he put into motion a plan to meet the owner of the post box. One night he offered to relieve the guard at the post office door, and that evening he saw me take mail from my post box. The next day I returned, and Mohammed made his move. He approached me and asked me questions about quotations he had read in my mail. He wanted to know who Isaiah was. I explained that he was one of the prophets. Mohammed was surprised. He thought that all the writings of the prophets had been lost. It wasn't long before a friendship developed between us, and Mohammed was reading a copy of the Bible.

One night Mohammed arrived at my house, obviously agitated. After the traditional cup of tea, Mohammed closed the windows to my living room, and sat close beside me, speaking almost in a whisper. He was afraid and said that the "walls may have ears." As we huddled together he explained that he had a problem with a Bible passage. His reading of the Bible had progressed smoothly until he had arrived at I Samuel 2:8. It was Hannah's song of praise to God for giving her baby Samuel. When Mohammed arrived at verse 8, he found something that he couldn't cope with. Hannah said "He (God) raises the poor from the dust and lifts up the beggars from the dung hill; He seats them with princes and has them inherit a throne of honor" (rendered from the Arabic Bible).

Mohammed threw the Bible down on the coffee table. "No," he said emphatically. "This cannot be true. A beggar is a beggar, a prince is a prince. This is garbage."

As I stared at Mohammed's face, I suddenly saw a truth I had never seen before. This wasn't garbage; this was the Gospel. I Samuel 2:8 described the Gospel in the terms of God taking us from the shame of sin and raising us to being joint heirs with Christ. I was only 22 years of age at the time and just beginning my ministry in the Middle East, but God used this incident to start me down the path of understanding His plan for mankind in the area of shame and honor.

Today Western culture has lost most of its understanding of shame and honor, but the Bible is filled with it. The Bible begins with man's fall into shame and ends with man being anointed with glory and honor at God's right hand.

All through the Bible, references are made to shame and honor in various forms. The Bible tells us to honor God, our parents, elders, Christian leaders, and government leaders. It even talks about certain things being more honorable than others. In all, there are more than 190 references to honor in the Bible, while the various forms of the word 'guilt' are mentioned only forty times, and only seven of these are in the New Testament.

The Bible also addresses shame, mentioning it over one hundred times, but simply counting the word 'shame' is not enough. There are many underlying principles in the Bible that deal with shame and honor, and these demonstrate how God moves us from a position of shame to that of honor. The whole point of mentioning these numbers is simply to illustrate that shame and honor hold a place in the Bible alongside teachings about guilt and righteousness.

The main reason God allowed His people to fall into slavery in Egypt was to demonstrate to all the people of the world with a shame-based worldview that Jehovah God could raise his people from a position of shame in Egypt to one of honor among the nations. Leviticus 26:13 states, "I am the Lord your God, who brought you out of Egypt so that you would no longer be slaves to the Egyptians; I broke the bars of your yoke and enabled you to walk with heads held high."

This is the overall message of the Bible. It is not just the story of God redeeming His people (a legal thought), but it is also the story of God raising his people from a position of shame to the ultimately honorable position of joint-heirs with Christ.

In the following pages, I have outlined a series of topics from the Scriptures that teach us how God is moving us from a position of shame to that of honor. The position of shame is described in the Bible in a series of ways: disgraced, defiled, naked, sick, poor, accursed, ignorant and so on. Each of these topics is a powerful illustration of God's desire and power to move us from shame to honor. The bible is rich with illustrations, typologies and teachings that speak clearly to those with a strong mix of shame and honor in their worldview.

Almost everyone in a shame-based culture knows of someone who is acting more honorably than he or she really is. People laugh at them behind their backs. At one time, I was told by friends that an acquaintance of mine wasn't as big a man as he made himself out to be. He drove a Mercedes car, dressed in fine suits, and had four boys. He walked the streets very piously and in an honorable fashion, but everyone knew he was just a little man, holding a minor government position and had no special position in his tribe. He was not the big man he made himself out to be.

And so it is that we come to the message of grace in the Bible. God is the one who can elevate people from a position of shame to that of honor. No one can elevate himself. This is the unwritten rule of the East. Everyone knows their place, and must stay in it. The message of the Gospel is that God has the power and the desire to elevate man from his lowly position to a place of great honor. "See, I lay a stone in Zion, a chosen and precious cornerstone, and the one who trusts in Him will never be put to shame" (I Peter 2:6).

Each of the topics mentioned below illustrates this point and has numerous Biblical references which are relevant. These topics make great conversation starters, Bible study material, or even sermon outlines. They are the kind of thing that those ministering to people from shame-based cultures must be well versed in.

God moves us from being defiled to being cleansed

Many Eastern religions concentrate on ritual washings. Before a man can enter a mosque to pray, he must remove his shoes and wash. His shoes are symbols of the dirt that contaminates his life by living and walking in a defiled world. He removes his shoes and washes according to the age-old traditions and teachings of Islam. Then he can approach God in prayer, without shame.

In Muslim culture, shame and honor are attached to places and locations as well as to actions. Some places are more honorable than others. Some are more shameful. A man can pray at home or in the market, but it is better to pray at the local mosque as the mosque has greater honor. Holy sites have even greater honor, and the Ka'ba in Mecca is the most honorable of all.

Before picking up the Qur'an to read, a Muslim must wash. Living in an evil world defiles his hands. After washing, he has removed the contamination that disqualified him from reading and hearing from God. Now he is deemed worthy.

After having relations with his wife, a Muslim man must bathe in order to be clean. If he does not, the very ground he walks on will become defiled. Once again, after ritual washing, he can approach God, but not before purification has occurred.

In most shame-based cultures, the Christian can make an immediate connection between defilement and cleansing and the grace of God as revealed in the Bible. The Old Testament is full of this imagery.

In Exodus 30 we see that Aaron and his sons were to wash their hands and feet whenever they entered the tent of meeting or approached the altar; otherwise they would die. Their actions portrayed a picture of what was to come in Christ, who provided cleansing through the washing of the blood.

Leviticus chapters 13 & 14 are about the cleansing of a leper. Remember that lepers were in a tremendous position of shame, even to the point of being isolated and having to go around crying out, "Unclean, unclean." Yet, in Leviticus 14, God provides a way of cleansing at the instigation of the priest, not of the leper. It is possible to make many comparisons between the cleansing of the leper and salvation.

Also in the Gospels, Jesus turned to the lepers to heal them, demonstrating God's desire to reach out to those in a place of shame and restore them.

In the Old Testament, blemished or defective animals were not permitted for sacrificial use. Items used for worship had to be anointed or consecrated. Unclean animals could not be used. In Mark 7:18-23 Jesus challenged the Pharisees in their use and understanding of cleansing and dietary laws, affirming that man himself is unclean.

The issue of cleanness centers on man's basic condition. In the West, Christians list man's sinful condition with a variety of legal words. How many of us include in that list that man is in a position of defilement? The law was put in place not only to point out man's guilt and need of a Savior, but to also point out man's defilement and need for a Cleanser. Just as the Old Testament offerings drew attention to man's need for a sacrifice for sin, the acts of cleansing pointed out man's need for washing and purification from defilement.

Just as Christ's work on the cross once and for all removed our sin, it also, once for all, removed our defilement. "The blood of goats and bulls and the ashes of a heifer sprinkled on those who were ceremonially unclean sanctifies them so they were outwardly clean. How much more, then, will the blood of Christ, who through the eternal Spirit offered himself unblemished to God, cleanse our consciences from acts that lead to death, so that we may serve the living God?" (Hebrews 9:13, 14)

Cleansing is fundamental to understanding grace. Mankind is unclean. It is not just that man is totally depraved; mankind is totally defiled.

If you use this paradigm, then New Testament stories about the cleansing of the lepers (Luke 5:12-14), the Gentile woman who was defiled in the eyes of the Jews (Matthew 15:21-28), and the Jewish woman who bled for 12 years and was thus unclean for 12 years and unable to enter the temple (Mark 5:25-35) will become part of your teaching. These are the kinds of verses that speak loudly and clearly to people living in shame-based cultures, who need a Cleanser, a Savior, and a Redeemer.

From Naked to Clothed

In reinforcing our message of God's provision for shame, the illustration can be used of how God covers our nakedness and clothes us.

In the Garden of Eden, man's shame stemmed in part from man's nakedness. The New Testament tells us that our proper clothing is eternal, and that we groan and long to be clothed with it (II Corinthians 5:1-2). When Adam and Eve sinned, they lost their eternal life and immediately felt naked and exposed. Until we reach heaven and are clothed with our eternal clothing, we will be in a position of nakedness and shame. II Corinthians 5 is a very useful chapter in explaining the Gospel to those who are from a shame-based culture. Many of Paul's illustrations and the whole basis of his teaching in this chapter demonstrate to the reader how God will someday clothe us with immortality.

However you want to state it theologically, nakedness and shame go together and can be a useful tool to use when sharing from the Scriptures. The story of our nakedness and shame must start in Genesis 3. Job tells us in Job 1:21 that we were born naked, and the picture can be drawn of our shame and nakedness right from birth.

The Old Testament law contains many references to nakedness and gives many rules concerning whom one could marry. From the Old Testament law it is obvious that there can be many shameful relationships between people. Leviticus 18 is full of references to shameful relationships that were forbidden among God's redeemed people. The word used all through Leviticus 18 is "nakedness."

Isaiah also says, "I delight greatly in the Lord; my soul rejoices in my God. For he has clothed me with garments of salvation and arrayed me in a robe of righteousness, as a bridegroom adorns his head like a priest, and as a bride adorns herself with her jewels."

In the New Testament, Jesus told the story of the prodigal son who returned home full of shame for what he had done. When his father welcomed him home, the first thing his father commanded was that a robe be brought for his son (Luke 15:22). In the same way, the first thing God does for his returning children is to raise them from a position of shame to a place of honor by covering them with the robe of righteousness.

The ultimate picture of God bearing our shame is found in Christ who was stripped of His clothing when He was hung on the cross. Roman prisoners were often hung naked on a cross, exposed for the scoffers to see and ridicule. Consequently, even in this, Christ bore not only our sin on the cross, but also our shame. Once for all, Christ died on the cross, bearing our shame so that we might be freed from shame as well as guilt.

There are many more references to nakedness and clothing, but in the final pages of the Bible, we are told how the believers will be clothed in heaven. At the Marriage Supper of the Lamb, we will come forth in our wedding garments. Right from Genesis to Revelation we see the unfolding of God's plan for man, starting with noting his nakedness and shame, and clothing him with animal skins representing the grace that would be provided by Christ on the cross.

From Expelled (from Eden and God) to Visited by God

In shame-based cultures, everyone knows how important it is to belong to a family or tribe. This is part of the *group* mind-set. Your group provides you with what you need in life. Everything from fellowship, money, opportunity, education, a spouse, and security is obtained through the group. A man without a group is in an impossible situation.

A Jordanian television series several years back dealt with the issues that arose when a man found himself in the shameful position of no longer having a family. The very act of being thrown out of your family is considered the ultimate shame. It is worsened in many countries when the expulsion story is announced in the newspaper so everyone knows that the person has been shamed.

Man was shamed when he was expelled from the Garden of Eden. The very act of expulsion added to man's shame. He was cast out of his home and away from the presence of his Father.

All through history man has lived separated from God. Even the Muslim can tell you that you cannot go into the presence of God, because God is honorable and you are in a position of shame.

The whole message of the Gospel revolves around the restoration of the relationship between God and man. Man is not in a position to elevate himself. Only God can restore the one who is ousted. Second, God used a mediator. Mediators must be able to speak on equal terms with both God and us, and so Jesus became human, in order to mediate between us. It is only through the person of Jesus that a way is made so that our relationship with God can be restored. Through Jesus man moves from being expelled to being accepted. We now have access to God's throne room. We are now called sons of God, and God even elevates us to the position of being a joint-heir with Jesus.

A friend in the Middle East once preached a sermon on John 17 where Jesus prays to the Father and says these amazing words, "I have given them the glory you have given me, that they may be one as we are one: I in them and you in me. May they be brought to complete unity to let the world know that you sent me and have loved them even as you have loved me." He went on to explain that Jesus has bestowed on every believer the glory and honor that God the Father bestowed on his son Jesus. Our position now is that of a joint-heir. Once we are in heaven we will fully enter into our inheritance.

The congregation had many questions afterwards. They couldn't believe that this type of honor was possible. Sometime after this the pastor realized that he needed to balance his teaching with Jesus' teaching on humility and preference for serving others, to keep his congregation from becoming too proud.

These concepts leave a powerful impact on those from a shame-based culture. People can accept that God honored Jesus, because He was the Son of God and sinless and thus deserved honor. But the Bible says that Jesus has also glorified us and has given us the same honor. This honor is ultimately demonstrated in heaven where we are rewarded and honored, even to the place of being joint-heirs with Christ. The heir always has the ultimate honor in any tribe, and we are included in this honor.

From Weakness to Strength

The Bible makes numerous references to weakness. Man is in a weak condition, and often unable to help himself. He easily succumbs to sin and falls quickly into temptation. Many people want to be stronger, but lack the will power.

As I have already mentioned, while traveling in taxis in the Middle East, the drivers would usually offer me a cigarette. I remember one occasion when I refused, the driver commented that I must be very strong to resist the pressure. This provided a wonderful opportunity to share about the one who makes weak people strong.

Isaiah tells us, "He gives strength to the weary, and increases the power of the weak. Even youths grow tired and weary, and young men stumble and fall; but those who hope in the Lord will renew their strength. They will soar on wings like eagles; they will run and not grow weary, they will walk and not be faint." Isaiah 40:29-31

Jesus, in his earthly ministry, displayed a kind of strength that is passed on to the believers. Jesus gives us strength to stand in the day of trial, strength to endure, and strength to withstand the enemy in Jesus' name.

Grace and strength are tied together in 2 Corinthians 12:9 when Paul says "But he (God) said to me, My grace is sufficient for you, for my power is made perfect in weakness. Therefore I will boast all the more gladly about my weaknesses, so that Christ's power may rest on me."

Peter adds in I Peter 5:10 "And the God of all grace who called you to his eternal glory in Christ, after you have suffered a little while, will himself restore you and make you strong, firm and steadfast."

The message of God's grace includes the concept that God wants to move us from a place of weakness to a place of strength; not our own strength, but Christ in us, the hope of glory, who is our strength.

From sickness to being healed

Why did Jesus spend so much time healing the sick? Part of the answer lies in the picture we have in the Bible of God moving man from a place of sickness to wholeness.

Part of the curse in Genesis is man's physical death. As soon as he is born, man begins the slow process of dying, and part of the dying process is sickness.

In Exodus 23:25, God told the children of Israel that if they obeyed his commands He would bless them and take sickness away from their land. However, in Deuteronomy 28:58-61 God warns them that if they do not obey His commands then God will bring sickness upon them as a punishment.

Sickness is one of the results of man's shameful and sinful position. It is part of the judgment of God on the entire human race. But through the person of Jesus, God demonstrates His power over sickness. In the book of Revelation, God tells us that in heaven there will be no more sickness and pain, (21:4) for they are part of the former things. Isaiah 53:5 says of the Messiah: "by his wounds we are healed".

God's ultimate plan of salvation can be demonstrated through God's plan to bring us from a place of sickness to a place of being healed, not only physically, but emotionally and spiritually as well. That is why we read that in heaven there will be no more sickness and no more tears.

As you can see from the examples above, there are many ways of explaining the Gospel to people without using legal terminology. Instead of expounding on more topics, I will simply list a number of others that I have heard ministers from shame-based worldviews use to explain the Gospel message to their own people.

From dying to being raised

From a place that is far from God to being indwelt by God's Spirit

From imprisoned in the flesh to being set free by the Spirit

From spiritually poor to having riches in God

From failure and falling short to being made complete in Christ

From being illegitimate children to being children of God

From ignorant to being taught of God

From blind to seeing

From darkness to being enlightened by God

From stumbling to being strengthened and encouraged

From accused to being exonerated and represented

From cursed to being blessed

From tiredness to being renewed

and finally...

From guilty to being redeemed

Yes, we should not forget this one. Legal concepts should be explained using the legal terminology of the culture. If a redemption analogy can be found in the culture then it can be useful to help demonstrate how God provides an answer to sin through the substitutionary death of Jesus on the Cross. However, redemption is a legal concept and other analogies could be sought to also explain the gospel to those in shame-based or fear-based cultures.

Once the person has understood how God is moving us from a position of shame to a position of honor, he may be able to also gain an understanding of the expression of God's plan to move us from being guilty to a place of receiving redemption.

Conclusion

When working with people who do not have a clear understanding of guilt

I have discovered that if I explain the Gospel in terms of God wanting to lift us from a position of shame to that of honor, I get an immediate response. I usually have had to explain that the Bible is talking of spiritual riches, not physical and that when the Bible speaks of God honoring us, he does not want us to be filled with pride. In fact, Jesus makes it plain in the Sermon on the Mount that God honors the humble, not the proud. If God honors the proud, they only swell with pride, but when the humbled are honored, they simply grow more humble and turn the honor onto the one honoring them.

When sharing the gospel with those from a shame-based culture or worldview, it is important to also explain what the Bible teaches about guilt. An example of this if found in the book of Leviticus. Starting in Leviticus 1, God begins to define what guilt is, and how presenting a 'guilt offering' can make the person clean again. Many of us take the instructions in Leviticus for granted, but for those coming out of the Egyptian fear-power worldview, and living in the Semitic shame-honor worldview, clear instructions were needed to define guilt.

From the Scriptures we can see that God is not in the business of shaming his followers. Rather, He is in the business of exchanging shame for honor. King David discovered this and recorded those wonderful words in Psalm 3:3, "You are the lifter of my head." Many well meaning Bible teachers from a guilt-based worldview have inadvertently put great fear into believers from shame-based worldviews by teaching about God's judgment without mentioning that God will honor His children, and publicly condemn and shame those who have rejected Him. Romans 8:1 tells us that there is now no condemnation to those who are in Christ Jesus.

We see in Isaiah 57:15 that God "dwells in a high and holy place with him that is of a contrite and humble spirit, to revive the spirit of the humble, and to revive the heart of the contrite ones." James continues this thought with, "Humble yourselves in the sight of the Lord, and He shall lift you up." (James 4:10) God's action of lifting the humble is all part of the outpouring of His grace. Grace is far more than forgiveness. It must also include God's work of restoring the honor of His followers. This is the work of glorification that Jesus refers to in John chapter 17.

In the following chapter, I would like to examine what happens when worldviews clash. Then in later chapters I would like to look at Islam in the Middle East as a case study of how a shame-based culture works. Finally I would like to draw this section to a conclusion by examining what a clear presentation of the Gospel should contain if it is to address all three aspects of fear, shame, and guilt.

Questions for Reflection or Discussion

1. Read Leviticus 26:13. What do you think this verse would say to your target culture?

2. Is the concept of cleansing important to your target culture? What parallels could you draw from Aaron's need to wash in Exodus 30:17-21, or the cleansing of lepers in Leviticus 13 & 14? How could you apply Hebrews 9:13, 14?

3. How important is clothing in your target culture? What parallels can you draw between nakedness and shame, and fine clothing and honor? Use II Corinthians 5:1-2, Isaiah 61:10, and the prodigal son in Luke 15:11-32.

4. Is belonging an important part of your target culture? What stigma is put on people who are banished? What can you teach from this concept, using our expulsion from the presence of God? Use Genesis 3 and Ephesians 2:13.

5. Are there other ways you can think of illustrating the gospel truth that God wants to move us from a position of shame to a place of honor?

6. Which of your core beliefs have been challenged or strengthened though reading this chapter? Why?

Chapter Eighteen
Clash of Worldviews

In the last chapters we have been examining what I believe are the three common-ancestral worldviews. In each of these paradigms there is a basic tension between two extremes. The three paradigms are:

guilt .... innocence

shame .... honor

fear .... power

It is possible to define logical thinking using each of these paradigms. When analyzing a culture I have often used the question, "How are decisions arrived at?" as a useful tool for determining how much of each of these paradigms is operating in any given culture.

While it is possible to find all three dynamics in most cultures usually one or two are more dominant. Some cultures, however, operate almost entirely within one major paradigm. Additionally, cultures and worldviews are constantly shifting. The shift may be slow or fast depending on the events of history.

For example, in the Western Canadian culture that I experienced in my childhood, guilt and innocence played an almost exclusive role. Almost everyone I knew made decisions based on right and wrong. Shame and fear played a very small role in our world. I believe that the roots of this worldview go back to the early pioneers. When the settlers arrived on the prairies of Canada, no one cared what family they came from. The desperately poor of Europe homesteaded beside families from well to do European backgrounds. None of that mattered in the harsh new world. Those that worked hard survived, those that did not, died in the cold Canadian winters. This reality shaped a worldview where hard work, and doing things right were the most important elements. Family honor, old traditions, and fear of others were scoffed at. The harsh new world created a new man with a new worldview. But once a few generations passed, honor and shame began to grow in importance, although it still plays a very small role.

During the founding of the Roman Empire, the citizens of Rome operated almost entirely within a fear-power worldview, worshipping a pantheon of gods. As their civilization developed, they introduced the idea of law being higher than the emperor. With this one step they accepted the concept of guilt and innocence as an important element in their worldview. As their civilization developed, they moved almost completely away from the fear-power worldview. However, as their empire expanded, they also slowly introduced into it shades of the shame-honor worldview.

One only has to watch the Godfather movies to see how fear-power and shame-honor are the two paradigms that many Italians moved in during that era. South European culture had almost entirely lost its guilt-innocence perspective on life.

The Freudian question, "Why do you have so much guilt?" is not the question society is asking today. Now people are asking, "Who am I?" People are seeking to discover who they are, and want to find an identity because their worldview is in flux. Thus, many questions can consume us: "Who am I and how can I express myself?," "How can I enjoy myself?," "Am I fully exercising my rights?," and "What are my options in life, and am I able to choose?"

Dr. James Houston of Regent College in Vancouver, Canada, thinks that in our post-modern North American culture, guilt is being replaced by shame. As I mentioned earlier, the concept of something being "cool" or "not cool" seems to have many similarities to shame and honor-based thinking. Others that I have spoken with feel that American culture is moving more towards including a greater mix of fear-power based culture. I believe this is illustrated by the award winning American documentary "*Bowling for Columbine*" and in the American reaction to the destruction of the World Trade Centre.

We must be careful here not to try and make all cultures fit into one of the three categories: guilt, shame, or fear. Cultures are made up of a mixture of all three common ancestral worldviews. Individual families and even individual people may identify with a different mix of worldview.

As an example, in one family you may have an individual who is an evangelical Christian with strong traditional roots. This person may relate much of life to guilt-innocence thinking. A teenager in the same family may not quite see everything as

162

so black and white and may be reluctant to accept things as being right or wrong. Rather, he or she wants to be seen as cool and desires to act and dress as cool. To be anything less would be humiliating. At the same time, a third member of the family may be into the occult, psychics, and horoscopes. He or she may see life as being influenced by the stars and occultic powers. Thus, in one family, you may have people who have been differently influenced by the three common ancestral worldviews.

Digging deeper, we may find that these people do not hold strictly to one or the other of these mega-trends, but that they have adopted some of each of them into their lives.

This can be illustrated by looking at culture among North American First Nations. Most of these cultures are made up of a mixture drawn from shame-honor and fear-power common ancestral worldviews. One North American native I spoke to seemed to be torn between seeking revenge against someone who had shamed him, and wanting to pray for him in the Indian sweat lodge.

The sweat lodge and the shaman religious leaders point us towards the fear-power based worldview of the native peoples. However, the tradition of honoring or shaming people through songs at tribal powwows can help us see the importance of honor and shame in their society. As I have read about aboriginal culture and history, and as I have interacted with missionaries working among North American First Nation people, I have been amazed at how clearly these cultural traits are part of everyday life.

Likewise, Hinduism and Shintoism are mixtures of shame-honor and fear-power paradigms. Even Russian culture is a mixture, one part being the shame-honor worldview of the East and the Eastern Orthodox Church, and the fear-power worldview of tsars and later the communists.

Clash of Cultures

In many cases where guilt-innocence cultures have contacted shame-honor cultures, they have clashed. As an example, the early settlers in North America could not understand or appreciate the North American First Nations perspective on life. In the end, many First Nations people chose to die rather than face the shame of living on a reservation.

In North America in 1889, a young Paiute prophet known as Wovoka gave a message from his home in the Nevada desert. His disciples sent it to all the First Nations peoples across Western America. The message from their prophet simply urged the Indians to "Dance everywhere. Keep on dancing. You must not ... do harm to anyone. You must not fight. Do right always." Soon village after village of Sioux began to perform his "Ghost Dance" with its promise of a return to the old ways in a world from which whites would have been erased by a flood.

The dancing appalled and frightened whites and they wired to Washington for protection. Army troops fanned out to round up the Ghost dancers and to settle them on reservations. Among the last to be caught was a group of about 350 Sioux under Chief Big Foot. They were led to a military camp at Wounded Knee Creek where they set up camp under a flag of truce. An incident triggered gunfire. When the firing ended, more than 150 First Nations people, men, women, and children, lay dead. Others fled or crawled off wounded. Chief Red Cloud said of the incident, "We had begged for life, and the white men thought we wanted theirs."

The guilt-based values of the settlers dictated that First Nations people must obey the law and live on special reservations. Fear-Power based values of the natives said that the Ghost Dance would change the situation. Sadly, it ended with a massacre.

It is said that the Nez Perce tribe could boast that since Lewis and Clark first encountered their friendliness in Oregon country, no Nez Perce had ever killed a white man. Even when their treaties were broken and settlers crowded into their lands, they avoided retaliation. In 1877 they were given thirty days to move to a distant reservation in Idaho. Hoping to escape, they began an epic flight to Canada. They were caught 40 miles from the border and turned back.

In this case, shame-based cultural values clashed with guilt-based values. Being cooped up on the reservation was a terrible shame and the ultimate humiliation for Indian chiefs. Leaving the reservation was breaking the law.

In 1878 a band of northern Cheyenne left the reservation to return to their old lands "where their children could live." Overtaken by soldiers, a chief said, "We do not want to fight you, but we will not go back." Clearly the shame of living on the reservation was too much for them. As they had broken the law by leaving, and now refused to return, the troops opened fire. Some Indians escaped and continued their journey. They met up with soldiers at Fort Robinson where they faced an ultimatum. "Go south or go hungry." Court records tell us what happened next. "In the midst of the dreadful winter, with the thermometer 40 degrees below zero, the native peoples, including the women and children, were kept for five days and nights without food or fuel and for three days without water. At the end of that time they broke out of the barracks." Troops hunted them down. They chose death over returning to the shame and humiliation of reservation life. Today many natives still feel the sting of shame. Many have turned to the numbing effects of alcohol, and others have immersed themselves in their native religions as they seek answers to their problem of self-esteem.

Western civilizations have now turned their attention to more global issues. Global travel and trade have forced the west into a position of trying to understand people from different cultures.

When researching the material for this book, I became aware of the large number of books in print in the Western world that deal with the Muslim or Arab mind-set. These books exist not only in the religious sector but also in the political and business sectors. Westerners, for whatever reason, struggle when they encounter Arabs and other Muslims. Western businessmen struggle to know how to do business in the Muslim world. Western politicians are often confused and unprepared for the actions and reactions of Muslim leaders. Political misunderstandings and blunders have created hardships and even wars. Christian missionaries have not fared much better in their efforts to communicate the Christian message.

Throughout the history of Christian outreach to the Muslim peoples of the world, Christians have faced tremendous struggles in knowing how to communicate clearly the Gospel message. Most of the church's efforts at communication have been received like water off a duck's back. The message is proclaimed, and the hearers are completely indifferent, sometimes resistant, and occasionally hostile.

Over the years, countless misunderstandings have developed between Christians and Muslims. Muslims often view Christians as immoral idolaters and blasphemers holding to old documents of untrustworthy heritage. Many Christians are suspicious of Muslims, viewing them as dangerous and unpredictable. Some go as far as thinking that all Muslims are violent and oppressive.

The battle lines have been drawn. Many believers in the Lord Jesus find missionary work among Muslims undesirable, a waste of money, and perhaps even offensive.

The secular world has had its fair share of troubles. Political tensions and issues create misunderstandings on both sides. Many Muslims view Western countries as expansionist and threatening. Many Western nations view Muslims as terrorists and their governments as oppressive. The average Western person reacted very negatively to leaders such as Ayatollah Khomeini, Muammar al-Qaddafi and Saddam

Hussein. Oil-rich Arabs are viewed as a threat to the economic stability of the West. Desperately poor and oppressed Arabs such as the Palestinians are looked upon as terrorists. On a political level, Muslim nations and Western nations have fared no better than Muslim and Christian clerics in understanding one another.

As a consequence of such misunderstandings over the years, Westerners have tried to understand the Arab Muslim mind. This is why there are many books and articles currently in print on the topic of the Arab mind.

Everyone realizes the importance of this topic. A St. Louis Post Dispatch revealed some of the US military thinking when it stated "Pentagon Threat-Assessment Officer Major Ralph Peters believes intelligence officers must set aside their preoccupation with numbers and weaponry. Instead, he says, they must start reading books that explain human behavior and regional history."

The religious world has reacted much the same way. Theologians from all backgrounds are now crying out for a greater effort at understanding each other's view points, and for a renewed effort in accepting one another's views.

The problem of understanding one another is not easy. When we meet another person whose system of beliefs is different, we tend to interpret that system according to our own framework of understanding. It can take months and even years of living in another culture to begin to understand that culture, but not everyone reaches a point of understanding. Many Westerners living in an Arab culture simply define the worldview around them according to their own understanding and perspectives. They assume that the other person thinks in a similar pattern as they do. They then try to understand the culture from their own framework, based on their own worldview. Years ago I started out this way, but soon realized that I could not fit everything into neat packages. There was something about Arab society that I did not understand.

My wife and I entered the Arab culture when I was a twenty-two year old student. At that point I had read many books about Arab culture and thought. My move to the Arab world was not so much a conscious decision to understand them as it was a conscious decision to become part of their culture and worldview. I initially concentrated on language learning and cultural adaptation. We began by living among the Arabs in the Levant. After two years, we moved to the edge of the Empty Quarter. Several years later we moved to what was then the Yemen Arab Republic. Many years later, we returned to the Levant and made our home there. Our last years in the Middle East were spent living among a nomadic Bedouin tribe. All together we have spent more than thirty years either immersed in the Arab culture while living in the Middle East or living in the west and doing research into Middle Eastern topics.

I say this only to point out that our personal experience with the Arab world has been based on a wide variety of exposures over a long period of time. Along with our personal experience, we have cultivated friendships with foreigners and nationals living in a host of other Muslim countries, stretching from North Africa to Indonesia, and have spent several years traveling and teaching seminars on shame-based cultures.

During our years in the Middle East, I was involved in various types of employment and mixed with different levels of society. I have visited the marble palaces of oil-rich Arab sheiks. I have also sat in the tents of the poorest Bedouin Arabs. I worked for a number of years as a liaison officer for a Western organization, interacting with varying levels of government in the Yemen Arab Republic. In the Levant, I worked with charities reaching out to the poor and handicapped. As a rule, we have made our home in lower to middle income neighborhoods.

In whatever situation we have found ourselves, we have endeavored to understand and communicate our beliefs to those around us so that they could better understand us, our religion and the society we come from.

One of my initial personal goals was to discover how the Arab mind worked. And so, with my Western training ingrained in my thinking, I started asking, "What is going on now?" That seemed to be my favorite question, and for many years I was curious to know what was going on in my neighborhood, in my city and in my nation. I even wanted to know what was going on in my neighbor's head.

During all of these years, I began to notice patterns emerging. The oil-rich Arabs of the Gulf, the mountain people of Yemen, the Bedouin of the desert, and the city dwellers of the Levant all held similar codes of conduct. While each region had its peculiarities, there was an overall pattern of similarity between the cultures.

These patterns, however, were not always clearly noticeable. Often there were many confusing and seemingly contradictory events. It was hard to work out what was happening, but in time, I moved on from trying to understand what was happening to trying to understand why what was happening was happening. I refused to believe that people acted and reacted unpredictably. In fact, the longer I lived in the Arab world, the more I recognized the predictability of the Arabs. During the Gulf War years I was able to predict certain events in the war days and sometimes weeks, before they happened. I found the Gulf War tremendously stressful. Watching Western news, I could understand the actions and re-actions of the Western nations. Having lived in the Middle East, I could understand the actions and re-actions of the Arab nations. On one side was Western understanding, and on the other was Muslim understanding, and in the middle was the yawning chasm of misunderstanding. As a result, countless millions of people paid the price with their lives, their wounds, and tremendous economic loss.

It was during this time that I began to realize how far apart Western and Muslim thinking patterns really are. The West sees events and interprets them one way. The Arabs see events and interpret them another way. It isn't that one was right and the other was wrong. Thinking in terms of right versus wrong is a Western thought pattern. During the Gulf War, Western governments poured their resources into proving to their citizens that they were on the side of right, and that Saddam Hussein was on the side of wrong. Numerous instances were relayed to the Western public to prove the wrongness of the Iraqi leaders. The people of the West watched their TV's and interpreted the news according to rightness and wrongness, with the majority supporting their government's actions.

In the Middle East, the situation was less clear. Many Arab nations initially supported Saddam Hussein, and only in the face of tremendous Western pressure did they start to withdraw their support. Almost all of my Arab friends told me that Saddam Hussein acted predictably and strove manfully to protect his honor and the honor of his nation. Not one of them ever discussed the rightness or the wrongness of the war.

And so, my study of the Arab Muslim mind became more intense. What was it that made this mind-set so different from my own? During this process, I also wrestled with the concept of cross-cultural communication. My role in the Middle East has always been that of a cross-cultural communicator of the gospel. I have always sought to find ways of clearly presenting the message and teachings of the Christian Church as found in the Bible.

As I wrestled with Muslim thought patterns, I began to question my own culture. How did we develop our own thought patterns? Were they right? Is my own culture "balanced" in its view of life on planet earth? During the course of history, what forces have molded my own worldview? I spent many hours studying history in order to understand how events in history molded our Western thinking and also Muslim thinking.

Eventually I arrived at conclusions that have been helpful in aiding me in communicating the Gospel of Jesus Christ to those with a Muslim mind-set. As I shared this information with other missionaries in other settings, they reacted positively, and began to contribute ideas from their cultural setting. Eventually I was asked to speak in a variety of settings taking me from Asia through Europe and eventually to the First Nation people of my native land. Having said this, I also realize that worldviews are changing. As the world is impacted by globalization, people with very narrow or simplistic worldviews are being challenged. This clashing and altering of worldviews is leaving many people uncertain and afraid because many of the foundational principles of their lives are being challenged.

This is happening on every front. Traditional Islam is being challenged. Islam in the West is struggling to find bridges between Western cultural norms and the Muslim mind-set. In my interaction with Muslim clerics in Britain and North America, I have been amazed at their reinterpretation of certain verses in the Qur'an. These Muslim clerics have arrived at these new interpretations because new interpretations are necessary if Islam is to have any real impact on Western guilt-based society. But Western culture is also changing as it adapts to the pressures of globalization.

In the next two chapters we will look at shame and honor in Arab Muslim culture as a case study of how shame-based cultures operate. In doing this, I will not deal with the typical parts of Muslim culture that are often addressed. I will not dwell on, "How much coffee goes into the coffee cup?" nor "How many times it should be served?" We will not look at body language, rules of etiquette, nor the unspoken rules of the desert. These are all part of culture and vary from setting to setting. In these chapters, however, I want to go deeper and look at the basic fundamental mind-set of Muslims. I want to examine the issues that are most important to the Muslim worldview and upon which their culture is built.

Questions for Reflection or Discussion

1. Most people's worldview is changing, especially now that globalization has brought about massive changes in every part of the globe. Do the Worldview Analysis (chapter 16) for your target culture or have a national brother or sister fill it in. You may have to explain the three common-ancestral worldviews to them before they do the analysis. If you have time, have both young people and older people fill one in. What do you think is changing in the culture? What is being reduced and what is being added in terms of guilt, shame and fear?

2. If you are a North American, view the movie "Bowling for Columbine" and then discuss how you feel American and Canadian cultures are changing.

3. Think about some of the clashes your target people group have had with other people groups. How much of this was influenced by a clash of worldviews? Are these wounds still felt in their society today? How can you speak to them or minister through them?

4. Today Muslims are often not only misunderstood but their character is also maligned. How is this manifested in your situation, or in your extended family or church? Are the accusations fair? How much of this is due to a clash of worldviews?

5. Does the exposure to teaching about guilt, shame and fear based cultures make it easier or harder to live in today's world? Explain your thoughts.

Chapter Nineteen
Case Study: Islam and Shame

"Arab society is a shame-based society," says Dr. Sania Hamady, an Arab scholar and one of the greatest authorities on Arab psychology. "There are three fundamentals of Arab society," she goes on to state, "shame, honor and revenge."

A few years ago, Arabs were loath to talk about their culture. Most Arab people had never interacted with outsiders to the degree that they would start to examine their own and the others' cultures. That has changed, and today you will find Arab psychologists and Arab media speaking out about their own culture. There are a number of issues that they raise as being important to them.

Group Mind-set

Arabs have always lived in groups and they tend to do everything from a group mind-set. The larger extended family makes up one's group, and the gathering of all of one's relatives makes up the tribe.

As I mentioned in the beginning of this book, Arabs have defined their relationships with others in terms of near and far. Those who are related to you by blood are near, and those from other tribes are far. People can be brought into a near relationship through marriage or adoption. If a foreigner is adopted as a "son of the tribe," a great honor has been bestowed upon him.

Arabs usually demand a high degree of conformity from those who are near to them. This conformity brings honor, social prestige and a secure place in society. The individual who conforms to the group has the advantage, in that all the members of his group are bound to demonstrate concern for his interests, and they will defend him unquestioningly against "outsiders."

Relationships

From top to bottom, Arab society is permeated by a system of rival relationships. This is because in the Arab value system, great value and prestige are placed on the ability to dominate others. In the constant struggle to dominate and to resist domination, the rivals of a given group quickly seize on any "shame" that can destroy the other group's influence. Isolating a target and thereby destroying it often achieves this, as an individual could not survive in the desert outside of the group setting. If one tribe insults the honor of another tribe, the entire tribe will respond in order to protect their place of honor.

Arabs fear isolation because in their view an individual or small group can only function effectively when he or it is identified with a group or a large body that can offer support and protection. This fear of isolation can be attributed to the fear that the Bedouins had of being isolated and left as individuals or small groups to fend for themselves in the harsh, hostile desert environment. Isolated individuals could easily be taken as slaves by other tribes and could spend the rest of their lives in low and mean positions. By sticking together, individuals could offer each other protection. Thus family units and firmly established relationships became paramount in knowing whom you could trust and who would stand by you if an outside force attacked you. Proverbs 14:28 shows similar thinking when it states: "A large population is a king's glory, but without subjects a prince is ruined."

Shame

There are many types of shame in Arab society. For an Arab, failure to conform is damning and leads to a place of shame in the community. This is often hard for Westerners to understand. We in the West value our individualism, but Arabs value conformity. The very meaning of Islam is to conform to the point of submission. The object of public prayers and universal fasting is to force conformity on all. There is an Arab proverb that can be translated, "Innovation is the root of all evil." If one fails to conform, he is initially criticized. If he continues to refuse to conform he is put in a place of shame by the community.

Shame can also be brought on by an act. Raping one's sister is considered by all as a shameful act. However, few things are considered right or wrong.

Right and wrong in Islam are usually defined in terms of what is forbidden by the Qur'an. But the Qur'an doesn't provide a nice list of rights and wrongs, so Muslims often talk about society. Society dictates what is acceptable and unacceptable. If you act against society, you may be acting shamefully, but not necessarily wrongfully in God's eyes. After all, the Qur'an tells them that God created good and evil.

Muslim men use this rationalization when living in what they consider an immoral Western nation. They can drink alcohol and partake in sexual escapades because the society they are living in doesn't define this as shameful. Something may be shameful at home, but when in different circumstances, the Arab may react differently. There is a proverb that states, "Where you are not known, do whatever you like."

Beyond this, shame is not only an act against the accepted system of values, but it can also include the discovery, by outsiders, that the act has been committed. Dr. Hamady puts it this way: "He who has done a shameful deed must conceal it, for revealing one disgrace is to commit another disgrace." There is an Arab proverb that says, "A concealed shame is two thirds forgiven."

A Syrian scholar, Kazem Daghestani, tells of an Arab husband who caught his wife in bed with another man. He drew a gun and pointed it at the couple while addressing the man. "I could kill you with one shot," he said. "But I will let you go if you swear to keep secret the relationship you have had with my wife. If you ever talk about it, I will kill you." The man took that oath and left and the husband divorced his wife without divulging the cause. He was not concerned about the loss of his wife or her punishment but about his reputation. Public shaming and not the nature of the deed itself or the individual's feelings had determined his action.

The story is told of a sheik who was asleep under a palm tree. A very poor Arab saw him and stole his expensive cloak. When he awoke the sheik was angry and his family hunted down the thief and brought him to trial. When asked for an explanation, the accused said, "Yes, I did steal this cloak. I saw a man asleep under a tree, so I had sexual relations with him while he slept and then I took the cloak." The sheik immediately asked to reexamine the cloak. After quickly looking it over he replied "This is not my cloak," and the thief went free.

The possibility of failure in some way also fills Arabs with dread, as failure leads to shame. Often an Arab will shrink from accepting challenges or risk when others are observing him. However, when away from his family this can change drastically. A meek Lebanese businessman at home can become a shrewd risk taker in the middle of Africa.

When there is failure, often outside forces are blamed. Anger, resentment, and violence are focused on outside elements in order to shift the blame to them.

In the case of other Orientals with similar shame-honor type cultures, failure is often focused on the individual. For example, a Japanese businessman may take his life when faced with tremendous shame. In an Arab situation, the Arabs will assign blame to someone else and react violently towards him.

As a result, it is easy to unintentionally offend an Arab. They have a very detailed code of conduct, and breaking that code can result in offense. This can be as simple as pouring too much coffee in a cup, making your visit too short, or serving unequal amounts of cold drink in visible clear glasses.

Shame can also result when each Arab is not treated as a special case. He expects rules to be bent to suit his convenience. He expects to be the favorite, and his friends have to constantly assure him that he counts more than others.

For example, when interviewing a number of businessmen, each interview should be conducted exactly the same length of time. I once heard of a man who accused an interviewer of spending five more minutes with the previous man. The interviewer got out of the situation by explaining that the extra time was necessary because the previous man could not express himself as eloquently and therefore took longer.

There are lots of little things in Arab culture that matter greatly. Everything in the culture has meaning, and an action as simple as stretching the left hand towards a person's face, as a Westerner might do in casual gesticulation, could be tantamount to telling many Arabs that he has the evil eye and that your hand was used defensively against it.

It is important to realize that shame is not attached to all of the actions that we would call wrong. While raping one's sister is a very shameful act, things like lying can be either shameful or honorable, depending on the circumstances.

Al Ghazali, the medieval Muslim theologian stated, "Know that a lie is not wrong in itself, but only because of the evil conclusions to which it leads the hearer, making him believe something that is not really the case. Ignorance sometimes is an advantage, and if a lie causes this kind of ignorance it may be allowed. It is sometimes a duty to lie... if lying and truth both lead to a good result, you must tell the truth, for a lie is forbidden in this case. If a lie is the only way to reach a good result, it is allowable. A lie is lawful when it is the only path to duty... We must lie when truth leads to unpleasant results, but tell the truth when it leads to good results." (Ahmad ibn Naqib al-Misri, *The Reliance of the Traveller*, translated by Nuh Ha Mim Keller, Amana publications, 1997, section r8.2, page 745)

The rule for telling the truth, or not to, is bound by honor and shame. If shame can be avoided, or honor obtained, then lying is more honorable, and therefore the thing to do.

Shame as part of culture

The most common Arabic word for shame is *ayb*. It is used repeatedly in child raising and usually means "shameful." In most cases it is not applied to very young children, because it implies a degree of prior knowledge and instruction that should have been followed. Older children who have disobeyed or have behaved disrespectfully are usually given a lecture which begins and ends with *ayb* or shame.

The instruction about shame is not restricted to just relatives. Almost anyone can instruct children, telling them that what they are doing is shameful, and usually the children will respond positively, not negatively. The power of the negative use of shame enforces positive reactions in people's lives. Children learn very early on that their personal behavior represents a part of the whole of family honor. Once this sense of honor is acquired, it remains with the person throughout life.

Sometimes when greeting an Arab and asking, "How are you?" one gets the answer "*mastur al-hal*" or "the situation is covered." This means, everything is all right as all shame is covered.

On the other hand, there are many ways of evoking violent reactions from others, using verbal abuse. This verbal abuse usually insinuates something shameful about a family member and thus evokes violent reactions from the listeners. This can result in bloodshed if someone does not intervene. In many ways it is similar to the old American West where the gunfighter exclaims, "You called me a liar! Those are shooting words." He pulls his gun and kills the person who implied that he was a liar. People in the old American West determined whether this was right or wrong if the other man also had a gun on his body. If he was armed but slower, it didn't matter. The fact that he carried a gun made it "alright" for the offended person to kill him.

People in the Western world seldom realize the powerful reactions that public shaming invokes in shame-based cultures. When President Bush Jr. of the USA called a number of nations the "Axis of Evil", those nations reacted very violently, even to the place of starting to produce nuclear weapons. The leaders of those nations felt that they must do something. They had been publicly shamed by the most powerful man in the world. If they did not react in a face-saving manner, they would lose the respect of their own people. So massive reactions took place in Iraq,

North Korea, and Iran. Much of this was lost in the Western media reports that focused on the alarming character of their actions rather than realizing what sort of offense took place.

In Arab culture, shame must be avoided at all cost. If it strikes, it must be hidden. If it is exposed, then it must be avenged. At all costs, honor must be restored, even if it means the loss of one's own life in the attempt.

Fear of shame among Arabs is so powerful because the identification between the individual and the group is far closer than in the West. Because Arabs think in a group mind-set, the importance of the group outweighs the importance of the individual. If an individual is in a position of shame, he loses his influence and power, and through him his entire group will similarly suffer, perhaps to the point of destruction.

Revenge

Shame can be eliminated by revenge. This is sanctioned by the Qur'an (Sura 6, 173). "Believers, retaliation is decreed for you in bloodshed."

It may also be eliminated through financial payment by fellow kinsmen in their group, or by the public treasury. In the case of a killing, the price of the blood must be settled between whatever groups are involved.

This need for revenge is as strong today as it ever was. In Egypt in 1972, out of 1,120 cases of murder, it was found that 25 percent of the murders were based on the urge to "wipe out shame," 30 percent on a desire to satisfy "wrongs", and another 30 percent on blood-revenge.

In the small country of Jordan, honor killings (killings to preserve honor) have come to public attention. The Jordanian penal code in the 1950's stated: "He who discovers his wife or one of his female relatives committing adultery and kills, wounds or injures one or both of them is exempt from any penalty." Some years later a penalty of one year imprisonment was instituted as many murders were being classified as honor killings.

In January 2000 the Jordanian government rejected a bill that would increase the punishment for someone who commits murder because of protecting the honor of the family from one year to life imprisonment. Then in the opening months of 2000, members of the royal family in Jordan joined a demonstration of young Arabs protesting the laws and attitudes about honor killings. Growing numbers of Jordanian young people are being educated in the West, and Western thinking and culture is beginning to clash with traditional Eastern thinking and culture.

Peace

In traditional Arab culture, peace is a secondary value when compared to the degree of feelings that shame and revenge invoke. This has led to the Western impression that peace in the Arab context is merely the temporary absence of conflict.

In Arab tribal society where Arab values originated, strife was the normal state of affairs. In the past, the ideal of permanent peace in Islam was restricted to the community of Islam and to those non-Muslims who accepted the position of protected persons and paid tribute to Islam. On the other hand, Islam instituted jihad (holy war) as the accepted relationship with non-Muslim states and made no provision for peace with them as sovereign states. Only a truce was permissible, and that was not to last for more than ten years.

This form of thinking then influences all aspects of life. As it has commonly been stated, "There is honor within Islam, shame without."

Questions for Reflection or Discussion

1. Do your target people have a 'group' mind-set? Do they make decisions in groups or as individuals? Who is included in the group or in the decision making process?
2. How important are relationships for your target people? On what basis are most relationships formed? e.g. Blood lines, common allegiances, religion, culture, common interests, politics, etc.,
3. Are people outside of the group treated as outsiders or in some way alienated from the decisions the group makes?
4. Do individuals in the group have enemies because they are perceived as enemies to the group in general?
5. Do people in your society fear isolation? Why or why not?
6. In what ways is shame brought upon people in your target group? Think about things such as bad acts, being different, failure, etc.
7. When people are away from their group, do they act differently? How much does the group affect how they act and react when they are with others of the group?
8. What vocabulary or proverbs do your target people have that focuses on shame

and honor? How are these concepts expressed? Is there a rich vocabulary or set of proverbs?

9. Are there acts or words that cause people to react very strongly?

10. What are some of the ways that you see perceived shame being hidden in your target culture?

11. If a major shame cannot be hidden, how do people react in your target culture?

12. How do the local religions deal with the shame-honor issue? What do they teach?

13. List some of the characteristics of Jesus that would demonstrate that he was an honorable person.

14. How did Jesus confront the shame – honor system of his day? What did he teach?

15. The Bible challenges the way people consider honor and cultural honor systems. What does the Bible say should be the basis of esteeming honor rather than simply adhering to an honor system?

16. Should missionaries focus on destroying the honor-shame basis of culture, or should they seek to address what gives honor, and any abuses that may arise from the current system?

17. Do guilt based cultures have abuses, follies and vices? Is this cultural system any better or worse than shame-based cultures?

Chapter Twenty
Case Study: Islam and Honor

"Honor is understood in a complex way as the absence of shame, for honor and shame are bound to one another as complementary, yet contradictory ideas." (Carolyn Fluehr-Lobban, Islamic Values and Social Practice, 1994.)

The other side of shame is honor, and every Arab desires and strives to be and become more honorable. The relationship between shame and honor has long been recognized by sociologists of Arab and Muslim cultures and has also been attributed to the generalized Mediterranean social complex.

In many cases the absence of shame conveys the idea of honor. Many times I have heard Arabs describe their families as being honorable because they don't do or act as others might. Conforming to social mores is of utmost importance to maintaining one's honor.

Honoring Elders

Arab storytellers tell the story of a father who is working in the hot sun with two of his sons. When he needed a drink, he asked the older of the boys to get him some water. "No, I will not," the elder son replied. The father then asked his younger son who said "Yes, certainly father," but he did not get the water. At this point the storyteller always asks his audience, "Which is the better son?" To give the wrong answer would be shameful, but the storyteller knows that his listeners will give the correct answer. The younger son is the better of the two because he had saved his father's face by not defying him.

In the West we would point out that both boys were wrong. This answer does not make sense to the Arab. What he regards as wrong is determined differently, i.e. namely in terms of shame and honor. To say no to your father's face would be to dishonor him, so that would be utterly wrong. To agree with him while in front of him is to honor him and that is good and right. Only one boy has done wrong according to this thinking. When Jesus told a similar story in Matthew 21:28-32, he added that the first son, who refused, later went and did what the father asked. In this way he restored honor by obeying his father. Jesus used this illustration to show that repentance covers shame. He also contrasted how those with worldly honor responded to John's message with how those without honor (the tax collectors and prostitutes) responded. The latter were preceding the former in entering the kingdom of God because those without honor believed and repented. That must have rankled some of his listeners.

Honorable acts

If there are shameful acts in the Arab culture, then what are the honorable ones?

In most Muslim cultures, hospitality is one of the most important ways of demonstrating honor. Hospitality honors the guest and the host alike. When you visit an Arab home, great effort is made to be hospitable. Rather than shame you, Arabs try very hard to honor you with hospitality. Everything is done to honor the guest and to present an honorable image of the Arab family.

The reverse is also true. If you don't want someone to visit you, simply talk to him or her outside your door, where everyone will see that they are not invited inside. They will immediately feel shamed and will never return to your home.

If hospitality is first, then flattery must be second in the Arab way of honoring someone. Arabs are often quick to flatter people they suspect are honorable. It is a way of pouring extra honor onto a person while demonstrating to others within earshot that they are honoring that person.

Third, if you admire something in an Arab home, they will be quick to insist that you have it as a gift. Even if you do not admire something, they will offer you gifts, demonstrating their willingness to honor someone else with a gift.

As the above three demonstrate, a visit to an Arab home is full of expressions of honor. Where you sit in the room, how you are fed, what you are fed, the hospitality shown, the flattery expressed and the gifts that are offered all express various levels of honor.

Moreover, the reverse is true. If someone visits your home, you are obliged to be hospitable. It is even expected that you will be overly hospitable to the point of demanding in your insistence that your guests eat, drink and accept your gifts. You must insist that people eat your food. Small friendly fights break out over food, and guests must demonstrate their appreciation for the hospitality that is shown.

Honor is attached to your family and your history

As long ago as 1377 Ibn Khaldun wrote, "One feels shame when one's relatives are treated unjustly or attacked, and one wishes to intervene between them and whatever peril or destruction threatens them." He continues, "The affection everybody has for his allies results from the feeling of shame that comes to a person when one of his neighbors, relatives or a blood relation in any degree is humiliated." In other words, Arabs are drawn together when defending the honor of the group, be it a neighbor, relative or any blood relation.

An Arab proverb states, "Learn as much of your pedigrees as is necessary to establish your ties of kindred." Another adds, "Many a trick is worth more than a tribe."

This is the reason that Arabs strive so hard to maintain the honor of the tribe. It is the duty of the eldest son of each family to maintain the honor of the family. If someone greatly offends the tribe, he will be the one to oust them, or, in the case of irreparable damage, execute them.

Nowhere is the honorable status of family and tribe more evident than in the differences between religious beliefs. During the Yemeni War (1962-1965), two Egyptians, a Coptic Christian and a Muslim, both members of well known and upper class families, had been lifelong friends. They were wounded in the same action; the Muslim in the arm and the Copt in the leg. Disabled, they lay awaiting treatment and removal from the battlefield. A half-empty truck arrived and picked up the Muslim, but left the Christian despite his desperate pleas for help. The truck crew had orders to collect the Muslim wounded before the Christian wounded. One word from the wounded Muslim friend could have saved the Copt. It was never uttered and the Coptic Christian died on the field, probably slaughtered by Yemeni tribesmen. The wounded Muslim soldier refused to acknowledge before others his friendship to the Christian, who would have been considered from a lower class.

Education

Education bestows honor. If a man gains a doctorate degree, he receives a great deal of honor in an Arab society. It is for this reason that Arabs strive to gain high educational standing. Many poor families sacrifice almost everything and work very hard to help an elder son make it through higher education. The elder son will work hard to honor the family. In the end, his achievements will raise the entire status of the family, and ultimately that of the tribe as well. What is valued is the awarding of the degree, not the hard work, ability or intellect involved in the process of gaining the degree. Because honor is so highly valued, cheating is often seen as dishonorable only if one is caught. Attaining the degree and its status is what is sought rather than competence gained though study.

Marriage

A young man has little status in his family until he is married. Suddenly he gains status and has a voice in tribal affairs. Once his first son is born, his status rises even further. An Arab proverb states "A man's wife is his honor." While this sounds like a compliment, the opposite can be true. If a man's honor is injured through his wife's misbehavior, swift judgment will come upon her.

Language

Albert Hourani, one of the great modern Arab scholars has said that his people are more conscious of their language than any people in the world. This consciousness is obsessive. Language is everything to the Arab. It is a divine expression and stems from the pre-Islamic era where Al-Kutbi was the god of writing. Today, classical Arabic is considered the language that God speaks, and those who speak it well are more honorable than those who do not. Language in the form of local dialects also separates those who are near and far. It separates the educated from the uneducated. It is an art form and for centuries was the sole medium of artistic expression. Every Arab tribe had its poets, and their unwritten words "flew across the desert faster than arrows." In the midst of outward strife and disintegration, these poems provided a unifying principle. Poetry gave life and currency to the idea of Arabian virtue. Based on the tribal community of bloodlines and insisting that only ties of blood were sacred, poetry became an invisible bond between diverse clans and formed the basis of a larger sentiment. It was poetry, the ultimate Arab art form, which bound Arabs together as a people rather than a collection of warring tribes.

When it becomes apparent that a young person is gifted as a poet, neighboring tribes gather together to wish the family joy. There are feasts and music. Men and boys congratulate one another, for a poet is a defense to the honor of the entire tribe and "a weapon to ward off insult from their good name, and a means of perpetuating their glorious deeds and of establishing their fame forever."

It is interesting to note that traditionally Arabs only wish one another joy, on three occasions: The birth of a boy, the coming to light of a poet, and the foaling of a noble mare.

The Arabic language is so powerful that Arabs will listen intently to someone speaking well, whether he speaks the truth or not. "I lift my voice to utter lies absurd, for when I speak the truth my hushed tones scarce are heard." Abu alAla, Syrian poet, 973-1057 AD.

Anyone wanting to understand Arab history and culture must be a student of Arab poetry. Arab poetry is full of glory. The poets glorified themselves, their brilliant feats, their courage and resolution, and their contempt for death. The Arab hero is defiant and boastful. When there is little to lose he will ride off unashamed, but he will fight to the death for his women and the honor of his tribe.

An example of the ideal Arab hero is Shanfara of Azd. He was an outlaw, swift runner, and excellent poet. As a child, Shanfara was captured by the Bani Salman tribe and brought up among them. He did not learn of his origin until he was grown up. He then vowed vengeance against his captors and returned to his own tribe. He swore that he would slay a hundred men of the Bani Salman and he had slain ninety-eight when he was caught in an enemy ambush. In the struggle, one of his hands was hewn off by a sword stroke, but taking the weapon in the other, he flung it in the face of the Bani Salman tribesman and killed him, making his score ninety-nine. He was then overpowered and slain. As his skull lay bleaching on the ground years later, a man of his enemies passed by and kicked it. A splinter of bone entered his foot; the wound festered, and he died, thus completing Shanfara's hundred. All of this is told in wonderful poetic language, skillfully blending the use of poetry with the honor of the hero.

Money

Arabs have a tremendous respect for wealth. Down through history, most honorable Arab leaders have been wealthy ones. Even Mohammed, the founder of Islam, rose to a position of great wealth. His use of wealth to help the poor and the masses is seen as very honorable and is often portrayed in Arabic literature and stories. Wealth allows the leader to be hospitable and generous, two elements that are extremely useful in obliterating shame and building honor. A wealthy leader can throw money around, gaining respect and covering a multitude of sins.

Heritage

Arabs are keenly aware of their heritage. Some can trace their heritage back to Mohammed, some back to other great leaders. Every tribe has stories of how individuals in their tribe achieved great honor or displayed honorable characteristics. Shameful figures in the tribal background are expelled or killed and ultimately forgotten in order to preserve the tribe's honorable heritage.

Wisdom

Arabs respect age and wisdom. Elders are listened to with respect. The language elders use is often more formal and elevated than young people are capable of. Elders are looked to for their wisdom, as they know all the old stories and can often give wise and good counsel. Elders often have more money and may have demonstrated their wisdom in acquiring riches or maintaining the tribal lands and tribal honor.

Charisma

Certain individuals have charisma. They are good looking, have a confidence about them, and carry themselves with honor. Often they have accomplished something of note and have been able to capitalize on it. Many times they are good at communication and at politically finding honorable solutions to problems.

Physical Strength

Arab lore is full of heroes who display tremendous physical strength. Most Arab boys are brought up to think highly of being manly and strong. Physical strength, as well as charisma and financial strength are a winning combination in Arab culture.

Alliances

Many Arabs look to leaders who have formed strong alliances. Since strength and riches are often found in a group setting, someone with strong alliances can rely on the combined strengths of many groups. Most political leaders in the Arab world use their alliances with tribes and families to put them into political power.

Bravery

Every Arab boy knows stories of Arab heroes who faced overwhelming odds. Whether he overcame or not is not the issue. The act of bravery, in itself, is very honorable. If one sits in an Arab coffeehouse and listens to the storytellers, or if you visit neighbors and ask, you will hear stories of brave Arab heroes.

Loyalty

Loyalty to the family tribe is considered paramount to maintaining honor. One does not question the correctness of the elders or tribes in front of outsiders. It is paramount that the tribe sticks together in order to survive. Once again, Arab history and folklore are full of stories of heroes who were loyal to the end.

Violence

Dr. Sania Hamady, one of the greatest authorities on Arab psychology and herself an Arab says, "Life is a fearful test, for modern Arab society is ruthless, stern and pitiless ... It honors strength and has no compassion for weakness."

In Arab countries between 1948 and 1973, a mere quarter of a century, no fewer than eighty revolts occurred, most of them bloody and violent. No wonder the West has a negative view of Arabs and Islam.

Violence in Arab history has been part of demonstrating one's honor and in removing shame from the tribe. "With the sword I will wash my shame away. Let God's doom bring on me what it may!" was written by Abu Tammam, a ninth-century poet in Hamasa.

You can see from the list of characteristics above why Arabs have a hard time recognizing Jesus as an honorable person. He did not display the usual characteristics that identify a person of honor. There is, however, one characteristic of honor that Jesus exemplified. Some Arab heroes demonstrate their honor by reaching down and helping people in need; namely people who don't deserve it.

If Jesus' character becomes an issue in discussion, then one needs to share about servant leadership and how Jesus displayed incredible honor by reaching down into our situation to help us and honor us.

For those Europeans and North Americans who criticize Middle Eastern culture for its views on honor and shame, I must remind them that Western history only a few hundred years ago was filled with honor and shame. The "high" French and German culture of the 18th and 19th century gave rise to dueling which carried over to the gun fighters of the American West. In Europe, a culture of honor survived for many years among the military and military families. These events are often forgotten as we tend to view history through the filter of our own current experience.

Conclusion

Honor in an Arab society is understood, in a complex way, as the absence of shame. Honor and shame are diametrically opposing factors, and the fundamental issue that defines society. In most shame-honor based societies, people accept that everyone has to deal with a measure of shame. The question is, "How is shame dealt with?" Few families or tribes can escape the birth of a handicapped child. The question then arises, what should be done with this child? Should the child be hidden away? Should it be killed? Should it be neglected, so that it eventually goes away? Is it more humane to quietly give it to an institution?

In some shame-honor based cultures, Christian societies have reached out to handicapped children in crisis, attempting to assist families that are reeling from the shame of having birthed such a child. Sometimes handicaps are not so easily noticed. The child grows and becomes a part of the family fabric. Then disaster falls when it becomes increasingly obvious that the child is deaf or has some other handicap that was not immediately noticeable. The discovery of such handicaps can crush whole families as they lose their place of honor in the community.

We encountered this in our own family situation. Our eldest son has cerebral palsy, and his presence in our family was of particular interest to our Arab friends as they tried to assess what this meant in regards to our honorable status, both in the church and in the community.

The question that always troubled me was, "Can a person move from a position of shame to a position of honor?" Arabs have trouble with this one. Almost all agree that someone can honor you, but you cannot honor yourself. However, people with honor seldom honor others without cause.

This is where we must be bold in proclaiming the Gospel. The Gospel that Jesus brought is simply this: God wants to lift man from a position of shame to a position of honor. When Jesus said, "I am the way," this is what he was referring to. Jesus is the only one who can bring us into the presence of God the Father. This is why Jesus had to be God. No one else would do. Only God could reach down to mankind. Jesus Christ was God displayed in the flesh, bringing us the message of reconciliation, a message of hope. God was providing a way to lift us from our place of shame to a place of honor.

Jesus taught us that the man who loves his life will lose it, while the man who hates his life in this world will keep it for eternal life. He went on to say that 'whoever serves Me must follow Me, and where I am, my servant also will be. My Father will honor the one who serves me." (John 12:25-26) Jesus clearly taught that it is God who gives honor, and he gives it to those who renounce worldly honor by dying to self and following Christ.

Questions for Reflection or Discussion

1. Who does the Bible teach us to honor?
2. What acts bring about honor in Christian circles?
3. How do these differ from those of your target culture?
4. Is education a way to gain honor in your target culture? How does education affect people? How much emphasis is put on trying to do well in studies?
5. Does marriage bring honor or status to a young man? Why?
6. Does marriage and children bring honor or status to a young woman? Why?
7. Is there a way to tell an honorable person from an ordinary person through the use of language? Are there special ways to address honorable people? Is there special language that honorable people use?
8. Does money bring honor among your target people, even if it was gained dishonestly? How can you explain this?
9. How important are family lines, or family heroes? Does honor or shame extend along family lines, and is it passed down from generation to generation?
10. Are wise people looked up to? How does one identify a wise person? Are they partially identified through their use of language, proverbs, stories etc?
11. How can you express or bestow honor on others, such as the elders in your community?

Chapter Twenty One
The Three-Fold Message of Salvation

Many times over the years I have asked myself, "How does one effectively communicate the Gospel to people from another worldview?" As I have pondered this question, I have broken it down into two questions. First, what is the Gospel message, and second, how is it best communicated to those who live in another culture than mine, such as the shame-based cultures of Muslims in the Middle East?

Review

In order to communicate the Gospel to all cultures and worldviews, we need to first accept that the Bible deals with God's answer to sin in a way that is applicable and understood in all cultures and worldviews. Sin, as we have seen, has three profound effects on mankind: guilt, shame, and fear. These three effects are dealt with throughout the Scriptures. We in the West have taken the guilt theme and have traced it through the Bible. We have formed our understanding of the Gospel and our systematic theology around this theme. In the Garden of Eden, the Bible tells us that Adam and Eve became guilty and that all mankind after this is in a position of guilt before God. From the book of Genesis we can trace God's plan of salvation, to free man from guilt, right through the Bible. This is the standard Western way of explaining the Gospel.

The Bible also tells us that Adam and Eve were ashamed and hid themselves. This is the beginning of shame. And the theme of God's dealing with the shame that came on mankind runs throughout the length of the Scriptures. Along with this, Adam and Eve were afraid when they heard God's voice in the garden. The theme of God dealing with our fear also runs through the entire Bible.

So today these three reactions to the sin brought on by Adam and Eve's first sin form the basis for three common-ancestor worldviews and all subsequent worldviews that developed down through history. Shame and honor form the basis of the worldviews that span from Morocco to Japan. It is almost exactly the same area as is covered by the 10-40 Window. As the Church in the West became more preoccupied with guilt-based thinking, it struggled in its ability to understand and relate the Gospel to those living with shame-based worldviews. This struggle is so pronounced that the church has made little impact on those parts of the world.

Missionaries have worked for the last two hundred years in fear-based cultures such as are found in Africa and South America and other areas. Many of these missionaries have reported their frustration that the Gospel does not seem to penetrate very deeply into the lives of the people that they work amongst. These missionaries report that the worldviews among these same people is made up of mostly of shame and fear based thinking. The Gospel seems to have penetrated people's lives only as much as there is a mix of guilt-based thinking in their culture. On the other hand, Western Christian workers who have majored on fear-power teaching have had amazing appeal and response from these same people.

This should challenge us to reconsider the makeup of the Gospel message that we are preaching. As I have said before, when man sinned, three great conditions came upon mankind. When man broke God's law, he was in a position of guilt. When man broke God's relationship, he was in a position of shame. When man broke God's trust, he was in a position of fear.

Guilt is more than a sense of having done something wrong. It is a position we fall into when we break a law. Fear comes when we become afraid of a consequence. You might be afraid because of an action or even an inaction. Shame, on the other hand, is more than the feeling of embarrassment or a sense of unworthiness. It is a position we enter into because of our wrong doing or sin. Salvation has to do with saving us from God's judgment, restoring our relationship with God, and rebuilding trust between us and God.

The Holy Spirit

A question that we will have to ask ourselves near the beginning of our discussion of the Gospel message is, "What is the work of the Holy Spirit?"

Jesus tells us, "Nevertheless I tell you the truth; It is expedient for you that I go away: for if I go not away, the Comforter will not come unto you; but if I depart, I will send him unto you. And when he is come, he will reprove the world of sin, and of righteousness, and of judgment: Of sin, because they believe not on me;

Of righteousness, because I go to my Father, and ye see me no more; Of judgment, because the prince of this world is judged." John 16:7-11

What does it mean to reprove the world of sin? The word reprove is *elegcho* or *el-eng'-kho* in the Greek and means to admonish, convict, convince, rebuke, reprove, or expose. Those from a guilt-based worldview often think of the work of the Holy Spirit only in the light of conviction. Those from shame-based cultures often think of the work of the Holy Spirit in terms of exposure. John 3:20 (NIV) tells us, "Everyone who does evil hates the light, and will not come into the light for fear that his deeds will be exposed."

While all of us are affected by exposure, conviction and rebuke, those from some specific worldviews have stronger reactions to some of these aspects than others. Sometimes missionaries from one worldview expect to see a specific reaction to the message of salvation, and are disappointed when it is not forthcoming. I believe that this is because we are pre-conditioned to certain sensitivities, and thus while some feel guilt, others feel shame or fear or a combination of these.

The Holy Spirit may be at work in the lives of our listeners, reproving them of sin, but they may not be feeling conviction of the guilt of their sin.

If we ask ourselves, 'What is the role of the Holy Spirit?' then we must also ask ourselves "What is the role of the evangelist?" Does the evangelist have to work hard to evoke certain emotional responses, or do these responses come from the working of the Holy Spirit in people's lives? If the evangelist puts someone on a guilt-trip, shame-trip, or a fear-trip it is an emotional challenge, but not the same as happens when the Holy Spirit is poured out. Manipulation is not the work of the Holy Spirit. Conviction is, but what is conviction?

What happens if God is already revealing their sin to them in the form of feelings of shame or fear but the evangelist is looking for feelings of guilt? During the work of the Holy Spirit, guilt, shame and fear often blend to become something we call conviction. What that blend is made up of depends largely on how much of each of the three common ancestral worldviews make up the worldview of the listener. We must be careful to understand that sin is the real problem not guilt, shame or fear. These are only the results of the problem, not the problem in themselves. Over the years however, many Christians have been conditioned to understand that salvation has exclusively to do with removing guilt, but the Bible speaks in much wider terms than this.

Our Position

It is important for us to realize that we are dealing with the topic of position here. Guilt is a position before God. (Imagine a man who does something bad, is caught and then taken to court and found guilty. He is then taken to jail where he meets some inmates who are Christians. They witness to him, and he asks God for forgiveness and becomes a follower of Jesus. What is this man's position? He may be forgiven in the sight of God, and perhaps even by those he harmed, but he is still deemed guilty by society and he must serve his jail time, even though he knows he is forgiven. It is also this way with shame. Society may still consider us with disrespect, but we know that in God's eyes we have been raised to a position of honor. God has lifted our heads, even though we continue to suffer contempt by those around us. In the book of James, the writer points out that Christians in churches should not consider some more honorable than others. (James 2:1-9) We are all sinners, cleansed and raised by the work of God. The brotherhood of all believers should include forgiveness, honor, and empowerment, as these things not only demonstrate to the world what has happened to us when God removed our sin, but are the tangible effects that result when forgiven people get together.

One plan or three?

If the work of the Holy Spirit is to reveal sin to people, and the results of sin are guilt shame and fear, are there three plans of salvation in the Bible: one each for guilt, shame and fear? No! The problem is not our guilt, shame or fear. The problem is sin. We must never lose sight of this. The Gospel is all about how sin can be removed from our lives.

What is the Gospel?

The question that faces us is simply, "Are there three or more models that we can use to explain the Gospel?" Should we adopt one model for one setting and other model for a different setting? When working among guilt-based cultures, should we stick to our legal model of salvation? Do we develop a power model of salvation for use among the fear-based cultures of the world? Is there a special shame-honor model of salvation that we should use among the shame-based cultures of the world? What about cultures that demonstrate combinations of these three? Do we develop other models?

I think not. I don't believe there are separate models of salvation that we are to use in different settings. The Bible gives us no clue that God ever intended this to be. Rather, the three themes of salvation are woven together in the Scriptures to present a complete picture of what God wants to do with mankind.

I believe that every presentation of the Gospel should address sin, not just the three subjects of guilt, shame, and fear. In the Bible these are three specific topics that God uses to help us understand his dealing with sin. These three are: Propitiation, Redemption, and Reconciliation.

Propitiation

The word 'propitiation' is a theological term that refers to the act whereby someone's anger is either averted or satisfied. In the case of someone's anger being averted, propitiation results in mercy. In the case of judgment, propitiation provides the requirements of the law, which is then satisfied. The three verses below speak to us of propitiation.

Romans 3:25 - Whom God has set forth to be a propitiation through faith in his blood.

1 John 2:2 - And he is the propitiation for our sins: and not for ours only, but also for the sins of the whole world.

1 John 4:10 - Herein is love, not that we loved God, but that he loved us, and sent his Son to be the propitiation for our sins.

If propitiation has to do with the wrath or anger of God, then it could be charted this way: The sin of man causes the wrath of God which results in the judgment of God on mankind.

Sin of Man --> Wrath of God -> Judgment of God
    a -->   b ->   c

The verses below illustrate how the Bible ties these three topics together. Follow the 'a' which leads to 'b' which leads to 'c' in the verses below.

Exodus 22:22-24 - (a) You shall not afflict any widow or orphan. If you do afflict them, and they cry out to Me, I will surely hear their cry; (b) and My wrath will burn (c) and I will kill you with the sword and your wives shall become widows and your children fatherless.

Deuteronomy 6:14-15 - (a) You shall not go after other gods...(b) lest the anger of the Lord your God be kindled against you (c) and He destroy you from off the face of the earth.

Ezekiel 8:17-18 - (a) Is it too slight a thing for the house of Judah to commit the abominations which they commit here, that they should fill the land with violence, (b) and provoke Me further to anger?...Therefore I will deal in wrath, (c) My eye will not spare, nor will I have pity.

Zephaniah 1:17-18 - I will bring distress on men... (a) because they have sinned against the Lord... (b) In the fire of His jealous wrath, (c) all the earth shall be consumed.

Ezekiel 7:3,8-9 - Now the end is upon you (b) and I will let loose My anger upon you, (c) and will judge you (a) according to your ways; (c) and I will punish you (a) for all your abominations.

Numbers 16:41- (a) They murmured before the Lord so that ... (b) wrath has gone forth from the Lord, (c) the plague has begun. (The Israelites' murmuring kindled God's anger against them and, as a result, a plague came upon them killing 14,700.)

John 3:36 - Whoever believes in the Son has eternal life, but (a) whoever rejects the Son (c) will not see life, for God's wrath (b) remains on him. (NIV)

The anger of God rests upon all of mankind. Subsequently, the judgment of God is currently being poured out upon both individuals and groups of men and women whether in tribes, cultures or nations. We need to communicate that the work of Jesus Christ satisfies the anger of God and removes His judgment from us. This topic of wrath, anger, and the fear that we should live in is an important topic for many worldviews. There are many people who experience this fear in their lives, and when the Gospel is preached from a fear-power paradigm they understand and respond.

Sacrifice is God's answer to propitiation. God's wrath was poured out on the sacrifice. If propitiation is the removal of wrath by the offering of a sacrifice, then propitiation can be explained in terms of God's wrath being removed by Jesus' work on the cross. This concept is easily understood in most fear-based cultures.

Redemption

In the Western mind, redemption has to do with payment for our sin and clearing our guilt. This is also true in a shame-based culture, where redemption has to do with a mediator working out payment to cover our shame and to redeem the honor that was lost. In either case, God has been offended, and a payment must be made to restore the relationship between mankind and God. Most Westerners think of salvation in terms of redemption, where redemption has to do with guilt and the payment required by the law. Since we cannot pay our own debt, a mediator has worked out payment to cover the penalty of sin (death). God has been offended and Christ is our mediator. Since we cannot pay the price, the Mediator chose to pay it for us.

Once again, sacrifice is God's answer to redemption. The laws of God have been broken. We are pronounced guilty, but God has provided a Redeemer, (someone to pay our penalty). The work of Jesus on the cross fully paid the price. We are redeemed, not through our own works, but through the blood of Jesus. We have been bought with a price. (I Corinthians 6:20)

Reconciliation

This is the act of restoring the relationship between man and God. It is more than the legal action of removing guilt. It is the act of God bringing us into a personal father-son relationship with Himself. Reconciliation is all about wholeness. Shame is removed, and honor is restored. Fear is removed, and acceptance and love replace it. In this case a mediator has interceded on our behalf in order to reconcile us with our maker.

Once again, sacrifice is God's answer to reconciliation. We cannot restore the old relationship that was broken in the Garden of Eden. We cannot forge a new relationship. We are 'far' from God. Only the cross can bring us near.

Propitiation   -> God's Wrath   (fear - power paradigm)
Redemption   -> God's Justice   (guilt - innocence paradigm)
Reconciliation -> God's Honor   (shame - honor paradigm)

All aspects of propitiation, redemption and reconciliation are dealt with through Christ's work on the cross as a sacrifice for sins. If God has done all this for us, then what is our part?

Repentance

This is the act of coming to God and accepting His way over our way. Repentance can be viewed in various ways. It is more than just turning from sin.

It is turning from pursuing one's own honor, one's own innocence, or one's own power and accepting what God has done for us. It is also turning from a life of fear, guilt and shame to a life where one is trusting in Christ's victory on the cross to defeat the enemy.

Sacrifice

Christ's sacrifice on the cross deals with our sin. When sin is removed, our shame, guilt and fear are dealt with. The answers to all three lie in Christ's sacrifice on the cross to deal with our sin. Satan however, tries to convince the believer that he is still suffering from the consequences of sin, so that we will doubt the work of God.

Where to start

The secret to sharing the Gospel, if there is such, is to use one or two of the three common-ancestral worldviews as the initial expression of the Gospel as it correlates with the worldview of the culture you are dealing with. If you are working in a guilt-based culture, there will be a felt need to deal with guilt. If you are working in a shame-based culture, there is a felt need to address shame. The same goes for a fear-based culture, needing to address fear.

It is important to look beyond the general culture to try and understand the person you are dealing with. On one occasion a fellow missionary and I were trying to share the Gospel with a Bedouin in his tent. After our first visit we realized that this man was struggling with a very acute sense of fear. He feared demons, the evil eye, and curses. When we returned to share the Gospel with him, we focused on God being able to overcome those things that we are afraid of.

Several miles away we were visiting another man and his family. This man had stooped to the place where he began to market his wife as a prostitute. As a result he was held in low-esteem in the community. This man had seen the Jesus film, and was attracted to Jesus who sat with prostitutes and sinners. In this case we started sharing the Gospel from a shame and guilt viewpoint. What we shared wasn't a "different Gospel" but rather the same message tailored to the felt needs of the listener.

I believe that the methods of the church around the world must be flexible enough to change depending on the culture that is being addressed. We have done an excellent job in communicating to the Western world that the church offers God's forgiveness for sin. In an Eastern setting, the church needs to communicate the message that God is offering respect and worth to those in a position of shame.

In a fear-based culture, the Church must communicate the message that God offers freedom from the bondage of fear. In every case, however, we must not limit our message to just the one facet.

As I have traveled in North America, I have tried to concentrate my preaching on the fact that God not only offers forgiveness of sins, but He also offers freedom from fear, and wants to restore our worth and value. I have been amazed at the positive response to this message. People have come to me telling me that they have asked for forgiveness for their sins, but they still carried shame. Others are stricken with anxiety and fear. Our focus in the West on guilt has left us with only a partial understanding of the Gospel, and some Christians are suffering because they are still bound by shame or fear.

We who communicate the Gospel message must share the full three-fold message of salvation. It is like a braided chord or rope. The three parts wrap around each other, strengthening each other. All three should be present in our Gospel presentation. Which one will be our starting point in sharing the Gospel will depend on the culture in which we live.

In animistic cultures it is natural to begin our message of salvation with something that focuses on fear. Man fears because man rebelled and did his own thing. We have a message of hope for those living in a world of fear. This message of salvation would not be complete, however, without fearful people learning to understand that Christ came to remove our guilt, and lift us from shame. Once someone understands all three views, they have a fuller understanding of what was involved in the removal of sin through Christ's work on the cross.

In the same way, those living in shame-based cultures need to have a complete view of salvation, but the door through which they will most easily come will probably be one that starts with man's shame in the Garden of Eden. This is the world they understand. Shame comes when people get found out. We are all exposed to the eyes of God, and thus in a position of shame. Every time we fail, we continue in a position of shame, because God's eye is upon us. Those that pursue the honor of the world have a false or shallow honor. The only honor that counts is honor before God. God calls us to repent of seeking worldly honor and to turn to him to have our shame removed. Even though we start with how God deals with shame, we must also go on to share the full message of salvation, explaining how God deals with our guilt and fears. All of these are accomplished through the removal of sin through the work of Christ on the cross.

Paul was fully aware of this when he wrote about making the message understood to the Jews, the Greeks, and the barbarians. Even in Paul's day, the world was split into three great worldviews. The Jews were a Semitic people who lived in a shame-based culture. The Greeks were the ones who were developing a guilt-based culture, and the barbarians were those who lived in fear-based cultures.

Paul did not preach three separate messages of salvation. He preached only one. Paul, however, used different techniques when addressing different people. In his letter to the Romans, he speaks to people who lived in a more or less guilt-based society. In his letter to the Romans, he addresses man's guilt as a result of man's transgression of God's law. On the other hand, when Paul was on Mars Hill, he addressed the Greek's who had a pantheon of gods. He drew their attention to the unknown god and to Christ's resurrection from the dead as demonstrating that God was dealing with the human race differently. God was setting up a new order that started with the resurrection of the man who would judge all men. (Acts 17:1-34). Just as Paul used different starting points, we also should be sensitive to our audience, and start with things that are familiar to them in order to bring them to the message of the cross and the resurrection.

In Romans 1:16-17, Paul describes the Gospel message in light of these three aspects when he states, "I am not ashamed of the Gospel for it is the power of God unto salvation to everyone that believes; to the Jew first, and also to the Greek. For in it the righteousness of God is revealed from faith to faith: as it is written, The righteous shall live by faith." (ESV) His reference to both Jew and Greek indicates that the Gospel dispelled all discrimination or positions of shame and honor. In this passage the Gospel is not described in terms of guilt, shame, and fear, but rather by using their counterparts, power (fear), righteousness (guilt), and no discrimination (shame).

Paul goes on to tell us about our new bodies that will be given to us in the resurrection from the dead (I Corinthians 15:42-43, KJV). "So also is the resurrection from the dead. It is sown in corruption; it is raised in incorruption. (from guilt to innocence). It is sown in dishonor; it is raised in glory (from shame to honor). It is sown in weakness, it is raised in power." (from a position of fear to a position of power). The glorious future that we look forward to is expressed to us clearly in terms of guilt, shame and fear. Once sin is defeated, we will be raised innocent, honorable, and powerful. Our innocence will be God's innocence placed upon us. Our honor will be God's honor raising us up. Our power will be God's power living through us. The message of salvation in the Bible is clearly expressed to us in terms of God dealing with guilt, shame and fear, as He effectively frees us from the hold and bondage of sin.

Cross-cultural contextualization of the Gospel is simply knowing how to start the Gospel message from a place of common understanding with our audience. It is knowing how to relate the Gospel message in a language and form that is meaningful to its listeners. Finally, it is knowing how to bring the person to a full understanding of Christ's work on the cross.

In many cases, new believers drift away because they have not grasped a complete picture of salvation. They need teaching in order to grow because they have responded to only one of the aspects of salvation and may see the work of Christ on the cross in a very limited way.

It is the responsibility of the person sharing the Gospel to address all three aspects of guilt, shame, and fear, tracing God's message of salvation throughout the Bible. It is there. It is clearly demonstrated in the Garden of Eden. It is pictured in the various acts of worship in the Temple. It is addressed by the prophets and is clearly presented in Isaiah 53. The three-fold message of salvation is seen in the work of Christ at Calvary. It is present at Pentecost and in the daily empowering of the Holy Spirit in our lives. Finally, it will be addressed with the return of our Lord Jesus Christ. We will experience it personally at the resurrection of the dead and ultimately in our position and experience in heaven.

Unfortunately, all too often, missionaries from guilt-based cultures have busied themselves with pointing out the sins of people living in shame-based cultures, but the people they are addressing never feel guilt. They may, however, feel that the missionary is shaming them by drawing attention to these areas of their lives. Missionaries can go even further, unintentionally shaming people by asking why they weren't in church and encouraging them to attend. In the end, it may cause them to attend, but they may do so simply out of a desire not to shame their missionary friend.

Many of our well-meaning Western ways of ministering can be misunderstood in other cultures. There are cultural "mine fields" that must be carefully negotiated, as we challenge people with the claims of the gospel. It isn't enough to simply use the right popular approach in vogue in that culture. We must also be aware that we are calling them to go against the flow in whatever cultural setting they live in. There is always a point of conflict as the gospel challenges all worldview systems.

I trust that through the message of this section, you have been challenged to dig more deeply and learn more effectively how to share the Gospel with people from other cultures. I have not attempted to explain everything. The purpose of this book is simply to unlock the door and open a world of new understanding when it comes to sharing the Gospel with people from other cultures.

Questions for Reflection or Discussion

1. Go back and view your answer in chapter five about what you would include in presenting a gospel message. Would you change your answer after reading this chapter? Why or why not?

2. How can we get people to see that sin is a major problem that needs to be dealt with?

3. "If people cannot see their sin, they will not have a need or desire for Jesus" Is this true? Why or why not?

4. How do people feel or experience sin in their lives? How can we show them that they have sin?

5. Read John 16:7-11. What is the work of the Holy Spirit?

6. Are feelings of shame, fear and guilt the result of the exposing work of the Holy Spirit? Why or why not?

7. What is conviction?

8. What is the role of the evangelist and of the Holy Spirit? Who does what?

9. If guilt is a position before God, are shame and fear also a position?

10. How does salvation change our position before God?

11. Does salvation change our position before society? How?

12. Does salvation change our position before the church?

13. Should the topic of fear be a part of our salvation message? Is God only love or can an element of fear also be involved? Deuteronomy 6:14-15, Zephaniah 1:17-18, John 3:36. How does this fit into your salvation message?

14. Can you find a local illustration where someone's anger was averted because of something that was sacrificially given by someone else?

15. Can you find a local illustration where something was redeemed or paid for through the sacrifice given by someone else?

16. Can you find a local illustration where a relationship was restored through the sacrifice given by someone else?

17. What does repentance mean? How can this be illustrated in your target culture?
18. Think of a person wrestling with a shame-based issue. How would you go about sharing the gospel with them?
19. Think of a person wrestling with a fear-based issue. How would you go about sharing the gospel with them?

Chapter Twenty Two
The Continuing Story

In this section (The Message) we have discovered that when building worldview models we should consider the three common ancestral worldviews as described in the Bible. Understanding these three fundamental building blocks will help us understand the foundation upon which worldview is built. As a worldview model is then constructed, many of the actions, values and beliefs of people can be better understood and appreciated.

Over the last three thousand years of history, great historical periods have come and gone. In the years before Christ, the world was torn apart by competing armies. The Egyptians, Assyrians, Babylonians, and others vied for power. Vast armies moved back and forth over the world with first one, and then another civilization becoming dominant. Despite their linguistic and cultural differences, most of these civilizations held a similar worldview. Gods and demons controlled their universe, and man lived in fear of these powers, doing what he could to appease them. The first chapters of civilization on earth were in the hands of those who lived in cultures built upon fear and power.

However, by the time of Christ, guilt-based cultures had risen to power, and they strove to take over the Western world. First Greek and then Roman armies marched across this part of the world, seeking to subject everyone to their worldview. While their civilizations still had many fear-based qualities, their new emphasis on the law helped them develop the first great civilizations based on using guilt as a controlling factor. The millennium following the birth of Christ belonged to these guilt-based cultures. These civilizations were known as the Greek, Roman, and Byzantine Empires. While these empire ruled around the Mediterranean, they were continually challenge by huge shame-based empires to the east.

In the last days of the year 999, civilization was following a clear course. The future of world politics lay with Islam. It seemed an unstoppable force that would eventually control much of the world, including whatever parts of Europe they chose to occupy.

The Muslims had energy, confidence, and imagination. Their society was now far superior to that of Europe. Bernard Lewis, the renowned historian of Islam, has written that the Muslims of those days "neither feared nor respected the barbarous individuals of northern and Western Europe, whom they saw as uncouth primitives." Islam at this stage was probably the most sophisticated and cosmopolitan civilization in the world.

So, how did it happen that Christian Europe and the colonies it established in America eventually dominated the world? What started out as Islam's millennium, became Europe's, in the end. Islam grew until 1669 when the Muslim Ottoman Empire, after a long war, took Crete from the Venetians. That turned out to be Islam's last acquisition. Fourteen years later it became obvious that history was reversing itself. In 1683 the Muslim Ottomans, after trying to conquer Vienna for 60 days, withdrew in disarray. The fighting that followed destroyed much of their army and crippled the military wing of Islam.

A Polish man named Kulyeziski had been instrumental in defending Vienna and for his efforts he was rewarded all the coffee the Turkish army left behind. Gifted in the ability to capitalize on things when the opportunity presented itself, he opened a café in Vienna and commissioned a baker to create a unique new pastry to accompany the coffee as a way to celebrate the great victory over Islam. The baker produced a crescent shaped pastry that the Viennese could eat to celebrate the defeat of Islam. It was called the croissant.

From the Muslim perspective, however, Europe soon ceased to be an invasion target and became an alien force whose armies and cultures began to trespass on Arab lands. A key year in European history was 1492. The date is well known as the year when Columbus arrived in the Americas. In January of that year, Granada, the last Islamic city in Spain, surrendered to European armies. Before the year was over, Columbus had arrived in America and Europe started its great expansion westward across the Atlantic.

Islam now turned its attention to the shame-based cultures of the East, reinforcing it's position as far as Indonesia, Malaysia, and deep into China. In the outh, they began moving against the fear-based African cultures, penetrating deep nto Africa. However, by 1918 the Muslim caliphate collapsed, and virtually the whole Muslim world experienced some form of colonization. It has only been since he 1970s that Islam started recovering as a political entity.

Over the course of time, history has moved from the early civilizations that were ear-based (BC), to the rapid expansion of the guilt-based cultures (100 BC -900 AD). During the next millennium from 900 AD till 1500, shame-based cultures eem to have had the upper hand. After this the ball was passed to the guilt-based ultures of America and Northern Europe.

At the end of the second millennium, a new force had grown on the face of the world: the evangelical church. By the end of 1999, evangelicals were the fastest growing religious force in the world. They had penetrated almost every country of the world and today continue to grow rapidly in many Third World countries.

Patrick Johnstone, in his book, The Church is Bigger than You Think, tells us that evangelicals are growing at over three times the population rate and are the world's only body of religious adherents growing rapidly by means of conversion.

The question remains, will the next millennium belong to the evangelicals? Will we be able to relate to all worldviews? All of the great civilizations of the world have failed to move out of their particular worldview with any success. Islam is struggling to move out of a shame-based world into the Western one. They are working on it, and are making certain advances. Christianity, on the other hand is struggling to relate to those in the shame-based world. However Christianity was not birthed under one worldview.

It was not by mere chance that Jesus was born into a stable in Bethlehem, and that his death on the cross took place in the city of Jerusalem. The cross of Christ stands firmly at the crossroads of the world. To the west are the guilt-based cultures of the world. To the south are the fear-based cultures, and to the east the shame-based cultures. And in the midst of all of them, the cross of Christ stands as a strong bold message of peace on earth and good will to all mankind.

The Church of Jesus Christ has the message and the methods to relate to every worldview and every culture in the world. In this book I have simply attempted to unlock the door to our understanding of guilt, shame, and fear-based common ancestral worldviews. It is my hope and desire that soldiers of the cross of Christ will open the door, and with the Bible in one hand, and the Holy Spirit guiding them, they will enter into a world that few soldiers of the cross have entered before. The millennium that might have belonged to the shame-based cultures is now over. Evangelicals must struggle to understand and relate to all worldviews, and secondly to battle secularism that rides fast behind every kingdom advance.

It is now your duty, as a servant of the Lord Jesus, to explore further and discover that the fields are indeed white unto harvest, but the laborers are few. May God bless you as you labor in his harvest-field.

Questions for Reflection or Discussion

1. Summarize in a couple of sentences what you learned in the "Message" section of this book.

2. What new skills would you like to practice?

3. What core beliefs have been challenged or strengthened through this section?

4. What do you want to change or address in your life or ministry?

5. What fears do you have?

6. What is one main goal you want to work on after reading this chapter?

7. Are there issues your team should address? Which ones?

8. How will you go about working on this as a team?

THE COMMUNITY

Introduction to *The Community*

When I finished writing the first two sections of this book, I felt that I had finished writing what I knew about planting churches in a cross-cultural situation. My family and I then returned to the Middle East to continue our ministry based on the concepts we had previously learned, this time in a fresh new setting among nomads. It was during this time that we came up against the third hurdle. While we had always known it was there, we were confident that with the principles we had gleaned from others, and from the wisdom that God gives in specific situations, we would be able to see our way through. We were wrong. Once again we discovered that we really were very ignorant.

The most frustrating thing was that while we knew we were making mistakes, we didn't know how to correct them. During this time, a fellow worker with more years of experience in gathering new believers together shared his findings with us. During his years of struggling to plant churches he had started to analyze the problems he was facing from the viewpoint of the new believer, rather than from the viewpoint of the frustrated Western missionary. He then listed the issues and steps that the new believers were going through as they moved from simply having contact with a messenger to that of belonging to a functioning body of believers. As I examined his list, I initially found it confusing. There were so many things I had taken for granted that were now being challenged. My whole view of the Church and the role of the Church in the community was being challenged. Out of the ashes of failure, with the help of my friends, I began to see a way forward.

In the next section of this book, I want to examine the material that was shared with me and try to explore with you how new believers from a non-Christian culture might view the Church, and how they might approach the gathering together of believers. What are they expecting? What are they looking for? What are the important issues from their perspective? What new concepts do they have to learn? What advice can they offer us?

Once again I don't offer all the answers, only some of the questions and some of the attempts that others have made in trying to build vibrant communities of believers that love Jesus.

Chapter Twenty Three
The Importance of Biblical Community

The word community is a commonly used English term to describe a group of people living in some sort of relationship with each other. Webster's dictionary describes community as "A group of people living in the same area and under the same government." While this is technically true, community is something more than this. In effect, our community is where we live, work, play, worship, and educate our kids. In general terms, it is the group of people that we rely on for support in the daily activities and challenges that life brings us. Our communities provide us with certain services, and we in turn have certain obligations and bonds to our community. We pay taxes and participate in the various societies, interest groups and action groups that help form our community. While this is one definition of community, it is not what many people mean by using the word today.

In the West, the term "community spirit" is used. This is where people participate together in activities for the good of the community. In the interest of "community spirit" we are encouraged to buy our goods within the community, and to participate as much as possible in the daily life of the community. We work together to keep our streets clean and safe and to provide sports and leisure facilities for our families. Community spirit is seen as good and positive, and those who refuse to cooperate are usually branded as outsiders, and even seen as selfish and self seeking.

During my years of ministry in the Middle East, I have frequently lamented at the lack of community spirit around me. Streets are often dirty, and people seem to be happy to throw their garbage just outside their homes. No amount of encouragement seems to work in getting people to take care of the community outside of the immediate confines of their homes.

Many of the more "modern" or "Western" nations in the third world are making great strides in the Western concept of community spirit. Efforts are being made to encourage villages and towns to have a town council, and for the council to take action concerning the issues of the community. In the Hashemite Kingdom of Jordan, the government often refuses aid to villages and towns unless they have a functioning council that will take responsibility. Government funds are available for kindergartens, roads, garbage collection, and even mosques, if the people of the town can demonstrate that they can work together. All of this is seen as being modern and progressive, but it is not necessarily seen as building community. Community, from an Eastern point of view can be quite different.

When I arrived in the Middle East, I discovered that Muslims described Islam as a "community of faith." By this term, they meant that Muslims living everywhere act as a community. They have common bonds through the religion of Islam which dictates how the community should live and how its members should relate to one another. This is also very true in many Hindu setting. Communities are made up of those near to you. These are your immediate family, not necessarily people who live close to you in a physical way. Traditionally, the family or tribe has acted as a person's community, and religion acts as the glue that keeps these communities functioning. So in fact, despite my lament about the lack of community spirit, I discovered that there was indeed a strong community spirit; it just operated differently and showed itself differently.

Who are our Neighbors?

Years ago when studying the Arabic language I told my language teacher the story of the Good Samaritan. I then alluded to the idea that Christians and Muslims could be "neighbors." This seemed to be a revolutionary idea to my teacher. The word neighbor in Arabic means "one who you are near to." To the Easterner this obviously referred to blood relations first and marriage relations second. It had nothing to do with physical nearness. When I pointed out that the Bible tells us that the Jews and Samaritans were not "near" in the Eastern sense of the word, but rather were enemies and had no dealings with each other, my teacher was puzzled. As we discussed it, it became obvious that Jesus was teaching an important lesson about "nearness." The Samaritan who took pity on the Jew was deemed 'near' by Jesus because of his actions and the attitude of his heart. This is a very important lesson for the church planter. Nearness is a very important concept in the non-Western world. Building fellowships of believers that are 'near' to each other is an important concept that the church planter must grapple with. The Bible encourages us to build communities of

208

believers, where the "nearness" is based on faith in Christ rather than blood relations.

The Eastern Community

The Eastern model of community is quite different from the Western concept of community. For instance, when a young man desires to find work, he turns to his extended family/community, and expects to find work within that community, if at all possible. He will initially look to his uncles and to distant relatives to see who might employ him in one of the family businesses. In his mind, employment within the tribal community is best, for he can participate in the building of this community, as well as gaining a salary. If he cannot find work within his own community, he will then look farther afield, but usually with the idea of earning money and bringing that money back into his own tribal community. Each year, thousands of Arabs work outside their communities, some venturing to other countries. They will work hard and excel in their jobs, but they will also funnel funds back to their community, where they can build a house and eventually set up some sort of business within the security of their extended family community.

The concept of community being built around the extended family unit has been in existence for many centuries. When you ask a Palestinian refugee where he is from, he will tell you the location of his home community. He will often name a village in Palestine, even though he has never been to this place, and his father may not have been there. It is still the location of the family community, even though people from another nationality occupy their houses and farm their lands.

On one occasion my wife witnessed community in action while traveling by public transport in the Middle East. When she entered the vehicle, the driver was busy on his cell phone. During the course of her trip, she observed this man participating in "community." Someone near to him was in the hospital, needing money for an operation. This man, along with others, then got busy on the phone to try and raise the funds that were needed. During the entire journey this man telephoned his friends and acquaintances to ask them to pledge help. He collected some money here and there. In between he would call back to the hospital to report his progress. No one was missed, not even the passengers. Everyone was given the opportunity to participate in this community action, and people responded. Everyone seemed to understand that if a lot of people gave a little, then the total could be reached, so people gladly dug into their pockets to help this stranger. Those who were closer to the situation gave more, but everyone felt good about working together, in the spirit of community.

209

Traditionally, ancient cities were made up of a collection of communities. Individual areas of a city were known as Quarters, such as the "Armenian Quarter" or the "Jewish Quarter." (The word quarter refers to living quarters rather than a fourth of something.) This is still true of many ancient cities today, where the older sections of the city are named after the place where the inhabitants came from or the ethnic makeup of the people who first settled there. In one city where we lived, our home was near the edge of a section of the city known as "Hai al Hajazeen." (The Hajazeen Quarter). The Hajazeen tribe was a nominal Christian tribe that had emigrated from the area of Saudi Arabia known as the Hejaz into the country of Jordan.

The existence of communities of families within a city is much older than Islam. It goes back to Biblical times, and has been a common element in most shame-honor based societies. For example, in the Biblical book of Nehemiah, chapter 3, we read of the various communities within Jerusalem working on different sections of the city wall. This was a very ancient tradition that is still found in some areas of the world today. While visiting the walled city of Sa'ada in Yemen, I was told that the city wall was maintained by everyone in the city. Each family-community had a section of the wall that they were responsible for. If the wall fell into disrepair, the honor of the responsible family-community was at stake. So it was in Nehemiah chapter three. When the call came for the wall to be repaired, the various communities within the city each took responsibility for a section of the wall. Community spirit? Yes, this is community spirit, functioning well within the framework of an honor-shame based community.

When the religion of Islam arrived on the scene, it came as more than just a new religion. Islam not only identified Allah as the exclusive God, it also brought a whole new set of religious customs. The teaching in the Qur'an was not limited only to teaching about religious practices. The Qur'an provided teaching about how the community would function. Islam was a total way of life, giving direction to individuals and also to family-communities. Islam's strength is that it was formed in the honor-shame part of the world, with honor-shame based communities in mind. Islam recognized family-based communities and provided guidelines of how these communities were to operate.

But Islam went one step farther. Islam saw itself as the glue that held these communities together. While cities were collections of family-based communities,

Islam itself was a religion of family-based communities. So Islam calls itself a "community of faith." In effect, it is a community of communities, a religious community made up of family-based communities. "You are the best community that has been raised up for mankind." (Qur'an 3:110)

Islam is very specific about how people and communities should relate together. For example, the Qur'an and the Hadith (The Traditions) give very specific instructions concerning the forms that need to be followed in every setting. Detailed instructions are given about how men and women should relate. All manner of subjects are dealt with and rules, regulations, and guidelines are given, even down to the direction one should or should not face when going to the bathroom. (Baring one's bottom towards Mecca would be to dishonor the holy place.)

While most Western researchers use terms like brotherhood, solidarity, equality, and unity to describe the community spirit in Islam, in actual fact it runs far deeper than this. Muslims believe that it is their responsibility to care for one another. While this is sometimes overshadowed by the Western media portrayal of various forms of hatred and violence, the attitude of mutual care is genuinely fostered and felt within Islam. The whole concept of belonging is important to Eastern communities. Belonging is not just something that you opt into for a short period of time; it entails commitment to, and responsibilities for others in the community. This is why communities made up of a combination of blood ties and faith ties are very strong.

When a Muslim or Hindu approaches Christianity, he considers religion as a community of communities. This thinking influences the opinions that he will form about Christianity. Thus, he is interested in Christian community with its rules, regulations, guidelines, forms, and customs. This is a normal part of what happens when another religious system is examined.

If a person is really seeking answers and exploring Christianity, he or she may well be interested in our Christian community. If the seeker has accepted that the messenger might be a valid messenger, and has then accepted the message might be a valid message, then the seeker has one last step to make: that of accepting the Christian community as a possible valid community, and herein lies the problem.

For instance, a Muslim's concept of community and a Western Christian's concept of the Church are two very different things. The Muslim seeker is looking at the Church through the eyes of Islam, wanting to find a community of faith that he or she can fit into. However, the Western Christian's concept of the Church has been molded by years of immersion in cultures based on individualism and a guilt-innocence worldview. Usually there is little room for the things that the Muslim desires to find.

In most cases, what we Christians have to offer to Muslims, as far as a community of believers is concerned, is something very unattractive. At least this is how it often appears to those Muslims who are seeking a viable Christian community of communities. Muslims, who are cautious thinkers, will explore our communities first, looking for a new home where they can live and function. If they cannot find it, they will usually turn away. This is a very sad situation, especially when they have accepted the messenger as a valid messenger, and when they have listened to and accepted the message as being a valid message. That is why many Muslim seekers turn away with sadness and maybe even bitterness.

On the other hand, there are Muslims who are not so cautious and who readily accept a messenger and their message. Most of these have not thought through the issues of community. From my experience, most of them naively imagine that they will discover their place in a warm, loving, and accepting Christian community, with support structures much like they had in the community they left. Some are so disappointed that after years of searching they leave the Christian faith.

Many others move from church to church, seeking their place but never finding it. Eventually they may accept a Western view of the church and community and settle somewhere, but often they have a feeling that they are missing something. Some, unfortunately, even after years of Christian living and involvement in the Church, return back to their old community. They do so, not out of a change of theology, but simply from a desire to be part of a community as they know it.

This leaves us with several burning questions. First, what are the essential elements that are needed to build a functioning Biblical Christian community of believers? Second, how does one help an existing church to become one of these functioning Biblical Christian communities of believers? And finally, how can we assist Muslims, Hindus, Buddhists and others in their move from one community to another?

These questions may sound simple, but they are fraught with difficulties. For instance, when working through the Biblical basis for community, a number of important questions have to be answered. How closely does the Biblical model have to correspond with the popular models used today? If we propose an entirely new model of Christian community, how can we offer it to seekers as a viable alternative, especially if it doesn't exist anywhere else in the world? Then, if we create these unique communities, how do the members of these communities relate to the rest of Christendom? Do we view Christianity as a 'community of communities,' and do the believers in our new communities have a sense of belonging to a wider community of faith? On top of this, how closely should our new communities reflect the models found in the surrounding setting? Should our churches (or Christian communities) of believers from a Muslim background be "Christianized forms of Islamic community," or "Islamitized forms of Christian community?" As you can see, the issues are numerous and difficult.

In trying to answer these questions, I would like to propose a much simpler middle path. First, we should examine the Biblical principles of Christian community in order to understand some of the essential elements. Second, we should examine some of the steps that seekers take when exploring and analyzing our community. Finally, we should examine our own community and allow the believers in any given context to create or change their own community while adhering to the essentials as they adapt them to the local culture.

Questions for Reflection or Discussion

1. What expressions of 'community' do you see expressed by the people you work among?

2. What expression of community do you see lacking in the people you work among?

3. Do you think that Christianity can be described as a "community of communities?" What would this mean to your target people?

4. How large a role does religion play in community life?

5. Do you think that people find an expression of community through their religion? How and why?

6. If they came to Christ, would they find the same expression of community? Why or why not?

7. At what level do people care for one another and look out for others?

8. Do you think that new believers are accepting Christian community as a valid community for themselves? What are the attractions of Christian community and what are the barriers?

9. In your church planting efforts, would you say that your church is closer to a Western model of Christian community or closer to a local model of community? Do you think your model is the best one for your situation?

10. How important do you think 'community' is to church planting? Is it something that your target people group greatly desire? Does your church meet or exceed their expectations?

Chapter Twenty Four
Biblical Principles of Community

I have discovered something interesting about Christians. Whenever I talk about the early Church they tend to warm up. There is something about the early Church that we all like. It was fresh, new, and full of zeal. The book of Acts contains thrilling stories about the great exploits of the apostles and the first missionaries. While these exploits are exciting and commendable, most believers are attracted to the early church because they see "community" in action.

In this and the following chapters we want to examine the Biblical principles of community, seek to understand just what it was that the early church enjoyed, and what it is for which we long for when we read the Scriptures that describe these believers to us.

Concepts

In order to do this, I would like to focus our attention on four concepts that the Bible teaches us about the church. For the average Western reader, the idea of living by concepts is a natural one. Many believers from a Muslim background, however, have difficulty drawing concepts and principles from scripture. The Qur'an is seen as God's Word for mankind, in which God dictates how he wants man to live by laying down clear and simple direction. Muslims seldom concern themselves with principles and concepts in the Qur'an. The Qur'an speaks to everything directly. It tells people how to pray, how many wives they can have, and how to treat them, and so on. Muslims go to the Qur'an or the Hadiths to understand how they should act and what is permissible in a specific setting. For example, since smoking isn't mentioned, smoking is permissible.

When a Muslim comes in contact with Christianity, he is introduced to a new kind of thinking. Christians seldom look for "legal direction" in their Bibles. They understand that the Bible lays out principles and concepts that we need to live by. Therefore, Christians understand that the concept of our bodies being a temple of the Holy Spirit brings us to the principle that it is important to look after our bodies, and thus smoking does not please God since it aids in the destruction of the body. While Christians formulate principles to live by, the Muslim simply shrugs and comments that if God didn't mention it, then it is probably OK to do.

So we come to the principle of Christians and community. In one sense, the Muslim has an easier time of it. He simply obeys the letter of the law and participates in community as far as the Qur'an and his local culture dictate. Christians on the other hand, have the tough work of drawing principles out of the Scriptures that can be applied across all cultural settings. In effect, a Christian who is discipling a new believer needs to explain how the local Christian community operates. I believe that when community is explained, confidence is imparted.

As churchplanters we must be very careful not to encourage new Christians to develop definitive rules for everything. Sometimes we do this by describing the Bible is an instruction manual. If that is what it is supposed to be, it is the worst one ever written. Instruction manuals are systematically and logically laid out for the benefit of the ignorant with easy step by step explanations. The Bible is not like this, because it is not an instruction manual, it is a rich source of principle and experience.

Community is built around bonding

All of us have bonding capabilities. We can bond to all sorts of things such as people, activities, and ideologies. If we are to build a community, we need to provide things that people can bond with. There must be vision, goals, principles, friendships and other common elements that the members of the community can bond with. Bonding is an act of the soul; something within us that desires to reach out and bond.

Some people, however, resist bonding. There can be various reasons for this. Individuals with little bonding experience, or who have experienced negative bonding, may fear bonding itself. This is a common occurrence in Western society where individualism is looked upon as a strength rather than a weakness. In order to overcome this, community must be explained and then experienced. For many people, explanation is not enough. Once true community is experienced, a thirst will be awakened that only community can satisfy.

There are some people who have something pathologically different about hem and they cannot seem to bond. There may be several reasons for this. The person may be held in strong satanic bonds, or they may have suffered psychological damage sometime in the past. They may fear bonding, or fear the hurt that one can encounter if they bond with someone or something that has the capability to wound them. However, I believe bonding is part of God's plan for man. People who describe themselves as 'loners' are really comparing themselves to the majority of people who bond with others. People who have hurts and have been disappointed usually have had deep strong expectations which they may never have defined, but yet still shape their existence. Once these hurts and painful issues have been addressed, people who seem to react negatively to bonding, can learn to experience and appreciate bonding again.

What is community?

Community is the desire to be one with others. It stems from our bonding capacity. This bonding capacity/ability never goes away. Even when we are old, we are still reaching out to those around us. We will in fact bond to everyone we meet in some fashion (and even to some we don't meet). This bond is generally expressed in an emotion. As it happens, there are two major bonds available. Either the bond will be love, or it will be hate. Once a bond is made, there is an expression of community, even if the bond is hatred.

Community can be experienced at a number of levels. The normal pattern for this is as follows: maternal -> paternal -> sibling -> extended family ->ethnic community (tribe) ->non-ethnic community -> local community ->national community -> international community -> spiritual community.

Depending on our circumstances, we can experience community at any of these levels, but seldom do we experience community at all of these levels. In many cultures community is experienced at the following levels: maternal, paternal, sibling, extended family, & tribal.

The religion of Islam tries to add the further levels of international community and spiritual community.

This explains how a Muslim Arab can experience community at these levels, but still holds prejudices against certain other groups, such as rival clans, or people of a different national or ethnic background. Islam holds tribal communities together, but still allows conflict at the ethnic and international levels.

In the West, many people have missed experiencing community at a family level. Broken homes, divided marriages, isolationism and individualism have robbed many of the 'community experience.' Today many young people experience community only at non-family or non-ethnic levels, such as school, in social groups, over the Internet, or with people in the entertainment world. Powerful bonds are often formed at this level because young people have not experienced community on a family level. Many times young people try to replace the earlier missing family bonds with bonds built around their social group. For many Western Christians, "church" is simply a meeting/worship place where individuals meet. Bonding is usually very superficial, as deeper bonding takes place in other social settings.

In an Eastern setting, bonding usually starts at the family level and often stops at the tribal/ethnic level. This is because when they get past the ethnic level they run into things such as different skin color, language, culture and worldview. This is often a hurdle that the cross-cultural church planter will experience both in his own life and also in the lives of those he is ministering to.

Building Christian community can therefore be difficult. Western people can resist community because of negative or missing experiences. Eastern people can resist community past the tribal level, usually because they have never imagined that community extends that far. Yet the Bible calls us to community that is built on deeper foundations.

Image

Another issue is identity. One of the issues with which we struggle is a desire for the world to be molded in our own image. By this I mean an expectancy that other people should conform to our own understanding of how things should be. All of us seem to go through this phase of wanting the world to be in our own image. We want friends and family to be in our image, spouses want their partner to be in their image, pastors and leaders want the church to be in their image, Americans want the world to be in their image. So, of course, do the Christians, and so does Islam. Hence the failure of community everywhere.

Everyone, including Muslims, need to learn to appreciate diversity in our communities. God loves diversity. He has made it part of all creation and he has made it an essential ingredient in community. It is one of the important lessons for the new convert.

Biblical Community

The Bible uses four terms to describe Christian community to us. These terms are not simply metaphors, but rather Biblical descriptions of how God wants us to view community. If we can understand these four, we have gone a long way in learning how to create or encourage true Christian community.

1. The Kingdom

Jesus conducted his ministry in Palestine for a period of three years, and for those three years his teachings prepared the way for the formation of the first Christian community. It is important to note that from the beginning of his ministry, Jesus taught his followers about the kingdom. When John the Baptist arrived on the scene, his message in Matthew 3:1&2 was also very simple. "In those days John the Baptist came preaching in the wilderness of Judah, 'Repent, for the kingdom of heaven is at hand.'" (ESV) This message announced the beginning of something that was to be known as the *kingdom*.

This kingdom was not some far off event, but was something that was very imminent. When Jesus started preaching, a short time later he also focused on this same message about the kingdom of God. Even before he called his disciples, Jesus had already started his ministry of preaching the kingdom of God. "Now when John was arrested, Jesus came into Galilee, proclaiming the Gospel God saying, 'The time is fulfilled, and the kingdom of God is at hand; repent and believe in the Gospel.'" Mark 1:14-15 (ESV)

Jesus continued to use the concept of the kingdom right through his teaching ministry. Even in the days before his death, he was still teaching about the kingdom (Matthew 25).

The concept of the kingdom was a useful one in describing the new community's relationship with God and with one another in community. It was a concept that people could understand, for governments at the time were made up of kingdoms, republics, democracies and dictatorships. (Herod the Great was a king. The Romans had a republic. The neighboring Nabataean empire exercised democracy, and many other nations were under dictators.) Jesus however, used the example of a kingdom to represent best what it was that he was coming to begin.

The King and his Subjects

The first lesson we should note is that there is a special relationship between a king and his subjects. Kings have absolute authority, and subjects are just that: subject to the king. This is a very important principle that must be present in our Christian communities. We are not democratic groups of believers. Rather, we are all subjects, and Jesus is Lord of us all. The entire community and everyone in it is subject to the Lordship of Jesus. We live, act, worship, and function as subjects of Christ. Everyone is welcome to join the community, but they must understand that in joining the community, they are placing themselves under fealty to a king. (Matthew 7:21-22; 22:2-14; Luke 14:16-24) It is for this reason that the community must meet together for prayer and waiting on Jesus. It is for this reason that the community reads scripture, prays and listens to each individual member and to what God is saying through each other as they seek to understand God's will together. There is no hierarchy in the kingdom. No one is greater than another or lords over another. Each of us stands before our God and King as a subject of the kingdom. This is an important lesson for the new believers to learn. Each of us has value and worth, but each of us is still a subject of the King.

The Kingdom and Stewardship

Once the Lordship of Jesus is established, it is important to understand that the king has bestowed certain responsibilities on his subjects. These vary from individual to individual. We can see this in the story that Jesus told in which a king called his servants for an audit (Matthew 18:23-35), and the story of the landowner who hired people at different times during the day (Matthew 20:1-16), and also in the story of the man who traveled into a far country after calling his servants and delivering his goods to them (Matthew 25:14-30; Luke 19:12-27). Everyone who swears fealty to the king becomes a subject, and thus a steward. Each of us is responsible for what God has given us.

Christian community will not work if we do not recognize the overall authority of God and the individual responsibilities that God has given to each and every member of the community. If members of the community shirk their duties, the community will struggle and ultimately fail. Joining Christian community signifies that we agree to carry our portion in the community. We agree not to join the community only for our own benefit, but to become active members in the community, thus benefiting others.

2. The Bride

The spiritual picture of a bride and groom is first introduced to us in the Old Testament in Genesis, and later in Psalms and Ezekiel. Later in the book of Hosea, God relates to the Israelites as a husband seeking his unfaithful bride. (Hosea 2:2). God, the husband, seeks to win his unfaithful wife (the Children of Israel) back to himself. (Hosea 2:14)

In the New Testament, the emphasis changes slightly. John the Baptist refers to the coming Messiah as the bridegroom. (John 3:29) Jesus later referred to himself as the bridegroom (Matthew 9:15) and used the illustration of the 10 virgins waiting for the bridegroom to come, re-enforcing the concept of bridegroom and bride. The marriage relationship is used in Ephesians 5:22-32 to demonstrate both our relationship to God and how a husband and wife should relate to one another.

Then in the book of Revelation, the concept of the bride of Christ is taken up more fully. In Revelation 19:7-9 we are told that the wife has now been prepared and is coming to the Marriage Supper of the Lamb.

God calls us "the bride" for several reasons. First, we are entering into a love relationship with the bridegroom. It is on this basis of love and mutual pleasure that we build bonds with Jesus. Second, we enter a relationship of mutual loving service through clearly defined roles, in which we will serve in joyful submission to Christ. Interestingly enough, the relationship in the Bible is always that of bride and bridegroom, never as wife and husband. The image used is one of anticipation.

Lastly, our whole identity is wrapped up in our relationship with Jesus. We are the bride and we will spend eternity with Christ, relating together in a Biblical community of love and mutual respect. We must recognize that we are all at different places in our walk with Christ, each of us working on a different area of spiritual development. Without this understanding, our efforts at community will fail.

3. The *Ekklesia*

As early as the fifth century before Christ, the Greek word *ekklesia* was used to refer to an assembly of people. This assembly was not necessarily religious. In Acts 19:39 the word *ekklesia* refers to the lawful assembly or group of men who settle disputes. In verse 41 the same word is used to designate the mob. Both of these are an assembly of people, and in both instances the word *ekklesia* is used.

Paul chooses the word *ekklesia* to describe the gathering of the believers together, and it is this Greek word that is often translated into the English word *church.* However, the original word meant an assembly of people, not a building or institution. Church buildings were not constructed until later in the second and third centuries. In the early church some homes became regular meeting places, while at other times the people moved from house to house.

In the Bible *ekklesia* usually indicates a popular meeting especially a religious congregation such as a Jewish synagogue, or a Christian community on earth, or even the saints in heaven. It is also translated as assembly. The important concept behind this term is that it is an assembling of the believers together. The Bible assumes that the community of believers will meet together. It is interesting to note that the Bible is not specific about how this meeting should take place, what its focus should be, what forms we should use, or how often we should meet.

What should happen when we meet?

While the Bible doesn't give us a specific list of what should happen when the Body of Christ meets, it does give us a number of important principles to work from. Acts 2:42 tells us that the church devoted themselves to the apostles' teaching, fellowship, breaking of bread and prayer.

a) Scripture Reading and Teaching - Since the word *ekklesia* was already in use and understood by the Jewish people, we should start with their understanding of the word. The *ekklesia* was the meeting together of people. This started in earnest when the Jewish people were in captivity in Babylon. The temple and its rites and rituals were no longer accessible, so the Jewish people started gathering in various places, and eventually they constructed halls known as synagogues. In the synagogue, the Scriptures were read and commented on. (Luke 4:16-20, Matthew 13:54) The Bible tells us that the ekklesia is a place where we should gather to receive spiritual nourishment (I Timothy 4:13 and 1 Corinthians 14:26) It is also called a place of exhortation (Hebrews 10:25).

b) Fellowship & Edification - Paul emphasizes that believers meeting together should strive to edify one another (I Corinthians 14:4-13). Our focus should be on others and building them up. We don't come to get something out of our meetings but to give our part so that the Body of Christ is alive and functioning well. When emphasis is put on spectator religion, then a few highly gifted people demonstrate their ability to make music, sing, lead, teach and preach, while the others sit back and enjoy. This creates wrong attitudes and limits the ability of the body to function properly. People start attending meetings to get something from them rather than o bless someone else. If everyone is striving to bless someone else, then everyone will receive a blessing in return. While this has to do with attitude, the forms (how we pray, worship, relate) in our meetings may differ widely.

c) Breaking of Bread (I Corinthians 10:17) - The Bible encourages us to break bread together as believers. This is a "community rite" or ceremony. Baptism on the other hand, was often a public event, taking place in the open at a river or pool. It was done apart from the community on several occasions (Acts 8:3-39).

d) Prayer - Jesus was very specific when cleansing the temple, telling us that his house should be a house of prayer (Matthew 21:13). Then the time of the physical temple came to an end. The veil was torn in two, and eventually the temple was completely destroyed. Today there is a new temple. It is the community of believers when they come together. The old temple was first and foremost a dwelling place for God, now his dwelling place is in us, not in any building. If the old building was intended to be characterized by prayer, how much more should the new ones be characterize by prayer? This was amply demonstrated in the early church, where men and women would meet, sometimes for days at a time for prayer and seeking God. In effect, corporate prayer was an act of the believers coming together before their king. (Acts 1:14, 12:12)

The Role of Music

Music does several things for the community. It can be an individual or corporate expression of prayer, and it can also edify and build up the believers. We are given a glimpse into some of the things that Jesus did when he met with his disciples in Matthew 26:30. They ate together, fellowshipped together, and at the end of their meeting in the upper room sang a hymn and then went out. While music was not always part of these meetings (and never mentioned in Scripture as the central focus) it did play a part. Music was used by Old Testament prophets, and it seems that it will be a part of our worship in heaven. Interestingly enough, music has become an integral part of Christian worship around the world. No other religion makes the same use of music as does the Christian Church. It is interesting to notice that when the body of Christ is truly functioning together, new music bursts forth. Church historians have noticed that when God's Spirit moves in history, it is usually accompanied with an outburst of new music. Along with this, music is also a community exercise, where everyone, even the less talented, can do something together to join with the rest of the community.

4. The Body

The Apostle Paul introduces us to the concept of the *body* in his first letter to the Corinthians. The term *body* is very unique, and not a concept that is easily understood outside the Christian community. It is important to understand why Paul refers to us as the Body of Christ (I Corinthians 12:12, 27). We are not just a body of believers, a group that meets together; we are specifically called the Body of Christ. This term is very unique to Christians. People who work at Microsoft are not considered the *body of Bill Gates* any more than the followers of communism are the *body of Karl Marx.*

Paul, however, is very specific in coining this new term *the Body of Christ.* There are two aspects to this term. First, Paul addresses the various body parts (I Corinthians 12:12-26) and points out that the body has many different members, (eyes, ears, nose, hands, etc.) This reinforces the concept of stewardship in the kingdom. Jesus is the head of the Body. (Colossians 1:18) None of us is greater than the other. Each of us has different functions and responsibilities that must be exercised and worked at in order for the body to function properly.

Paul then goes on to apply a second part to the concept of Body when he tells us that we are part of the Body of Christ in Corinthians 12:27. If we were simply a group of believers, we might have a president, treasurer, secretary, committee members and so on. But because we are the Body of Christ, we have different responsibilities and functions. As I have examined these verses over the years, I have come to believe that these gifts and functions are all part of what Christ did when he was here on earth. We can understand how to use the spiritual gifts of apostleship, prophecy, teaching, miracles, healing, helping, administrating or gifts of the diversities of tongues if we look to Jesus. The principles that Jesus laid down in his life and ministry are the basis of how we should use the gifts of the Spirit, for the very same Spirit that was in Jesus is in us. God is one, and He does not change.

Over the years I've heard preachers admonish their listeners to live and act as Jesus did. While this is true in one sense, it is impossible when one considers all that Jesus did. As I understand the Scriptures, we as individual Christians are not expected or equipped to do everything that Jesus did. Jesus did not leave behind millions of followers who are each an imitation of Jesus. I don't see this in the Bible. Rather, Jesus left behind groups of believers known as "The Body of Christ." If they function together, and each does his part and exercises his spiritual gifts, then Jesus is alive in their midst in a very special way. I believe that the local body of believers can do everything that Jesus wants to do in that setting. Spiritual gifts are nothing less than the abilities that Jesus had, divided up among his believers. Thus, when a Christian community functions as the Body of Christ, Jesus is alive and ministering among and through them (Ephesians 1:22-23). Groups of believers that do not function as the Body of Christ are missing something. They have fellowship, teaching, and a measure of spiritual life but they are not what God desires them to become.

Rather, God desires the world to be full of functioning communities of believers who act as the Body of Christ to those around them. Where this happens Jesus is alive and well in that part of the world. This is why Jesus told his disciples the astonishing truth: "Whoever believes in me will also do the works that I do, and greater works than these will he do, because I am going to my Father." (John 14:12, ESV) I believe that this has a double meaning. First this means that we are to bring people to a knowledge of Christ and see people born again and filled with the Holy Spirit. This could not happen until the Holy Spirit was given to the church. However, I also believe that it implies that when Jesus was present on earth, he was only physically present in one place. Today, through the Bodies of Christ around the world, Jesus is alive and well and operating all over the world.

Today Jesus' ministry is often restricted by the quality of the Christian community that is present. I believe that Christians should function in a way similar to the radical Christian communities portrayed in the book of Acts. Unfortunately sometimes the Church often looks more like a respectable country-club.

By working together we are to carry on Christ's own ministry and be his physical presence on earth. As the Body of Christ we should also see ourselves as the temple of the Spirit of God (I Corinthians 3:16, Ephesians 2:19-22, I Peter 2:5). In the Old Testament the dwelling place of God was the temple (2 Chronicles 6:1-2). When Moses received the commands to first build the tabernacle (Exodus 27), it was known as the "tent of meeting" where God would meet with them. (Exodus 29:43-44) The same should be true of the Body of Christ wherever it is functioning. When it functions, the world will see Jesus alive and well, and they will discover a setting where they can meet with God.

In effect, when we gather, we are to do whatever Jesus would have done when he was on earth. He prayed, taught others, cared for others, and demonstrated the love, power, and wisdom of God. We are to enter into this ministry. I Peter 2:9 tells us that we are a holy nation and a royal priesthood. The priesthood describes our function and highlights the priesthood of all believers: which is every one of us serving God together. The Greek word for 'nation' in this setting is *ethnos* (from where we get our English word *ethnic*). We are a new family, a new tribe, and a new ethnic group. Christian community is to be a gathering of believers where we can function together in a visible, demonstrable way. Galatians 3:27-28 (ESV) tells us, "For as many of you as were baptized into Christ have put on Christ, there is neither Jew nor Greek, there is neither slave nor free, there is neither male nor female, for you are all one in Christ Jesus."

Conclusion

So far we have identified four Biblical terms used to describe the community: Kingdom (the Lordship of Christ and our role as stewards), Bride (we are loved and we enter into an eternal love relationship) Assembly (*ekklesia*, we should gather together in some form to exercise being the body of Christ, and Body (each member has a part to do; when we function together, Christ functions in our midst.)

Now, how do we put these things all together into a living, functioning community? There is still one important ingredient that we must examine. This will take a whole chapter to cover. Then in the following chapters, having established the Biblical definition of community, we will look at the steps that people often take when switching communities. We want to do this as it will highlight a number of other important issues that we will need to address before we can tackle the job of planting churches that are living, spiritual communities.

Questions for Reflection or Discussion

1. How easily do your target people work with abstract concepts? Do they prefer to have simple directions or do they like to wrestle with issues?

2. At what levels do your target people generally develop strong bonds? (maternal, paternal, sibling, extended family, ethnic community (tribe-clan), non-ethnic community, local community, national community, international community, spiritual community) How does this differ from your own experience?

3. How will your church fit into their bonding pattern?

4. At what level do you expect people to bond in your new community? What are you offering them?

5. In what ways does your new community reflect the teachings of the kingdom of God? How do people learn about lordship, stewardship and servant-hood?

6. In what ways do people in your target culture understand the relationship that we can have with God? Do they find pleasure in coming before God? Do they worship with all their hearts?

7. How central are your meetings and teaching times to the life of the church? Is there a sense of community outside of meetings and teaching?

8. Do you think new believers are becoming excited about the role that they can play in the Body of Christ? How can you encourage them in this?

Chapter Twenty Five
Others

You shall love the Lord your God with all your heart and with all your soul and with all your strength and with all your mind, and your neighbor as yourself. (Like 10:27 ESV)

When Christians think of the sense of community demonstrated in the first chapters of the book of Acts, they generally think in terms of the love, support, and care that the believers expressed for each other.

This expression of community was evident from the very first day of Pentecost when the early church was birthed. The Bible records for us this amazing narrative in Acts 2:41.

"So those who received his word were baptized, and there were added that day about three thousand souls. And they devoted themselves to the apostles' teaching and fellowship, to the breaking of bread and the prayers. And awe came upon every soul, and many wonders and signs were done through the apostles. And all who believed were together and had all things in common. And they were selling their possessions and belongings and distributing the proceeds to all, as any had need. And day by day, attending the temple together and breaking bread in their homes, they received food with glad and generous hearts, praising God and having favor with all the people. And the Lord added to their number day by day those who were being saved." (Acts 2:41-47 ESV)

This amazing spirit of community continued on for an extended period of time. Two chapters later (Acts 4:32-37) we get more of the story.

"Now the full number of those who believed were of one heart and soul and no one said that any of the things that belonged to him was his own, but they had everything in common. And with great power the apostles were giving testimony to the resurrection of the Lord Jesus and great grace was upon them all. There was not a needy person among them, for as many as were owners of lands or houses, old them and brought the proceeds of what was sold and laid it at the apostles' feet, and it was distributed to each as any had need. Thus Joseph, who was also called by the apostles Barnabas (which means son of encouragement), a Levite, a native of Cyprus, sold a field that belonged to him and brought the money and laid it at the apostles' feet." (Acts 4:32-37 ESV)

Later in Acts 6:1-2 we learn that there was a daily distribution of food to widows who were in need, and that the church leaders were involved in serving tables. It seems that they had really taken Jesus seriously when he taught them about servant leadership.

Community, not communism

There is a difference between commune and community that confuses many Western readers. A commune may be an expression of community, but it is not the only viable form of community. In the Biblical narrative it is obvious that people were selling some of their goods and distributing these proceeds to those who were in need. It is not clear if all of the people sold all of their goods or just some of them. Acts 4:34 - 35 notes that those who "were owners of lands or houses," (note the plural) "sold them and brought the proceeds of what was sold and laid it at the apostles' feet." Acts 4:37 seems to make a particular point about one individual, Joseph of Cyprus who sold one of his fields and brought the money to the apostles. The fact that the Scriptures mention this one particular incident seems to illustrate that this was a particularly noble gesture, somewhat uncommon, and worthy of special mention. The scriptural account also points out that he sold "a" field, not "all his fields." If the early Christians had sold all of their houses and land, there would have been no place for them to meet together. The Bible points out that they met in homes, and even mentions some of the homes by name, such as the house of Mary, the mother of John.(Acts 12:13). Obviously this woman did not sell her house. Rather, the emphasis in the Scriptural account is on the spirit of love and sharing that was evident among the early church, in which those with much, liquidated their extra assets and shared with those who had little.

The early church did not practice communism, nor did they live communally. In Acts 5:4 Paul says to Ananias, (who bragged of giving the entire proceeds of his land to God, while he secretly kept a part) "While it remained unsold, did it not remain your own? And after it was sold, was it not at your disposal?" In a commune everything belongs to the group and nothing or very little belongs to the individual.

So it is clear that they were not practicing communism or communal living. Whereas in a commune the people and their things belong to each other. In a Christian community the people and all they have, belong to the Lord. They are in a position to share what they have because they are stewards of their possessions, not owners.

The Role of the Community in Modern Society

It has been argued that since modern society takes care of the poor through welfare programs, this type of financial sharing among believers is no longer needed. While this may be true, it has had unfortunate results. Society in the West does not often see church community in action, and so this part of community ceases to exist. The role of the government in helping individuals in need should not, however, deter us from reaching out to lonely people, needy students, single parents, the disadvantaged, and the downtrodden. It should not deter us from acting as a community that helps one another in such areas as networking together to help those in our community with services such as finding jobs, house hunting, providing childcare, aid in time of disaster or need, and whatever other needs the members of the community might have.

This community spirit in the early church stands in stark contrast to the institutionalism that seems to have invaded much of the Christian church around the world today. Somehow the church has become so focused on a business model of operation accompanied by theological exactness, that community spirit has virtually disappeared. I believe that some of this is due to the western church's pre-occupation with the guilt-innocence aspect of theology. This has colored how we relate to one another in the church, and to those who are without the church.

And so it is that when many seekers or new believers read the Book of Acts, they become excited with the powerful demonstration of community in action. But when they look at the reality of the church their old community (be it Islam or whatever) is often a closer picture of what a functioning community should be. Is it any wonder that some go back into their old way of life?

Bible Teaching on Others

In his first letter to the Corinthians, the Apostle Paul contrasts three types of people: the natural man, the spiritual man, and the carnal man. These are illustrated in the chart below. Starting on the left hand side of the chart, the natural man knows little of spiritual things and the things of God. This man must pass through a *cross experience* in order to be born again and come alive to the things of the Spirit.

230

Once the natural man has come to faith through the cross of Christ, he then starts on the path to becoming a spiritual person. As long as we are on this earth, God is in the business of teaching, molding and making us into better servants and eventually into the image of his dear Son.

As we move along this path of spiritual growth, we experience a series of small *cross experiences* in our lives. These experiences are used by God to help us see the difference between being alive to ourselves and being alive to God and others. Philippians 3:10 tells us that this is the process of "being conformed to the image of his dear Son."

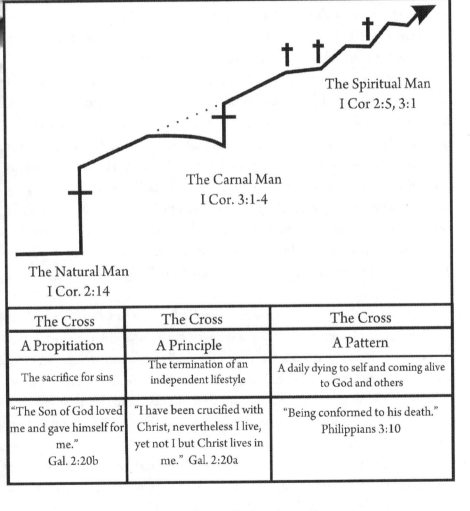

The Spiritual Man
I Cor 2:5, 3:1

The Carnal Man
I Cor. 3:1-4

The Natural Man
I Cor. 2:14

The Cross	The Cross	The Cross
A Propitiation	A Principle	A Pattern
The sacrifice for sins	The termination of an independent lifestyle	A daily dying to self and coming alive to God and others
"The Son of God loved me and gave himself for me." Gal. 2:20b	"I have been crucified with Christ, nevertheless I live, yet not I but Christ lives in me." Gal. 2:20a	"Being conformed to his death." Philippians 3:10

(Learning about Union with Christ, Stewart Dinnen, Christian Focus Publications, 2000, Used with permission)

Along the path between regeneration and becoming spiritual giants, believers sometimes falter. Usually this faltering happens when they are faced with a small *cross experience* (something that they should die to), and they rebel. Rather than dying to whatever it is that God has shown them in their life, they choose rather to disobey God. In this act they start down the path of becoming a carnal Christian.

While we may feel uncomfortable with the word "carnal Christian" in reality, being a carnal Christian is rather comfortable. Carnal Christians are concerned with their own welfare, security, and comfort. They have experienced regeneration through the cross, but they have refused to give up something in life that God has asked them to give up. They continue on as regenerated believers, but their focus in life moves from solely pleasing God to any number of other good things. They can become involved in their family, their church, and their community, but in reality they are alive to physical things rather than spiritual things.

Over the years I've come in contact with a lot of carnal Christians. In fact, I am carnal more often than I like to admit. As carnal Christians we are deeply in touch with our own wants and desires. When talking to a carnal believer about his dream car, house, or vacation, these believers can spend hours discussing in great detail what they would or would not like. Whatever the topic, carnal Christians demonstrate how focused they are on their own wishes. The crunch comes when the topic moves on to spiritual things, and we start to discuss what God wants and what He is saying. Suddenly these fine Christians, who are active in their churches and families, become quiet. Slowly questions start to come out: how do you know what God wants? how do you hear his voice? how do I know what the will of God is for my life?

Can you see the difference between a carnal believer and a spiritual one as Paul describes them in I Corinthians? Carnal believers are in tune with their own wants and desires. Spiritual believers are in tune with God's wants and desires. But there is another important aspect here. True spiritual believers are also in tune with the needs of others. As they walk and talk with God, they begin to feel the things that burden God. Suddenly their lives become focused on others, such as leading others to Christ, discipling them, and serving them.

This was the experience of the early Church. They no longer cared about their own personal success and status. Extra possessions were sold and the money was distributed to others who had little. It was not something that was organized by the disciples. It was a spontaneous act of concern for others.

This is the basic, fundamental building block for developing Christian community. Believers must learn to take their eyes off themselves and focus them on God and his love for others. This basic message of love for others is one of the themes of the book of Philippians.

Paul's Letter to the Philippians

Many years ago I sat under the teaching of Dr. Herbert W. Peeler, the president of Millar College of the Bible. Every student who passed through the school had the opportunity to sit under his teaching and enjoy the truths he expounded from the book of Philippians. In the section below I would like to share some of these truths with you, as they have profoundly affected my life and my view of community.

Paul begins his letter with a prayer for the Philippian people. He tells them that he is sure that "he who began a good work in you will bring it to completion at the day of Jesus Christ." Then he adds, "It is right for me to feel this way about you all, because I hold you in my heart" (Philippians 1:7 ESV). This was the secret of Paul's ministry. He had others and their needs on his heart, not himself. If he wanted to serve himself, he would have stayed in Jerusalem and led a comfortable Christian life as a leader in the churches. But it was his burning desire for others which motivated him in his missionary journeys.

Paul goes on to tell them that he is a prisoner of the Romans with a very serious charge against him that could result in death. He then writes that famous phrase: "Christ will be honored in my body, whether by life or by death. For to me to live is Christ, and to die is gain" (Philippians 1:20 ESV). Most of us are familiar with this statement, but few of us connect it with the next verses.

"If I am to live in the flesh, that means fruitful labor for me. Yet which I shall chose I cannot tell. I am hard pressed between the two. My desire is to depart and be with Christ, for that is far better." (Philippians 2: 21-22 ESV)

Paul presents us with a ridiculous scenario in order to get our attention, suggesting that he himself has a choice whether he should live or die. He points out that he really would like to die and be with Christ because that would be far better for him. Then in verse 24 he points out that to remain in this world "is more necessary on your account." In other words, while Paul would rather be with Jesus in heaven, the reason for his existence on earth is simply "others." Paul has no secondary interests in being alive, outside of serving others.

In the opening verses of chapter two Paul instructs us "Do nothing from rivalry or conceit, but in humility count others more significant than yourselves. Let each of you look not only to his own interests, but also to the interests of others." (Philippians 2:3-4 ESV) This is the golden rule for forming Christian community. All members of the community are to care for others first and for themselves last. The best example of this is found in the life of Jesus himself. This is why Paul writes the next verses. "Let this mind be in you, which was also in Christ Jesus"(KJV) What is this mind of Christ that Paul is talking about? It is expounded in the next few verses, "Who, though he was in the form of God, did not count equality with God a thing to be grasped, but made himself nothing, taking the form of a servant, being born in the likeness of men. And being found in human form he humbled himself by becoming obedient to the point of death, even death on a cross." (Philippians 2:6-8 ESV)

In order for Christians to form true community, our minds must be transformed. It is not enough to only come to the cross for salvation. God wants to take us further into himself and transform our minds and thinking so that we focus on others, not on ourselves.

A few verses later in the same chapter Paul mentions to them that he is sending one of his traveling companions, Epaphroditus, back to Philippi. Then he goes on to tell them that Epaphroditus had been so sick that he almost died. Paul points out that Epaphroditus was very concerned that the Philippians might have heard about his sickness and been burdened by it. How opposite this is to most of us! If we were so sick we almost died, we would almost certainly write letters home to tell others about our condition. But not Epaphroditus, because he had others on his heart.

In chapter three Paul points out that he had every reason to be satisfied with his Christian life in Palestine. But he counted everything as garbage in order to win Christ and follow him. Chapter four follows this thought with an address to two women who were at odds in the church. This is an example of how Paul solved problems in the community. Notice that he directs them to "be of the same mind in the Lord." He entreats them to look to Jesus and imitate his action of caring for others rather than for themselves.

Later Paul admonishes them by pointing out that he knows how to both have much and also to suffer need. He is content in all things, whether rich or poor, because he could do all things through Christ who strengthened him. And he ends up challenging them at the end of the book "my God shall supply all your need according to his riches in glory by Christ Jesus." If you pour out your life for others, God will in turn pour into your life all that you need.

234

Paul's message is that Christians must think of others. He uses many examples including himself as a picture of those who have abandoned the pursuit of personal happiness and fulfillment, and now preferred helping others. However, in his pursuit to serve others, he had discovered many great truths about how God would, in return, supply his own need.

Today, many Christians are focused on supplying their own needs. The needs of others they leave to the government, or to aid agencies. As churches focus on the legal aspects of salvation and as members pursue the "good things in life," the experience of community living has all but disappeared. The message of "others" is the forgotten message of the church today.

Community cannot function as long as we are self-centered and think only of ourselves. Community is not a win-win situation. It is a giving of ourselves to others. It costs us something. It feels like loss, but in the long run it will become a win-win situation as we learn to give and receive as a community of believers. The issue here isn't how to gain something, but rather how to lose it for Christ's sake. The goal is to give away what we have. We seek to serve others, for in doing so, we believe we are serving Jesus himself. (Matthew 25:37-40)

Most of our churches in the West have lost this sense of community. People often think of themselves rather than of others. We think about what we can "get out of the service." We focus on receiving a blessing from the Lord, rather than being a blessing to others. It is here that Muslims outshine Christians. Their religion insists that they give to others. It insists that they look out for others, for the unfortunate and the needy, and to extend hospitality to everyone who is around them.

While Islamic community is not perfect, it is a functioning form of community that is often better than the community experienced in many Christian circles. This is not because Christians are not capable of doing community. I personally think it is because we overemphasize theology at the expense of community. Oh that churches would wake up and start functioning as Christian communities! Islam has the potential to make great inroads into our midst, because our younger generation seeks to find relevant community experiences, and they are not finding it in many of our churches.

What we lack

Today, we in the evangelical church in the West sometimes have the feeling that we have arrived. We have everything we need. We are theologically correct.

We have the best teaching and preaching available to us in our church pulpits, in seminars and coferenes we attend and through the Internet. We have more excellent books and resources than the church has had all down through the centuries. Our hymn books and music programs provide us with the very best of godly worship music. And so, just like the Laodicean church we feel that we have arrived. This is as good as it gets. Yet we lack one thing.... community.

We have forgotten the words of Jesus, who asked the rich young ruler to sell what he had, give it to the poor, and come follow him. Somehow we have fooled ourselves into thinking that this was simply Jesus' test to show the rich young ruler that he was wrong. We ignore the fact that we too would fail the test if it was given to us. Jesus is looking for servitude expressed though helping others.

We seem to forget the qualifications of a pastor. I Timothy 3:1-2 (ESV) tells us, "The saying is trustworthy: If anyone aspires to the office of overseer he desires a noble task. Therefore an overseer must be above reproach, the husband of one wife, sober minded, self-controlled, respectable, hospitable, able to teach ..." Today, the ability to teach is considered far more valuable than the qualification of hospitality. We search for men who excel in the pulpit, but usually forget that they must first excel in hospitality. This trend towards theological and homiletical perfection at the expense of hospitality has cost the Western church dearly. While we have perfected our pulpit skills we have neglected the forming of community. Titus 1:8 tells us that our ministers should be "lovers of hospitality." Does this describe your minister or yourself? How easily can our ministers be approached today? How much do they encourage visitation, interaction, and the mutual support of believers? Fortunately, there are a growing number of evangelical ministers today who realize that one of the Western church's great weaknesses is "community" and they long to experience the freshness and the vitality of the early church as people cared for one another.

Let's be encouraged with the words of Romans 12:10-13 (ESV). "Love one another with brotherly affection. Outdo one another in showing honor. Do not be slothful in zeal, be fervent in spirit, serve the Lord. Rejoice in hope, be patient in tribulation, be constant in prayer. Contribute to the needs of the saints and seek to show hospitality."

Conclusion

While some of the evangelical churches of the world today are very self-focused this is not true of every church and every situation. God is continually raising up new communities of believers that emulate the early church in their zeal and their dedication to serve others.

In the next chapter We will examine some of the steps that people take when they "switch" communities of faith. While I will focus on the steps and obstacles that we have seen Muslims face, many of these issues affect Hindus, Buddhists and others.

Questions for Reflection or Discussion

1. Read Acts 2:41 – 47 and 4:32-37. How does this description differ from the atmosphere in your new church plant?
2. What common bonds can you build your community around so that people will love and care for each other?
3. Use the chart in this chapter. God wants us to move from being natural people to spiritual people. Natural people are mostly in tune with this physical world. True spiritual people are also in tune with the things of God. What is the main event that everyone must pass through to start on the road of growing spiritually?
4. What must happen daily in our lives to continue to grow spiritually?
5. If we refuse to die to something in our life, what begins to happen to us spiritually?
6. What type of things interest the carnal believer?
7. What must happen for a carnal believer to start again on the road to spiritual growth?
8. If carnal believers are in tune with their own wants and desires, what should spiritual people be in tune with?
9. On the basis of Philippians 1:19-24 why do you think God kept Paul alive on his missionary journeys? Was it for his own benefit? Why do you think you are alive today?
10. Read Philippians 2:3-8. Do you feel that you have the same mind that Christ had? How is this demonstrated in your life and ministry?
11. Read Philippians 2:19-20 and 2:25-29. What did Timothy and Epaphroditus have in common?
12. Think of the pastor of your home church. Does he fit the qualifications of I Timothy 3:1-2 and Titus 1:8 that mention hospitality? Do you?

Chapter Twenty Six
Steps to Switching Community (I)

Some people think that church planting consists of doing evangelism and then simply gathering believers into groups. In some setting this may be true, especially if people live in a spiritual vacuum and do not belong to a tight-fitting community. This is often the case in the Western world or the communist world where religious, family and tribal units have little value. In these contexts, church planting usually consists of attracting individuals to Christ, bringing them into the church fellowship and endeavoring to form community with them. The situation is very different in other parts of the world. Sometimes the people we are seeking to win are already part of a functioning community. As seekers from these communities explore the message that the messenger is presenting, they also want to explore the community that the messenger represents, because they realize that when they accept Christ, they will become part of the community of Christ. This is a normal part of the process of exploring a new faith.

In effect, the messenger calls for people to accept his message and join the community he or she represents. That community may be culturally close or it may be culturally distant to the hearer's community. However it is structured, it still represents a switch in communities. For example, a white American from Utah with a Mormon background will experience a significant community change if he or she leaves the Mormon community of faith and joins a white American evangelical community of faith. In many cases Mormons, Jehovah's Witnesses and other groups do better at forming community than evangelical churches. As a result people leaving these groups often struggle more with community issues than they do with theological issues.

In this and the following chapter I would like to examine some of the steps that seekers may take as they proceed to move from one community of faith to another.

The majority of these thoughts are taken from the Muslim world. Most of them come from a close friend and associate who has had many years of experience in aiding Muslims as they explore Christian community. His name has been withheld for security reasons because he continues to minister in Muslim countries. Again, even though much of this material has been gleaned from ministry in the Middle East, others have found it equally applicable across the 10/40 Window as well as in other settings.

Recognizing our Community

Before we look at the list of steps, we need to recognize that we are all part of a community, and perhaps more than one community. As John Donne, the English poet of the seventeenth century said, "No man is an island." All of us have networks of people with whom we function. Whether we like it or not, we are part of a community. Some Christian workers have thought that if they moved into a Muslim, Hindu or Buddhist country and effectively communicated the Gospel message, they would win people to Christ and form churches. They were surprised when those that responded to their message wanted to join their mission agency, live on mission support, and have the same standard of living as the Christian worker. What they hadn't realized was that while they as missionaries, were physically living in an Eastern setting, the community that they were relying on for their support included their church in the West, their friends and their supporters in their home country, as well as the other members of their team on the field. Thus, it was natural for the new believers to want to be part of the very community to which the messenger belonged.

Checking out the other community

From my own experience I have discovered that when Muslims start to respond to Christians as messengers and listen to their message, they usually want to move on quickly and explore their community. In one case several neighbor boys began asking our teenage sons about our faith. Eventually I sat with them and started to explain what we believed. Within a couple of visits these young men were asking about the place we worshiped, and they wanted to come and observe our community in action. At first I was frustrated by their interest in church rather than theology. As I talked with others however, I came to realize that this was a normal part of the process of exploring Christianity.

239

Now, put yourself in the place of a seeker. You become interested in the faith of the missionary, and so you look beyond the missionary to see his community. Wow! The community looks great! Almost everyone in the community sends their kids to the best international schools, drives automobiles, and flies abroad every couple of years. Everyone in the community meets together for prayer and fellowship, has each other's relatives visit them, borrows and lends things among them, and generally has a higher standard of living than the people around them. Wouldn't you want to be part of this community? This may be why some seekers express interest in accepting the message and becoming a Christian.

Everything seems to be going fine until the seekers discover that this community is closed to them. The international school and the automobiles are all paid for by people called supporters. If you want to join the community you must have supporters. And to get supporters, you needed to go to something called Bible College. After this you must join an agency. The hurdles are huge. What a disappointment it is when they discover that the community they want to join doesn't really want them.

And then they discover something even worse. The messengers want them, a small handful of unrelated people with limited resources, to form their own community. It soon becomes evident that there really isn't a community for them to join. The missionaries have their own community, and they expect the handful of believers, drawn from different backgrounds and different families, to create community on their own. Because the new believers have only experienced community with those that were "near" to them, the task looks impossible. And so many of them return to their old community, not because they didn't have a messenger, not because they didn't believe the message, but because they didn't have a community to join.

In discussing these topics with Christian workers in the Middle East, I realized that our initial focus should not be on "how to create the perfect community for Muslim, Hindu or Buddhist seekers." These are topics that concern specific cultural practices. Each missionary in his specific situation will have to analyze the local culture and incorporate meaningful cultural practices into the life and worship of the local Christian community.

I am very aware of a number of people who are working on creating communities for believers from a Muslim background. Each of these efforts use different theologies, philosophies, and approaches. Some want to build a very Islamic ooking community that will have few cultural hurdles for Muslim seekers to cross. Others want to build communities that can integrate more easily with existing Christian churches. Choosing the cultural practices which would help form the best community for people from a Muslim background is an interesting topic for discussion, but it may be a very academic one at best. Each of us has to recognize that we are already part of a community. When we come to Muslims, we come as part of an existing community. The question we have to ask ourselves is, how can we make our existing communities more accessible to seekers from a Muslim, Hindu, or Buddhist heritage? We may naively believe that we are creating a brand-new community, but at best we usually start from the framework that we know, and try to blend our experience of Christian community with the new convert's expectation of community.

Before we attempt to provide seekers with too many answers, we should stop and examine some of the steps that they may pass through as they enter into a Christian community, whatever that community looks like.

We want to begin with people who are simply contacts and track changes that usually happen in their lives, until they become disciples of Jesus functioning in a Christian community setting. The steps I outline are not given in absolute chronological order. They are provided as important points that usually occur in the life of the seeker. The order may vary and some things may happen simultaneously.

1. Dealing with Contacts

We start by classifying the person as a contact. This is a person with whom you have some kind of relationship, perhaps as a neighbor, classmate, or a regular business client. As messengers of the Gospel, we should desire to build personal relationships with people we meet so that we have a stronger basis from which to share the Gospel.

As you build bridges into the life of your contact, he or she will begin to trust you as a person and come to know who you are, what you stand for, and what is important to you. If you are an outsider, that is a foreigner, reaching this stage may take some time. A number of things should happen. For instance, the contact will have some questions about who you are, so you need to know who you are as well.

There are a number of things to consider as you answer this question. Are you a messenger? Are you an ambassador of the Most High? Or are you simply a businessman making money, a lonely foreigner in need of a friend, or a foreigner that can help the contact learn more about other countries, perhaps even helping him to emigrate?

Second, what is your role in society? Are you just a neighbor or business contact? Will you become a friend? Are you active in the community around you? Do you get involved when neighbor kids are fighting on the street? Are you a leader or a follower, a teacher or a learner, a passive or an active person?

Finally, what are the distinct marks of godliness that you are demonstrating? This is a bicultural issue. You may be personally satisfied that you are a godly person but do your neighbors know you are displaying godliness? What are the marks of godliness that your neighbors are looking for?

For example, you might attend religious services, and thus feel that you are demonstrating to your neighbors that you are religious. You may take time for personal devotions and pray regularly. Perhaps you can even quote your holy book. Does this demonstrate that you are a religious or holy person in your new community?

What about your kids? When a foreign family moves into a community the neighbors will want to know what impact the new family will have on the neighborhood. As they watch our children play and interact with their kids, will they see marks of godliness in the actions of our children?

As a missionary in a foreign setting, your role in society will also come into question. If you drive a late model car, have a big house, and have money to give to the poor, then you may fit into their concept of a wealthy person whose role is to give to the poor. In some settings everything comes from the hand of the sheik. Is this the role you are presenting? Do you hand out things? Despite our best intentions some people may seek only financial or social benefits from us.

It is also important to observe and learn how the community recognizes and sees someone who is spiritual. This may have good and bad connotations, but the information is very important to know. Do spiritual people know and quote holy books? Do spiritual people dress or act in particular ways? Will this help you in your role in the community? Do spiritual people speak about religious things in a different dialect, such as the way religious Muslims use classical Arabic? Will this help or hinder your message? How can you demonstrate true spirituality without being seen as uneducated and ill informed?

On one occasion while visiting a Bedouin encampment, several of us were waiting around for the sheik to arrive. One of our party moved off to the edge of the encampment and began to pray. He sat on some rocks and began talking with God. After some time he moved off to another location overlooking the camp to do the same. We Christians were all comfortable with this but it upset our Bedouin hosts. They asked what the person was doing. Someone in the party explained that he was praying. This created some discussion... What sort of demented person walked around and talked with God while strolling or squatting on the rocks? God must be approached with reverence and awe. In the end, some of the Bedouin decided that the person was not really praying. Perhaps he was casting evil spells on them! This misunderstanding did not help in the process of trying to build relationships with our hosts.

Once again, at this early stage of contact we must realize that we are working hard at building relationships so that we can earn the right to be heard. We need to be accepted as valid messengers.

Not everyone is accepted as a messenger. In one of the churches I attended in the Middle East, a particular man loved to get up and share things. Whenever he stood to pray or participate in discussion, people would yawn, look the other way, or even start talking to their neighbors. They were making it as obvious as possible that they would not listen to this man, no matter how valuable his contribution. As far as they were concerned there were things in this man's life that disqualified him from being a messenger.

When we foreigners enter into a cross cultural situation, we must be sensitive to cultural issues, and realize that it takes time to be accepted as a valid messenger. Relationships have to be built, and lessons have to be learned.

It is at this stage of ministry that the approach known as friendship evangelism is most useful. We build relationships so that we earn the right to be heard. We work at being seen as religious people so that we earn the right to speak about religious things.

Much of what is included in the first part of this book, (The Messenger) is aimed at helping the reader be the type of messenger that can not only communicate a message, but earn a hearing as well. How this is done will differ from culture to culture, but it is most important as it will determine one's ability to move forward to the next step.

2. Accepting your message as a valid message

Once you have earned the right to be heard, you need to be able to share an understandable message. There are a number of strategic issues that you will have to face and pray through at this stage.

First, it is often best to follow a plan to help you develop your skills in the areas of language and communication in order to present adequately a valid message. The first section of this book, (*The Messenger*) looks at this in greater detail.

Second, your message needs to be contextualized for the person you are speaking to. If the person you are speaking to is living a life filled with fear, then you should begin with a message that addresses the needs of someone in a fear-power paradigm. If the person with whom you are speaking is focused on gaining honor, or on preserving the family from shame, then you should begin with a message that addresses the needs of someone in an honor-shame paradigm. The second part of this book (*The Message*) looks at these concepts in greater detail.

One of the struggles that you will face at this stage is to find time when you can give a full and logical presentation of the Gospel. It is doubtful that you will be able to do this in one session. Careful thought needs to go into the various aspects of the Gospel message that you want to share. Prayer needs to be focused on seeing opportunities develop. Satan will do everything he can to keep you from having adequate and quality time. You need to prepare your sessions with prayer, and ask the Lord to take control of specific things when you next meet. These things should include things such as opportunities to share, others who might be present, and interruptions that will happen during the visit.

Finally, be prepared for the Lord to provide opportunity for you to share in more detail. Be bold and share. Don't be intimidated, but don't push ahead like a bulldozer. Be sensitive to what the Holy Spirit is saying to you. Take your opportunity and share the aspect of the message that the Holy Spirit has put on your heart.

On one occasion, my friend and I were visiting a very sick Muslim man, with whom we had shared before. We knew it would be a difficult visit, because there would be other visitors. We had made visits before, and we wanted to continue sharing various aspects of the Gospel with this man before he died. Prior to arriving, we specifically prayed that God would overrule, and that the people present at his bedside would be the ones God wanted to be there. When we arrived, there were several people gathered around. We tried to follow the correct social protocols for the visit. Then, after exchanging glances, we started to change the topic of conversation.

As one of us spoke the other would quietly pray. Eventually we got to our subject. One of the visitors was keen to provide the opposing Islamic view on things. We politely asked if we could share, and then he could have time to speak if he wanted. As the sick man concurred with this idea the Lord provided us with a wonderful window of time. After about fifteen minutes, the other man was starting to get agitated, and we started drawing our little talk to a close, trusting God for whatever came next. Then, suddenly, a fancy car arrived and an important sheik got out. All attention suddenly focused on the new visitor, and we politely excused ourselves, thanking God that we were able to share openly and clearly for a good period of time, without interruptions, and that our talk ended without any arguments.

The problem with a setting such as I have just described is that while the sick man had accepted us as valid messengers, those around him. This makes sharing particularly difficult. When working with a family situation, it is important that the husband, wife, and school age children all accept the messenger as a valid messenger. They will then listen to the message, and respect it as a message. The Holy Spirit can then do his work of convincing and convicting hearts. This work of earning acceptance takes time, love and perseverance.

3. Accepting the Christian community as a valid community

Sometimes the listeners accept our message as a valid message, but may not accept the message as truth. In other words, they understand us and our message, but do not yet accept it. It may be that the missing ingredient is the community of the messenger.

This is an important issue that many Christians fail to recognize. Somewhere in this process, the contact will begin to investigate the community of the messenger. It may start out of curiosity, but as aspects of the message slowly take hold of the contact's heart he will start to consider the messenger's community with deeper interest.

At this stage, the contact has usually moved from being a contact to being a friend. He has also moved from being simply a friend to being someone in whom you have confided and with whom you have shared your message. He or she may not have fully accepted the message as true, but they have accepted it as a valid message and will readily listen to you when you share things.

Somewhere in this process, your friend will start exploring your community. If this doesn't happen, you should start to encourage it, for it is a natural next step.

You can encourage this exploration by being transparent about your life, your relationships, the struggles you face, and how God helps you in them through your Christian community.

This is very important for those from a Muslim, Hindu or Buddhist background who are exploring alternatives to what they have traditionally believed.

Is Entering Community Important?

It is at this point that I and many of my fellow workers have failed. We have not grappled with the correct concept of community. For years I and others were totally unaware of how important this topic was. And thus, having brought the seeker this far, we failed to finish what we had started.

Part of this has to do with our view of how a person comes to Christ. In the West, most new believers come to faith outside of the church community. That is, they come to faith through a children's ministry, student ministry, a crusade, or an outreach program that may be sponsored by churches but are generally outside of the church. The new believers are then encouraged to find church homes where they feel comfortable. In the West, many new believers never make it past this point and so never successfully settle into a church. Those that don't, may spend years moving from church to church without finding one that feels like home.

Often our view of how someone comes to Christ is completely separate from how someone comes to the body of Christ. Many people believe that you can be a Christian without being part of the body. For them the body or church is simply an add-on that might help you grow in the faith, but is not really necessary.

On the other hand, believers from shame-based cultures will usually be interested in being accepted by the community of believers. They usually want to check out this aspect of following Christ before they make any rash decisions. And so they will start to check out the Christian community.

Usually they will start by asking you if you pray, how you pray, and where you go to pray with others. They usually don't have any clue about private worship, or corporate worship, so they start with what they know - formal religious prayer. Sometimes they will ask questions about various churches and how they relate to each other. This is not a diversion from the truth, but part of the process of learning about following Christ.

How you answer these questions is crucial. If you are not happy where at the church where you worship and they recognize this, the whole Gospel message starts to lose its appeal. If you glibly push the questions aside so that you can deal with real issues like sin and salvation, they will feel dissatisfied, or think that you are hiding something. Rather, take this as an opportunity to share about the body of Christ and how the members relate to one anothr.

If you have anticipated the questions and have prepared yourself with answers, you will be much better prepared to present the full message of God's love. Not only does He save us from our sins, but He brings us into relationship with God and with our fellow believers. Most likely your inquirer is not only interested in a relationship with God; he may be keenly interested in what kind of relationship with other believers this implies.

Your Community

First, it is important for you to examine your community of believers. Everyone has a community. It is vitally important that you examine that community and decide if it will help or hinder you in your message. Can you help your community so that they will welcome new believers from other religious backgrounds? This may sound simple, but in the Middle East we discovered that believers from traditional Christian backgrounds struggled to accept new believers who were coming out of Islam. It took several years of work and effort before they began to accept these new believers. If your community is totally unsatisfactory, can you cooperate with others so that you have something into which to welcome the new believer?

In many cases missionaries working together in Muslim counties have no believers from a Muslim background to include in their community, when they initially start to minister. So the missionaries form community with each other, meeting and worshiping in their own language, and visiting in each other's homes. As time goes on, they begin to enjoy very much the small Christian community that they have created in the midst of a Muslim setting. While this can be seen as a healthy thing for the personal needs of spouses and children, it does not create the kind of community that can readily accept new believers from a Muslim background.

It takes a great deal of effort to change your community from being exclusive (for like minded Christians/missionaries only) to being inclusive (for everyone, even those from other cultures and worldviews). It is my opinion, however, that this is the only way forward. New believers from Hindu, Muslim and Buddhist backgrounds need support, friendship-discipleship, a place of refuge, and much more. If it is not apparent that these things are available in the body of Christ he or she may turn away from the Gospel.

If the missionaries feel they need their own community in their own language and culture in order for them to cope with the stress of living in a Muslim setting, how much more do seekers and converts from Islam also need a community? If there is no national community, and if the missionary community is closed to them, then how will they survive? In every case in which missionaries have been involved in significant church planting movements among Muslims, those missionaries have opened their hearts and their homes to the new believers. Community has been inclusive, rather than exclusive.

Community Identity

At this stage you need to decide if you are going to work within your existing community, or try and create a new community. The drawback of working with your existing community is that some may resist your efforts in changing the community to be more inclusive. On the other hand, the problem with creating new community is that you have to pre-design it, and then find people to fit into it. If you are by yourself, you cannot have a community. It takes others.

New Community Questions

Is your new community going to be a sub-community of a Western entity (evangelicalism, Protestantism, your home denomination, or whatever), or is it an entirely new kind of Christian community? If you create a new community, will it be seen as an extension of the local religion (Islamic, Hindu, Buddhist, etc.), a new local community, an extension of a Western community, or some sort of international community? What sort of relationship does your community have to surrounding churches, supporters and governments? Personally, I feel that in most cases it is best to build some sort of international community, where each other's cultures are respected, but are not central to the fellowship and function of the community. If you are a cross-cultural communicator of the gospel, you may want your new community to look and feel more like the target community than your sending community.

In one Muslim nation, Christian workers created a multifaceted community of new believers. They met any interested people at a local restaurant (back room) on Thursday evenings to discuss religion and philosophy. Everyone was welcome, and it was a come-and-go event. The believers at these meetings tried to sense when it was appropriate for them to invite people to an inner circle that met on Fridays, the weekly religious holiday in the Middle East. The Friday meeting was an all-day event. The group initially met in the home of the missionary-teacher. His home opened in the morning, and was open until late evening. People came when they could, as most had obligations with their families. During the Friday event, people dropped in to chat, eat, and when there was a group of them to pray, sing, and study the Word. This might occur several times during the day when there were sufficient numbers. Otherwise the teacher would visit, talk and pray with the ones and twos that dropped in. The missionaries working in this situation told me that they found this to be very satisfactory, and that they were starting a third meeting for young couples, especially those with small children. They also told me that they received their sole spiritual support from this community. Thus, it was the kind of community where the new converts could also find their sole spiritual support.

Community culture and structure

Every community has its own internal culture. If you are working through an existing community, don't hide the culture, but examine it and decide if it is helpful. Will the members of your community accommodate new believers or believers from a different background? Don't assume that they will. Most church communities are built around something. Perhaps it is a family unit. Perhaps it was the founder. Perhaps it is a denominational tie. Don't assume that the members of your community will welcome new believers, especially if they are from a radically different background. This is especially true if your community represents a guilt-based culture, and you are trying to assimilate people from shame or fear-based cultures.

Structure and leadership style

It will be important for you to examine your community from the perspective of the new believers. What are these seekers seeing? What are they experiencing? They may accept that your community is a valid community for you, but will or can they fit in? Is this something for them? From their point of view is it realistic that they could make this community theirs?

If your church planting team has never discussed community, many of your contacts will reach this point and go no further, because there is no valid community for them. Others may go further if they can envisage themselves living like you do, and being part of the various communities of which you are part of. So don't be surprised when new believers want to join your mission organization, or travel and visit your friends and supporters.

From the seekers point of view, he will probably assume he is exploring the message as he works through understanding the community. The message and the community are usually one and the same to him.

Seekers from a Muslim, Hindu, or Buddhist background usually think we are bringing a completed message. On the other hand, we often think that we are bringing the religious part of the message, and that the new believers will adapt their culture and community around it. If you are expecting your new believers to create their own unique community all on their own by reading the Bible and applying the principles, then you should communicate this to them, and prepare them to understand the Bible in this context. This, however, is an almost impossible task. Most new believers from a Muslim, Hindu, or Buddhist background have no experience in studying religious things. Most have never read a religious text and thought about what it means. Islam does not require this. Discussion and questioning are often frowned upon as they fly in the face of submission.

New believers from Islam generally do not easily create Christian communities wherever they go. In many cases they continue to find their best support in Muslim community and eventually slip back into Islam.

It is important that we clearly present to seekers how our communities operate, and invite them to participate with us in Christian community. Let them experience the love of Christ as it is shared among the believers. The Bible tells us that they will know that we are Christians by our love for each other, and that they will be drawn into the faith when they see a loving Christian community in operation.

So when seekers start exploring your Christian community, share it with them. Be transparent. Allow them to come to your meetings and bask in the love of Christ. If your meetings are generally agency business meetings, separate the two... keep the business for those who are part of the agency, and offer worship, prayer, and fellowship for those who are part of the body of Christ. Worship should not be reserved for only those who are part of a mission agency.

Questions for Reflection or Discussion

1. In what ways do believers have to "switch" communities when joining your church plant?

2. Is your church-plant culturally close or somewhat distant from the culture of your target people?

3. Have you experienced new believers wanting to become 'Western' and experience 'Western culture?' Do you see this as healthy or harmful?

4. Do new believers have a sense of joining a new community or a sense of joining a new religion? Or something else? Explain.

5. Are there financial or other benefits that believers receive when joining your community? (Perhaps a chance to meet foreigners or spend time with the opposite sex?) Is this helping or hindering you?

6. Do you feel that you have earned a hearing among the people you are trying to reach? If not, what are some things you might want to do to earn a hearing? Do you need to learn more about their lives and livelihood? What else could you do to earn a hearing?

7. Have you had opportunities to share some parts of the gospel message? Do you feel that people are responding to you and interacting with the message you are giving?

8. Have people expressed an interest in knowing about who your friends are, or how you worship? How much do they play a part in your life and in the conversations you are having? Is there a way you can express your appreciation for the Christian fellowship that you have and the Christian community that you experience?

9. Do you feel that it is important for new believers to not only come into relationship with Christ, but to also come into relationship with his body?

10. Spend some time thinking about the Christian communities that you represent. Are these communities open or closed to the new believers? (For example, your sending church in your home country would be closed to these believers because of distance, language, and culture).

11. Are you part of several Christian communities on the field? Do you need each of these in order to survive spiritually? Do the new believers also have access to this spiritual support?

12. What sort of structure and culture does your new church plant have? Is this foreign or familiar to the new believers? Do you think they are comfortable with this? What might they want to change?

Chapter Twenty Seven
Steps to Switching Community (II)

4. Accepting the Forms of the Community

At this stage the seeker starts to explore your community to discover if it is a valid community for him, but he is neither fully a part of it nor feels a part of it. If you invite the seeker into your community, he will usually start adopting the forms and processes of the community.

One of the first forms that a seeker may participate in is the prayer of salvation. If you ask him to pray at this point, he will readily pray to accept Christ as his Savior. This may not be so much an expression of his personal identification with Christ as his desire to explore and be part of the community, and to follow the forms of the community.

Usually this exploration begins with an interest in the outward forms. How do you pray? What sort of words do you use, and what are the important body positions. He will become interested in what you do with your Bible. How do you hold it, when do you read it? If you put marks in it, why?

He or she will also observe how you relate to members of the opposite sex. How do you greet each other? How do you speak and relate together? He or she may have heard wild stories about how free Christians are with members of the opposite sex. Although these stories are false, they have their roots in truth. In the West, which is often seen as Christian, there are swingers who practice free sex. Male contacts may want to test this freedom to know if this is the kind of community he is entering into. His own community may have very strict laws on how members of the opposite sex relate. By entering into a freer atmosphere, he may assume that there is total freedom and may act very inappropriately. Some national believers from a traditional Christian background in Muslim countries have been greatly offended by this and assume that all Muslim young men are only interested in their women, and not in true Christian faith. You must be prepared for major misunderstandings.

Another question that will arise is, regarding what do you do on festive occasions, and religious observances. In many traditional settings, festive occasions are celebrated in similar ways, with people visiting each other, eating festive foods and drinking traditional beverages. He may miss this and misunderstand Western Christian events in which small family units meet together and exclude the wider community. (e.g. North American Thanksgiving and Christmas dinners)

He may also have heard false stories about what happens on Christian festive occasions. On one occasion I met a young man who was totally convinced that at our New Year's Watch-Night Services, the lights were turned out, and the men were free to mingle with, grope, and kiss the females who were present. Where did such an idea originate? Well, in our church, at the stroke of midnight, the lights were indeed turned off. Each member held a candle, and they knelt together to welcome in the New Year; men on one side of the room and women on the other. However, Muslim observers outside the church had put two and two together. Male and females were present, a party had been happening all evening, and then at midnight the lights went out, and everyone knows how Christians act in Western films.

Women seekers may have the opposite reaction. They may have heard the same stories, and may be very frightened to attend a worship service. Great care and sensitivity needs to be exercised in bringing these women into a Christian worship place. Women at the mosque usually occupy a totally separate room from the men. How will you handle this in your community?

Another issue that may arise is that of the process of discipleship. The seeker will need to learn what is expected in the discipleship process. He also needs to know how to present himself properly in the new community. Does he need a white shirt and tie for worship? If everyone wears these, and he does not own these, he will feel very uncomfortable. If you provide them, he will feel they are required. If his good clothes are in the wash, he may feel that he cannot come.

Your community needs to have a very clear idea of what community worship is. How is it done? Will you have musical instruments? Will you sing? Will you use a drum? Will you follow a traditional Western order of worship? Does everyone need to sit on a chair and have a Bible and song book? If so, will the new believer feel that he cannot worship God without these?

Other forms and processes

How does the community handle weddings, funerals, birthdays, tithing, and

253

helping the poor. What about helping the seeker if he has a material need? The seeker may ask questions, or he may even test the community in various ways to see how it reacts to him. This testing is usually an investigative process to discover the forms and processes of the community. The messenger may think he is dealing with a real believer at this point, but the seeker may be just testing community to see if it is trustworthy. He probably has heard that there is money in the community, and may be testing the community to see if financial help might be available to him. The messenger, on the other hand, may think the new believer is focused on money, has backslidden, or is now revealing his true motive. What is required at this point is an explanation of how the community helps others. If it is not explained to the seeker, he could reject the community and move on. This is really a learning stage, and should be handled as such.

5. Investigating the Power of the Message

The previous steps are usually taken through the initiative of the contact. He has let the messenger know he is interested in hearing the message and exploring the community. Now the messenger may have to take the initiative.

A Difficult Question

There is a lot of confusion at this point about the seeker's true spiritual status. He may have prayed a prayer of salvation long before this, and so the leadership may consider baptizing him.

For many Westerners, a personal relationship with God comes first, and a relationship with the community second. They assume that if the seeker has said a prayer of salvation, and if he is now participating in the forms of the community, (coming for worship, Bible study and fellowship) then he is a true believer.

For a lot of evangelicals, baptism is the evidence of obedience and evidence of a personal relationship with God, and thus declares one's intention of become part of the community. In the Muslim context, however, seekers may become part of the community, long before they have a personal relationship with Christ.

So the question of baptism is a difficult one. The decision to baptize may have a lot to do with your theology (i.e., a Presbyterian view versus a Baptistic view), but it also needs to be viewed in relation to seekers exploring the community.

Important Note

Please remember that the stages I am presenting here may not be happening one after the other. They may be overlapping, or taking place at different times. I am simply presenting what we have discovered to be a very common order. So, this stage that we are discussing is probably happening parallel with some of the previous stages. However, at some point, it becomes an issue.

A Change of Focus

In actuality, if the seeker has been generally following the steps we have outlined, he has still only grasped the physical, outward side of the Christian religion. Much of Islam, Hinduism and Buddhism are made up of observable activities, and so it is natral that the seeker's eexploration has been focused on these. Now the focus needs to change. Spiritual issues must be dealt with, not just community issues. The seekers need to personally experience divine power in some form.

If the community has not been practicing this, the messenger needs to start sharing stories of how God is working in his personal life. Transparency is very important in promoting growth in the seeker. It is imperative that the seeker begins to want a personal experience with God. You, as a messenger want to impart a desire to enter into the deeper things of God. As you encourage this, your seeker should then take some initiative to investigate the power of the message.

The first step the messenger should take is to reveal himself and his community. This step is the one in which the messenger is revealing the Spirit and spiritual things (external and internal). The seeker needs to be made aware of the way the Holy Spirit affects the messenger's life as well as the messenger's community.

Rather than openly teaching and telling everything, the principle that should be used here is to first introduce a topic and then allow the seeker to explore and seek out answers. Many evangelists and disciplers want to teach a series of lessons at their pace rather than at the seeker's pace, and in the process they leave the seeker far behind.

In the model we are introducing, the messenger introduces his message, and allows the contact to seek answers for any questions he might have about it. Then the messenger introduces his community and allows the contact to investigate this aspect. Finally the messenger introduces the Spirit and the things of the Spirit, and allows the contact to seek out answers in this area.

6. Seeing the Transforming Power of the Holy Spirit

Having explored the forms of the message, the seeker needs to experience personally the power of the Spirit in his or her personal life and in the Christian community. This requires dealing with core issues like transparency, repentance and forgiveness.

Your seekers will need to discover the transforming power of God to change them from being people who hide behind facades to those who are empowered by God to be transparent.

As the Holy Spirit is transforming, some cultural values will come into question. You need to be prepared to know how these should be dealt with. What you do with these issues is more important than what the issues actually are.

Some issues that will arise at this point

First, the Holy Spirit will begin to bring up issues in the seekers life. They may be volunteered by the seeker, or he or she may be put into a situation where these issues become evident. Whatever happens at this point, it should be the work of the Holy Spirit, not the accusation or prompting of the messenger or members of the Christian community.

As we have mentioned, most shame based cultures accept that shame must be covered. The teaching of the Bible is that sin needs to be confessed and dealt with. (I John 1:9) Reconciliation with others and God needs to be sought. This is a difficult process as different cultures vary the seriousness of confessions. What may be almost routine in one culture may become traumic in another. In some instances, confession can be done privately between an individual and God, in others, Christian leaders may be involved, and yet in others the whole community may need to agree on how to resolve an issue. They key is how the community feels about the issue, and not the perception of the individual seeker.

Old sins and background problems may need to be dealt with. Sins and issues that were hidden in the seeker's life should start to come out. It is not necessary to totally reveal all of these things to the entire community, but they still must be dealt with. Be prepared that you may start dealing with some shocking issues. Lying, stealing and moral sins may be revealed, and need to be handled sensitively. It is important here to deal with these issues, and not to leave them covered up.

Other issues need to be worked through. For example, what about attitudes towards the government, and other forms of authority? This can be a key issue in helping reveal deeper feelings about God and what he expects of us.

Attitudes to opposing religious views need to be dealt with. We are not at war with others; we are at war with Satan and his hosts, and are trying to rescue people from darkness. We do not lash out at individuals or religious systems, but rather at Satan. We try to reach out in love to those with opposing religious views. This is often a hard lesson to learn, as we may have been taught that we should oppose and lash out at evil people.

Attitudes to political leaders may need to be corrected. This is especially true if you are dealing with people from a suppressed minority background. They may need to learn about submitting to leaders and authorities as well as to God.

Another area that may need attention is business practices and attitudes. In a culture where lies and cheating are common, honesty and ethics in business may be difficult for the seeker to address.

These need to be dealt with by both the community and the seeker. Can you begin to see the transforming power of the Holy Spirit in someone's life? Does the messenger recognize God at work in the new believer's life, even if the issues are very different from those that the messenger may have dealt with when he became a believer?

7. Testing the Messenger and the Community

Around this point the seeker will face a serious challenge. Either the seeker will totally accept the message and the community, or the seeker will walk away. It is not uncommon for them to get to this stage and then test the community the messenger, or even the message. Will the community react as they have promised? Will God provide as he has promised? Tests come in many forms and situations and should be seen as part of the normal process of a person coming to Christ, not something strange or negative.

Sometimes the seeker or new believer does something that appears strange to the onlooker, just to create a test. Sometimes he brings a small problem he is facing and makes it a big problem to see how the community will react. Sometimes he creates a fictitious problem or acts out of character in order to create a test.

It is very important to note that many seekers are not fully committed to the community until they pass through this stage. We must not accept seekers as fellow believers until they have committed not only to Christ, but also to the community.

Interestingly there is a certain amount of tolerance in Islamic communities in allowing people to be either actively or passively involved in other communities. Some room is given to experiment and play. Young men, until they are married, can experiment with some freedom. They may be able to participate in your community, but in the end they may not commit themselves, or may be kept from committing themselves. Saying a prayer, attending meetings, and reading other books are not necessarily seen as joining another religion. Changing communities is the important issue. Once a seeker starts testing the community, you will know that he or she is starting to get serious about making a commitment to the community.

The Personal Character Test

Our missionary team had gathered at the home of one of our missionaries, who were involved in gathering Muslim background believers into a Christian fellowship. Our host's living room was full of missionaries who had gathered to hear our specially invited speaker from the West. The table was covered with baked goods that various individuals had brought. We had just sung a song and were about to listen to the speaker when the doorbell rang. My heart sank. Not now! Who could it be? Sure enough, it was a young Muslim man that our missionary host was counseling. Our host slipped out of the room. A few minutes later his wife followed him, so she could make tea. They were gone for the rest of the meeting. After our team meeting had finished and everyone was leaving, I cautiously broached the subject.

"You missed a great meeting!"

"Yeah, but Muhammad dropped in for a visit."

"Didn't you tell the guys that you were busy with visitors today?"

"Yes, I did."

"So he must have had a pressing problem to bother you today."

"No, there wasn't any problem, and his visit wasn't a bother."

"But you missed hearing our speaker!"

"I know, but I'm here for Muhammad," he replied. "I think he just wanted to discover if I would leave my other friends if he came by."

Sure enough, sometime later we came to realize that Muhammad had purposely come to the missionary's home to test him. Hospitality is a basic fundamental principle in the Middle East. When my friend dropped everything to attend to his guest, he had passed the test. It wasn't long before Muhammad started to bring his friends over to listen to the missionary.

On another occasion I was rushing out the door to a meeting when a young Muslim man dropped by. I explained to him that I was in a rush, and couldn't stay. I asked him to come back the next day when I would have more time. That young man agreed but never returned to my house, and his contact with Christians ceased. I had failed the Personal Character Test. I should have invited him into the house, offered him a drink, and then explained what was going on. By rushing out the door and down the steps, I had greatly offended him. All the neighbors would see me rush out, and the young man following a few minutes later. They all knew that I had rejected him in some way.

Other missionaries have also shared how their contacts have sometimes deliberately dropped in for a visit when they knew it was inappropriate. They were not demanding attention, they were simply testing the missionary, his sincerity, and the depth of his commitment, their friendship and his character. Hospitality is not the only test, but be aware that your personal integrity and your character will be tested from time to time.

The Ethnocentrism Test

There are great differences between Eastern and Western culture. A seeker may try to get you into a situation to test your reaction. Do you refer back to your Western culture to make decisions? They may set up a situation and personally take a position that would not be condoned in their own culture just to test you.

For example, in one situation a seeker invited a messenger/teacher to a restaurant with some of his friends. The restaurant was located beside a mosque, and the table they chose was directly opposite the mosque's loudspeaker. After a while, the prayer call started. At this point the young seekers started to complain about the noise. They began to say things like "Why are they permitted to make so much noise? The prayer call is a bother. Islam is a false religion anyway." They were simply trying to test the messenger to see how he would react. Would he agree to what they were saying, and thus prove that he was a typical Westerner?

In this situation the messenger responded, "My book teaches us to speak respectfully of all men, even when we disagree with them. Disrespect is a sin that God will judge." The young men grew quiet, and the topic changed. The teacher noted a new seriousness in their interest in the things of the Gospel after this encounter.

The Humanism Test

Does the messenger have a humanistic philosophy? The most obvious outworking of this in Muslim society is through issues like the human rights movement, women's rights, and the separation of religious and state affairs.

Humanism is often described as "the value of accepting the worth of the individual." A basic premise of humanism is that people are rational beings who possess the capacity for truth and goodness within themselves. The term humanism is most often used to describe a literary and cultural movement that spread throughout Western Europe in the 14th and 15th centuries. This renaissance revival of Greek and Roman studies emphasized the value of the classics for their own sake rather than for their relevance to Christianity. The whole humanist movement came to the forefront of Europe in the 16th and 17th centuries and made its way to America. Islam and most Eastern cultures on the other hand, hold views that are directly opposite to Western humanistic values.

In a missionary setting, your contacts may question your interests in them. You must consciously think about your focus. Are you so focused on making converts that you fail to recognize the people you are reaching out to as human beings with other needs as well? The people to whom we are reaching out may be caught in various traps. Women may feel abused or suppressed. Young people may feel frustrated with lack of opportunities. Men may feel that they are being exploited by their employers. Ethnic minorities may feel oppressed or persecuted. People of low esteem may want opportunities to advance. They may test you to see if you are interested in them as people, not just religious followers. Do you understand and enter into their struggles? If you do not, they may reject you as a messenger, they may reject your message, or they may refuse your offer of community because it does not address any of their felt needs.

The Materialism Test

As Westerners we often surround ourselves with material things. We enjoy good-quality, nice-looking things, and our houses are usually filled with these items. How important are these items to us? Are they more important than the souls of the people that we are trying to reach? Sometimes these items leave our friends and neighbors convinced that we are extremely wealthy. Our lives are often watched, and we are sometimes tested to discover how closely we are attached to these items.

Early in our ministry the neighbors began sending over plates of food to our house. Whenever they cooked something special, they would send one of the children over with a plate for us to sample. We usually filled the plate with Western baked goods and sent it back. Sometime later, my wife decided to send some of our food over to the neighbors. She placed it on one of our dishes and sent it over. They sent back food on one of their dishes. Every time we sent one of our dishes, it disappeared. Eventually my wife asked them about her plates. They apologized, but they had used it to give food to another neighbor and that neighbor hadn't returned it. At first we were frustrated. Our plates were wedding gifts and we had brought them from our home country. They were special, non-breakable plates, not like the cheap local products that our neighbors were sending to us. Eventually we had to make a decision about our respond to the situation. What was more important - our neighbor's souls or our precious dishes? We gladly continued to trade food with our neighbors, and eventually bought local plates in the market to replace them.

The Spirituality Test

Some of the people we are trying to reach are much more aware of the spirit world than we are. We talk about the spirit world, but do we really believe our own message? What are we saying when we talk about the spirit world, or the Holy Spirit? What do our listeners understand about spirits? How do you deal with the spirit world? Do you really hear the voice of God?

In one instance, a seeker invited the messenger to a very large restaurant. He asked him to meet him there at a very specific time. When the messenger arrived, the restaurant was very busy, but he found the seeker at a small table on the balcony overlooking the main floor. During their visit, the issue of hearing God's voice came up. The seeker challenged the messenger, asking him directly if God really did communicate with him. The messenger replied that on many occasions God did speak to him, sometimes through the Bible, sometimes through other believers, and sometimes directly. The seeker then challenged him on the last point, laying out a test. During the previous week, the seeker had explained the Christian message to a friend of his. His friend had prayed the prayer of salvation, and that friend was now sitting somewhere on the main floor of the restaurant. Could the messenger please ask God who this person was and then point to him?

How would you have handled this? In this case, the messenger, a friend of mine, told me that he prayed "Lord, this isn't about me and my relationship with you, it's about you and a possible relationship with this young man. Can you please show me who it is? I will point out the first person that comes to my mind."

Then he looked around the restaurant and he pointed to the first person that came into his mind. The seeker nodded, and then the discussion proceeded on to other issues. After that meeting there was a profound positive change in the seeker's attitudes and commitment to following Jesus.

The Financial Test

Will the community help me when I'm in need? The seeker may create situations in which he is in need, or he may make up a fictitious situation to see if the community will help him. In this case, he is not being untruthful because in his mind this was a fictional setting; he is simply testing the community, and this for him may be an honorable act.

On one occasion a young male seeker asked the Christian community for some money, as his sister was getting engaged and they needed money for the party. He would repay it as soon as he got his next paycheck. The community said it would consider it. When the elders met, one of them protested that he knew the family and as far as he knew the sister in question was not getting engaged. The Christian community immediately assumed that the young man was simply looking for money. There was a confrontation. Anger was expressed, and the young man reacted angrily. Later the missionaries found out that the young seeker was testing the community, and had planned to refuse any money that was offered. The question to which he was seeking an answer was whether it would be offered? The underlying issue was whether the community would be there for him if he had a need.

Many Western Christians struggle with financial issues and community. A good basic guideline to follow is to plan how you as a community will react when needs are presented. Rather than dealing with issues on an individual basis, tell those in need that your community will meet and discuss what can be done to help them in their needs. Then respond by helping people. Seekers will not test a community that they can actively see is helping others financially. It is only when they don't see this that they will test it. So be open about how you run the community. What do you do with offering? Do you have a fund for helping people in need? Who administers it? How quickly can decisions be made? What happens when the fund runs low? Who qualifies for help and who doesn't?

On one occasion a young neighbor man came to us asking for money. I explained that we had money to help people who were poor. I then asked him how one tells a poor person from a normal person. He answered that a poor person had no blanket and no food to eat. Since he had answered his own question, the conversation moved on to other things, and he did not ask for money again. However, when a family in our village later lost everything, he came running to us to tell us that there was a poor family in need. We responded immediately, as did others in the village. If the people you live among are all 'poor,' ask them how they help one another. Discover how they analyze situations and how they respond, and discuss how you as a community can also be involved.

Testing should not be seen as weakness of fiath. Rather, it should excite the messenger that the seeker is now at a point of wanting to make a decision. So much is at risk for the seeker. If the seeker whole-heartedly accepts the message, then he may lose his old community and all of his old support structures. He or she needs to be absolutely sure that they are making the right decision.

This decision is not something that the messenger should push. It is one which the seeker should make at his own pace. He must accept that the messenger is a true messenger, and that the message is absolutely sure and trustworthy. He or she must also be moving forward with no illusions and false trust in what the community is and what it has to offer.

8. Accepting the Authority of Jesus and the Holy Spirit, and Becoming a Disciple

Have you ever tried to cross a rope bridge? I had an occasion to cross one once, and found it fascinating to watch other people's first attempt at the bridge. Most carefully placed one foot on the bridge and tested it for strength and balance. That is often what new believers do with the Christian message and community. Once the seeker tests the messenger, the message, and the community, they should be at a place where they are ready for total submission to Jesus. They must accept the transforming power of the Holy Spirit in their lives. This is a humbling position to be in, and if possible it should be done in community with other believers who will accept and support the new believer.

If at all possible, the new believer should not be alone in his act of submitting to God. He should be joining the community in their corporate coming before God's transforming and empowering work.

As a person submits to God, he is filled with the Holy Spirit and will hopefully desire to express his commitment with baptism. The expression of baptism is more than just a step of obedience and identification with the death and resurrection of

Jesus. It is also a symbol of submission to God and a symbol of joining the community of believers world-wide that is expressed in and through the local community of believers.

At this point there should be plenty of support from the community to help the new believer grow into a disciple. His or her personal walk with Jesus needs to be encouraged and developed. The new believer needs teaching in order to grow. This is where the discipleship process (as we know it in the West) really begins, and an individual or a group should take on the responsibility of mentoring and discipling.

In the process of discipling, you might want to take the disciple through a series of materials that address specific issues and questions. A sample of this kind of material is found in the Growth Group Studies, found in The Church Planter's Handbook and on the resource page of the website (http://rmuller.com).

Questions for Reflection or Discussion

1. Have you experienced people wanting to explore your community? If this has not happened, why has it not happened? Is your Christian community isolated or considered strange by the local people?

2. Is your community open enough that you could invite seekers to come and explore who and what you are?

3. How 'user friendly' is your community? Do you explain which book you are reading out of, and what page number you are on? Are your services confusing for new comers? Is your location conducive to new people feeling at home and finding their way around. Try and put yourself in their place, and walk through a first time visit. Start at the street and think through each of the moves the person must make, and how frightening or welcoming each are.

4. Do members of the opposite gender relate much the same or very differently than in the culture around you? Is this a benefit or a distraction? Do you think that it might attract young men and alienate young women?

5. Have you considered various forms of worship? What should people do while they pray? Are you simply doing what you learned in your home country? How can you be more culturally sensitive in the various forms of worship?

6. How do the people in your target culture celebrate festive occasions? Are there some local traditions that you could incorporate into Christian festivals? Think in terms of how they visit, what they eat and drink, and things they do that might also have a Christian symbolism.

7. Consider the worship songs you sing. Are these all translated from other cultures? Have your new believers started expressing themselves through their own culture and language? Can you encourage some of them to start writing poems, prose, songs, or chants that are their own forms of prayer or worship?

8. How open is your community about how they help people in need? Can seekers easily understand who and how you help people? This is an important expression of community. Think of the early church that we studied in chapter 25. Their reputation as a fellowship was centered on how they helped one another. Can new seekers easily see this in your new church?

9. How does the community handle weddings, funerals, birthdays etc? Do any of your forms mirror those used in the local community? Why or why not?

10. Do you think there is a time that is too early to baptize? What indicators would you look for before approaching this topic with a new believer. Explain.

11. Does your team present a gospel message that focuses on accepting and believing? Does it also contain strong elements of confession and repentance? Are there culturally sensitive ways for repentance to occur?

12. Have you seen a change of attitude in the new believers? Think in terms of attitudes about religious things, politics, and business practices.

13. Think of ways that the personal character or depth of friendship of you or your team mates has been tested. How have you fared? What can you do to improve this?

14. Do people invite you to criticize their culture, religion or worldview? Have you joined them? Has this labeled you as an outsider? How can this improve?

15. Have you passed the Humanism test? Have you demonstrated that you appreciate people as much or more than your programs or ideas? Have there been times when you insisted on your good idea or program and have broken relationships?

16. How much does your financial status differ from the people in your target group? Are you seen as rich? How does your income compare with theirs? If you are significantly better off, do you share? In what ways have materials or money come between you and others? How have you handled this? How could you respond better?

17. Do the people you work among have a sense of the spirit world? Are there ideas that they will have to change in order to understand the Bible or are you introducing a whole new realm to them? Is your message based on spiritual realities, or is it limited to accepting historical facts and believing in them?

18. Do you think you have been tested by seekers or new believers? How have you fared? Are there other tests you have faced?

Chapter Twenty Eight
Some Considerations

Community first or personal faith first?

This is a common question that is asked in our seminars. According to the steps that I have outlined, the seeker may spend a lot of time exploring the community rather than dealing with his own personal faith. This is the opposite of what most Westerners expect. We usually expect to deal only with personal faith and theology and leave community issues to be worked out later. The model of spiritual growth that most Western Christians have subconsciously accepted is:

Evangelism -> Discipleship -> Joining a Christian community

In many cases, however, the seeker will want the question of community to be dealt with first, or at least alongside that of personal faith. In some cases the order is reversed.

Community (Belonging) -> Discipleship(Exploring) -> Evangelism(Accepting)

In Islam, faith is not only a personal matter; it is a family and community matter. The Muslim seeker may want to see faith dealt with on all levels before truly submitting to Christ.

This situation has often caused misunderstandings. Many missionaries have misunderstood what was taking place. They failed to address the issues that the seeker was facing. He was exploring or participating in the Christian community first, before making a commitment of personal faith. A great deal of this misunderstanding can be cleared up if the missionary recognizes what is taking place and helps the seeker deal with issues that the seeker feels are important, as well as the issues that the missionary feels are important.

Community-Based Evangelism

There is something about a properly functioning Christian community that is attractive to those outside it. Many of the "people movements" or "church planting movements" in history have had a real sense of Christian community. As the world sees Christian community in action, they are drawn to the community. Actually they are drawn to Jesus whom they can see in the community of believers.

In I Thessalonians 1:6-10 Paul tells the church in Thessalonica that they were examples to surrounding Macedonia and Achaia and beyond. Paul and his comrades did not need to go around preaching because everywhere they went people were telling them what had happened to the Thessalonians. This same principle has been an effective evangelistic tool all through history. When God begins to work in people so that a dynamic Christian community forms, others are drawn to God through the love and actions of the community. In effect, the same principle of the transparent messenger who allows Jesus to shine through him and thus attracts non-believers (discussed in the first section of this book) now applies to the community that the messenger forms. When the community is transparent and allows Jesus to shine through them as a corporate group it will attract non-believers.

Conflict of Interests and Missionary Compounds

Years ago under the colonial era, missionaries established missionary compounds where they could form a community which, in some ways, represented the community they left at home. Colonial governments wanted to demonstrate to the native people the advantages of Western culture. Missionaries sent under the colonial system adopted the use of compounds as they provided many advantages. As time passed, local people joined the compounds. Many came for employment, but others came because they were seeking something they saw in the missionaries. As they joined the community these seekers changed their outward form, wore Western clothes, attended churches, sang Christian songs, and even prayed to the Christian God. But many of them had only outwardly joined the community. When their lives didn't match the expectations of the missionaries they were called backslidden, rice Christians, and other demeaning names because they had not really taken the second step of investigating the personal relationship aspect of the Gospel. Meanwhile, when the seekers found out that the community spirit, which they had seen expressed in the missionaries' relationship with each other was closed excluded them, they became angry and bitter.

This misunderstanding of community created tremendous problems in Africa and India. The nationals wanted to enter the community, and the missionaries wanted to share spiritual things with those who entered, but not physical things. In their Western thinking, they assumed that when someone joined the community they already had a personal relationship with God. This is an assumption we should never make. If we keep our communities closed to seekers, they will struggle to accept our message, because they cannot also accept our community.

One successful ministry to Muslims in the country of Gambia is based on a "community" form of evangelism. The leading pastor opened the church compound so that housing could be constructed for any new believers that needed housing. Food and clothing were shared while new believers made the transition from a Muslim community to a Christian one. This community in turn attracted the attention of other seekers. If their own Muslim community reacted strongly against them, there was an alternative community for them. Suddenly Christianity was much more acceptable and possible for Muslim seekers and the numbers of new converts grew.

Accepting Communities

It is on this subject of community that we must understand and work with converts from shame-based cultures. Historically, these people have resisted the spiritual communities that Christians have offered to them. Most Western communities were restricted to Sunday morning worship services with some accompanying programs throughout the week. These types of churches usually had little real community-commitment and as a result were not seen as attractive.

In many of our minds, the ideal church has only believers in it. As Christians we want to get away from the world and worship, fellowship, and receive teaching in the company of other believers. Many Western believers want an exclusive club where they feel comfortable and where nothing threatens them.

In the Christian communities I have been describing in this book, the community may include large numbers of people at various stages of investigating the claims of Christ and the community of Christ.

For many of us, we assume that membership in the community entitles you to rights in the community such as leadership. Eastern communities, however, can include many people who are in the process of joining the community. Islam can embrace many quasi Muslim people, especially in Asia and Africa. In this way, Islam s very tolerant, and considers itself very tolerant. Our Western closed communities are often seen as very intolerant.

Many Christians in our evangelical churches in the West think in terms of believers inside the church, and unbelievers outside the church. Those who are outside might come to Christ in such places as evangelistic crusades, ladies meetings, businessmen's breakfasts, personal witness or cell groups or through the personal witness of a friend from work or neighborhood, but all outside of the church's circle of influence.

Some years ago I was attending a large church service in the West. In the middle of the service a drunken lady came staggering down the aisle. It was very embarrassing for everyone, and they tried to look away. I tried to help, even if I did feel uncomfortable. She had come to the church for help, and instead of receiving help, she discovered that she didn't belong there, and no one wanted her. The ushers told her she could sit in the back of the church if she was quiet. It seemed to me that they wanted her forgotten or ignored. I felt that she should have been taken into a side room by one of the ladies (or couples) of the church and helped to as far as her condition would allow.

This example illustrates the commonly held idea among evangelicals that non-believers can attend church only as observers. They are restricted in their participation. Some seekers, on the other hand, want to experience our communities before they commit themselves to a lifelong relationship to the community. Somehow we must find a way to allow seekers to experience real Christian community, and at the same time explain to them the theological beliefs of the community and the way of becoming a real follower of Jesus and not just part of the community.

The Road Into Our Community

How does your community accept new members? Is there a clear path into the community? Have you thought through how people should approach and join your community? In the 1970's, I attended a Brethren Assembly in Ireland, where I learned much about this important aspect of community. While many considered the Brethren to be "closed" they were actually very open if you approached their community in the right way. Their Sunday morning services (called Breaking of Bread) were closed, and only open to those who had been accepted as spiritual members. The Sunday evening service was the exact opposite. It was called a

Gospel Meeting, and the entire purpose of the meeting was to bring people into their Christian community. The whole concept of the Gospel Meeting was that the believers were hosting this meeting for seekers. Before the meeting, members would either go door-to-door to invite people to come, or they would hold open air meetings, or hand out invitations in public places. The Gospel Meeting was warm, lively, and friendly, and open to everyone who wanted to discover what active Christian community was all about.

When newcomers came to the Gospel Meeting they were invited to a home Bible Study in their area. Once they had accepted Christ, they were assigned a community member who would mentor and disciple them, usually for a year or more. During this time they continued to attend the Bible Studies and the Gospel Meetings. Then, at a certain point, the mentor would invite them to attend the Sunday morning 'Breaking of Bread' Service. This service was closed to everyone who had not entered into their community via the Gospel Meetings, Bible Studies, and the mentoring process, or who had not have a letter of recommendation from another similar Christian community. The strength of this approach was that the members all understood how their community operated, and that there was an accepted method of becoming an inner member of the community.

Now, consider your community. How do seekers experience community before they become Christians? Is this possible? Is there a clear path that seekers are directed along that is understood by everyone?

Existing Community

There is another issue that must be dealt with. How does the church-planter go about dealing with the seeker's existing community? In most settings seekers will already be experiencing some form of community. In some cases this is a very tightly woven group with particular ideas of how community operates. If the church-planter is dealing with a small unique community, then the best strategy may be to become part of that community in some way and win the entire community over to Christ. This is often the approach that is used in a tribal setting. However, when dealing with a larger group of people, the church-planter will probably have to deal with a small group of seekers who will end up leaving their old community. If this is the case, then this group will have to consider the type of new community they want to form. In the majority of urban church planting situations, the new Christian community may end up drawing members from several different types of backgrounds. In this case, it is important that they form a Christian community that is viable to all of the surrounding types of people.

Example: Existing Community in Liberia (West Africa)

The following material was related to me by a missionary to the Bassa tribe, which has existed in Liberia for many centuries. Before the arrival of the white man and the resulting Westernization, their community was expressed in a very particular way.

For as long as anyone can remember, everyone in a Bassa village understood that they had responsibility for each other in three specific areas: (1) Everyone built buildings together, (2) Everyone defended the village together (3) Everyone hunted together.

It was understood that these were the joint responsibilities of the men, and a system of accountability was in place.

The men of the village expressed their solidarity through their daily main meal which was eaten in the evening. All of the men of the village went to the house of one man to eat from a common dish. They would usually only eat a few spoonfuls or handfuls of food. They would then start to discuss the events of the day. After a few moments they would move on to the next house, gather around the common dish there and eat a few more spoonfuls, continue their discussion, and then move on to the next home until they had eaten in all of the houses. This was the outward expression of their community.

If a man was expelled or punished, he was ostracized. He could still live in the village but he was known as "the man who ate alone." It was a method of publicly shaming him. Restoration was expressed by restoring his right to share and eat the evening meal with others and thus publicly reinstating him into the community.

When the Gospel message entered the Bassa area, it was important that it could be introduced into this community setting. If every new believer was expelled from the community, then Christians throughout the area would be known as people who ate alone. If the Christian message could be introduced into the community, and accepted by most if not all of the men, then this ostracizing could be avoided. But more than this, the key to explaining the Gospel was found in explaining that we as humans are people who eat alone. We are separated from God, and from the fellowship at His table. It is through the mediation of Jesus that we can be invited back into fellowship with God, and into the community of believers from around the world. This is why we gather around the Lord's Supper and eat together, with Jesus in our midst.

Satanic Community

Almost everyone in the world relates to some sort of community. Most of these communities are not neutral, but already have a system of belief that needs to be addressed by the church planter. In Liberia, every four to five years the tribal leaders would hold a school in Shamanism, known as a "bush school." It was often 1 to 2 years in length. The teachers and students would live in a walled-in community learning witchcraft, tribal language, reading, secret hieroglyphics, herbal medicine, poisons, secret symbols, and signs of treachery. Boys and girls bush schools were held separately, but all attended. Girls learned about cooking, weaving, and sex. Boys learned to hunt, use bow and arrows, and activities that involved sex. Most of all, the students learned submission to authority. The larger tribe was divided up into several groups. The *Fish People* would learn useful skills like catching fish and clams using a diving bell. *The Snake People* had the responsibility to kill or use snakes, and so on.

As Christians entered the area, they were confronted with the existing community. It was more than just "people who ate together." There was the "bush school" and also a strong Satanic element that had to be dealt with.

The existing community is an important factor in all church planting. We must know what people are being called out of, as well as what we are calling them into. One of the important tasks that the church planter faces is understanding the existing community, knowing how to relate to it, and prayerfully considering what aspects, if any, of the existing community should be incorporated into the new community of believers in Jesus.

Questions for Reflection or Discussion

1. Read I Thessalonians 1: 5 - 10. Does this illustrate evangelism-> discipleship -> community or does it illustrate community -> evangelism -> discipleship? Explain your position.

2. What do you think of 'community-based evangelism'? Does this describe what is happening in your church plant? Are people attracted to what they see happening in the community of believers?

3. What draws people to an active Christian community? What makes the community attractive?

4. Do you live in a missionary compound or Western neighborhood? Does your living location help or hinder your message? Much might depend on how exclusive or inclusive the missionaries are.

5. To what extent have you experienced a clash between you wanting to share spiritual things and local people who want physical things? Do you think that your material possessions may be speaking louder than your faith?

6. Think for a minute about the history of missions in your target area. What sort of track record have church planters had? Are there some people groups who seem more resistant? Compare their idea of community with the Christian community that is being offered them. What differences do you see between these two communities? What reasons might they have in preferring their existing community to the Christian community?

7. How does your Christian community meet, accept and integrate new members? Is there a clear path into the community? List the typical steps that new believers might pass through.

8. Do the members of your Christian community understand these steps and are they playing vital roles in helping people pass through them? Is there a sense of welcoming new people and helping them through the process?

9. Can seekers experience Christian community before they commit themselves to becoming Christians? Is this possible in your setting?

10. Are you building a model of Christian community that is unique? Is it patterned after something used somewhere else? Why did you choose that model? How well do members of your Christian community mix with members of other Christian communities?

11. Is there a sense of community among the non-believing people you are working with? What is this community built around? Has Satan created a pseudo-community? Do you need to confront it, or simply do a better job of creating community?

Chapter Twenty Nine
Planting Churches (I)

Let's review. When one first starts out as a cross-cultural church planter, it is important to learn the language and culture, and to begin the process of being accepted as a messenger, learning how to share the Christian message. The new church planter should be conscious of the community he wants to form, even before evangelism is initiated. In many cases, language learners plant churches. When my wife and I first entered the Middle East, we became involved with a local Christian family and had a part in starting a church, while we were studying the language. That church has grown over the years and continues to minister today. Never assume that church planting will come later. Everything you do should focus on the church that will one day be in existence.

The Initial Steps for the Novice

Below is a short list of the type of basic goals that the new missionary might set as goals to reach. These can be adapted according to the local situation.

1) Language learning
   a) Shopping with ease
   b) Visiting neighbors with ease
   c) Telling Genesis 1-3 stories
   d) Collecting and telling proverbs and parables
   e) Teaching basic Bible stories and lessons
   f) Becoming indistinguishable from a local on the phone.
2) Evangelism
   a) Learn to say provocative things
   b) Learn the stories based on Genesis 1-3 and tell them
   c) Explain to people about objections to Christianity
   d) Develop your agenda and learn to use you tools.

Below are a number of strategies and issues that we have found to be important in the church planting situations we have worked in. These topics are only briefly mentioned here, as many books and articles have been written that address these issues in greater detail.

1. Define the location of your church plant

Are you planting a church in an area of the city or in a rural area? What are the boundaries that you will set for yourself? This needs to be done prayerfully as you determine where it is that God is calling you and what indications you have that God is at work. Make sure you know what God is doing in your area and join Him rather than starting your own activities. It is very important that you don't tackle too large an area. Start somewhere, but don't limit what God is doing. In one rural situation in which we were working, our evangelistic efforts covered an area hundreds of kilometers wide. As the Lord directed us to seekers and believers, it soon became apparent that it would be impossible to gather them because they were scattered so widely. We ended up encouraging these scattered believers but never planting a church.

2. Use pre-evangelism and salt-type tools

Having defined the area that you will work in, prayerfully seek ways of influencing people across the entire area. In a cross-cultural situation, take time to mix with people so that you are not frightening and strange to them. Talk to people in the shops, in parks and on the street. Visit neighbors and find ways of getting to know what is happening in your community. Prayerfully consider things that you will say and do to influence the community and introduce them to Christian concepts. This is a vital step in starting your church, and in discovering which people are 'somewhat interested' and who might be 'seekers'. It will also start to prepare the wider community for the new believers who will someday be in their midst.

3. Use Visitation

I have often advocated that visitation is the way to build a church. After many years of ministry, I am still convinced that this is one of the "golden keys" that many church planters miss. As you live in the community, seek ways to visit people. Most people would welcome a visit from you, but they don't know how to connect.

The first step in doing visitations is to clear your schedule of things that fill your day. Second, mix with people, and show an interest in what they are doing. Train yourself to become interested in the activities that are taking place in your community. I once dropped in at a small dirty shop looking for an electrical part. I discovered that the men in this shop were re-winding small electric motors. I chatted with the owner, and told him I had been looking for a hardware shop. I then asked if I could bring my washing machine motor to him if it burned out. We struck up a conversation, and soon I was seated beside him chatting about his shop and his involvement with the British army years before. Tea was offered, and I soon had a new friend.

I've discovered that if I am available, people often ask if I would like to come in for a cup of tea. Being available is the issue. When we lived in a rural setting, I would drive to the market in the morning. Along the way I would pick up people walking on the road or waiting for someone to come by and take them to market. After market I would load people's things into my car and drive them to their homes. Tea was always offered with friendly conversation. In an urban setting it is important to discover when it is that people sit around and visit, and then make an effort to join them. When my wife noticed what time the local women were free, she made an effort to visit with them. Usually this meant that her visits and mine were at different times, as the men were usually free for visiting in the evening, although many of them had time or made time during their work hours, especially if they were taking care of a store.

4. Move your visits to the next stage

There are a number of steps that should be recognized when trying to move the visit from a social visit (building relationships) to a spiritual one. (1) Learn about your host, their family and their culture. (2) Learn about your target community, (3) Introduce prayer or Bible truths into your visits, (4) Move towards having home Bible studies.

The most important step in the process is introducing spiritual content into your conversations. This can be done in various ways such as telling parables or proverbs, offering a prayer for a pressing need, or sharing biblical truths through telling a portion of a Bible story. You may need to create situations where you can tell a story. When there is a break in the conversation, you might be able to say "I heard an interesting story the other day ...." End the story by saying that it was a story told by Jesus. Don't comment or teach, just tell the story and let the Holy Spirit do his work of applying the story to the listener's hearts. These are non-threatening forms of communication and may open the door for leaving a Bible or video in the home.

5. Start Bible Studies

When visiting people, our initial interest is in developing friendship and building relationships because we have an interest in people as humans whom God has made and loves. As the relationship grows, we will naturally desire to share Christ with everyone, especially those who have become dear to us. Thus, once you have established visits that have spiritual content to them, you can start moving closer to starting Bible studies in the home. Mention the possibility of Bible studies, and invite those in the home to consider having a study. If they decline, you have lost nothing. Gracefully accept this, and continue to visit regularly. When you feel the time is right you can once again invite them to study the Bible.

Mass Media

If you have a small church planting team, made up of two couples and a single, then you can get five different visits in at one time. By doing three visits a day, your small church planting team can visit up to fifteen homes or businesses each day. If you do this six days of the week then over 90 families or businesses can be visited in the period of a week. Since your visits may influence two or three people, over 200 individuals can be contacted in the space of a week. As you find individuals who are interested in discussing spiritual things, those individuals will require longer and more frequent visits. The whole purpose for these visits is to find people who are open to spiritual things.

In the West we often assume that mass media means technology. This is not necessarily the only way the term can be used. Along with visiting, you might want to consider distributing booklets, tracts, videos, and cassettes. This kind of mass media is good for catching the attention of the public. This may be good or bad, depending on how hostile the general community is towards Christians.

In a closed country you may need to be creative as you distribute materials. In one country, Christians visited video rental shops at night, dropping the Jesus film into the video return slots. The following day, the Jesus film appeared in these shops for rent! In another country advertisements were taken out in the local paper giving people an address outside of that country to which they could respond. In another country they advertise a phone number with an answering machine that gives a short message and provides an opportunity for the caller to leave his or her name and phone number.

Sometimes mass media distribution (such as door-to-door, or stuffing mailboxes) has a negative effect. It can offend some people, especially if they feel they are the specific target of unwanted attention. On the other hand, newspaper advertisements might work, as people are used to ignoring advertisements that do not interest them. Those who are interested can respond. Sometimes, however, people who are offended also respond. I would classify these forms of distribution as "proclamation" types of evangelism. They may be very useful when the missionary does not speak the language fluently, or for attracting people to a seeker service or Gospel meeting.

Follow-Up

Mass media is usually connected to evangelistic efforts but it may also be useful for follow-up. There may be occasions when security issues limit the number of visits you can have with new believers. In one situation a single Muslim girl responded to the Gospel. Those doing follow-up with her up introduced her to a radio broadcast to which she could listen to in the privacy of her own home, usually after her family had gone to sleep. She would crawl under the blankets and listen each evening. In time she shared her faith with her sister, and after that they would listen together each evening. In this way, mass media can be useful for augmenting follow-up and discipleship. It also allows the teacher more time to focus on uniting the two faces and can especially be useful for secret or persecuted believers.

The downside of using mass media is that if it is not handled properly, new believers or seekers are not integrated into a local church, and thus may not move further on in their Christian faith. Our goal as church planters is to plant churches, not just win a few people to Christ. As churches are planted, more people will be drawn to Christ and a movement towards the gospel will begin. Therefore, we must not limit our efforts to just evangelism and discipleship, but church planting must be the goal from the very beginning.

Optimal Size of Groups

Sociologists tell us that there is a maximum number of people that most of us can relate to. It is often thought to be around a thousand individuals. Some of us can relate to more but others can only relate to a smaller number of people. Beyond this, we simply do not have the capacity to remember names and faces. This is important when planning your Christian community. While a thousand people may seem like a very large number at the beginning, it is always good to realize that when a group becomes large, it must contain smaller units, or it cannot survive.

Sociologists also tell us that most of us relate better to smaller groups of people, usually up to 150 in number. This was originally put forward in *Co-evolution of Neocortex Size, Group Size, and Language in Humans* by R.I.M. Dunbar in 1993. This number of 150 has since become known as "Dunbar's Number" and has been popularized by various business books. It has also become a benchmark number used in various social network services.

According to these writers, good group dynamics happen in meetings smaller than 150 individuals. If the number of individuals is greater than this, then group dynamics are often much more difficult or impossible. This doesn't mean that good group dynamics is not possible for a meeting o f 150 people or more; it simply helps us set the maximum number that should be involved in any one group. Researchers also tell us that the premium size for group interaction is 15 – 80 individuals and I believe that this should be the goal of the cross-cultural church planter.

On the other hand, in many cultures, group dynamics do not work well if there are less than 15 – 20 in the group, especially if newcomers do not have a natural relationship with other members of the group. When a newcomer enters a small group he may feel conspicuous, and have nowhere to hide, especially if he or she is shy. If church planting is done through relational lines, or through existing social networks, then the size of the group can be much smaller. People will not feel uncomfortable joining a smaller group, since they often meet these same individuals in smaller groups in their social networks.

However, if a seeker is exploring a new community, he may feel threatened if the group is less than fifteen individuals. Many Westerners on the other hand struggle to experience intimacy if there are more than ten or fifteen people.

These group dynamics have interesting effects on people, and the church planter should be aware that the optimum number varies from setting to setting and culture to culture. In one church planting situation we discovered that a group of eight was considered 'small and struggling.' When we reached fifteen people, everything changed. Now we were a significant and dynamic group and everyone's attitude was much more positive.

In light of this, it is important to consider the effectiveness of small cell groups.

In some cultures cell groups should be more like house-churches and contain at least fifteen to twenty people to enable good group dynamics to work. In other settings, smaller groups work just as well.

Along with this, it is important for the small church or cell group to feel part of the larger picture. Efforts should be made to make them feel part of what God is doing on a larger scale. Meeting every month or two with a larger group should be encouraged, or else members from other groups should be encouraged to visit the smaller group in order to stimulate and encourage the the smaller group.

Use Different Types of Gatherings

It is important to use both 'timed' gatherings and also "event" gatherings. The difference between timed gatherings and event gatherings should be obvious to those who are attending, and should be clearly spelled out so that they know what is happening. For instance, Bible studies should have a limited time frame. If they drag on for hours, people will lose interest no matter what culture they are from.

On the other hand, social events and day-long events should be just that: events with no time limits. It is generally a good idea to set a starting time and a set time for food, but the event can go on all day, longer if people so desire! Often people want to get away from the hectic life they lead during the week, and so an all-day, or one or two day event will be attractive. We have discovered that these events are usually remembered with great fondness for many years afterwards. Often these events have had only a little spiritual content, but they are powerful in building community. If you are planning a longer community event, then you might consider having a short spiritual element such as a special speaker, musical element, or media element. In some cases, we have discovered that taking our new church plant on a day trip or weekend trip out of the city had a very positive impact. First, many of our people had never been on such an outing, and had only rarely been outside the city. Your trip may be as simple as going on a picnic and sitting under some trees for the day, or it might be as complex as staying overnight. If there is no Christian camp or conference center, consider buying or renting some tents and heading for the country or even the beach.

We have found that these events cement friendships and greatly encourage the believers. Having one or two of these events each year can really boost the group and make them feel like a cohesive unit.

Questions for Reflection or Discussion

1. Analyze your church planting location. Are you planting a church in an area of the city or in a rural area? What are the boundaries that you have set for yourselves? How many different people-groups live in this area? How diverse is the income they earn? Are there cultural, historical, political or religious differences that divide people? How would you describe the community (even if it is part of a larger city)? What should you adjust or change in your focus as a result of your analysis?

2. Analyze your pre-evangelism program. How are you impacting the wider community? As you move through the community what are some things that could impact the lives of people? Don't think only in terms of mass-media; think in terms of activities, or other ways of impacting the wider community.

3. How effective is your visitation program? Are there homes that you regularly visit? Are there ways that you and your team members can meet people and start to build bridges into their lives? Are there people in the community who are just sitting around? (Women watching children, old people, guards, store keepers, unemployed, etc.) How would you approach these people?

4. Are there times during the day when people are visiting, or open to have visits? Can you make yourself available during this time?

5. Have you been able to introduce spiritual content into your visits? Are there homes where you can pray and talk about spiritual things? Is there a possibility of starting Bible studies in these homes?

6. Re-read the section on optimal group size. What do you think might be the optimal group size in your target culture? Why do you think this? Ask some of your friends and neighbors. Do you think you should plant a large or small church? If people prefer larger groups, can you build your church around groups of this size? Read chapter 31 from "The Man from Gadara." What did Abdalla discover about group size and how it affected the cells in his church?

7. Analyze your meetings. Do you have a variety of types and styles or do all your meetings follow a similar pattern? Can you plan outings for the new group that are not necessarily spiritual focused, but community-building focused? How about picnics, or outings where people just sit around and visit?

Chapter Thirty
Planting Churches (II)

Over the years I have been amazed at the number of church planters that have been sent to the mission field who have had very limited experience with churches let alone experience in planting one, training leadership, or developing church ministry. This is even more amazing when you consider that is difficult enough in any part of the world, but in the 10/40 window it can be tremendously challenging. There are few success stories from which to learn and few who have managed to get more than a handful of believers together. (Outside of South India, some areas of China and South Korea).

Now, despite their lack of experience and the absence of an abundance of successful models, I am also amazed at the number of new workers who think they know how to so this. Each of the experienced evangelists I spoke to in my survey felt that was the most difficult task they faced. Few felt they had ready answers, and most had only a limited success in getting converts to fellowship and worship together.

Trust

Everyone agrees that one of the most important issues in a closed country is the issue of trust. The most practical solution of which I have heard was the idea of bringing the new converts together in a social, informal, non-religious setting. They are not told that the others are believers in Jesus. In this way, they can meet and form unbiased opinions of one another without the pressure of trying to discover if each is sincere and trustworthy.

One mature Yemeni believer spent several years promoting friendships among a group of people he was discipling, and only after real trust developed between people did he reveal to each of them that they were believers. In some cases it may be advisable to inform the most mature convert about what is going on, and ask is opinion of the other individuals. This has several effects. First of all, it puts the responsibility of exposure onto the mature convert, allowing him to come out at his own timing. It also assures him that you are trustworthy yourself, and that you will not expose him to others without his permission.

In another setting, a teacher invited a group of people to his house for a party. Only the small fellowship of believers knew that the others attending were all new converts still in the initial stages of walking with the Lord. Several days after the party, the small fellowship met to decide who, if any, should be invited to join them. The teacher continued to work with those who had not been chosen until another party was arranged some months later, and the new converts were again assessed by the small group. In this way, the fellowship of believers felt protected and responsible for who could join their group.

If the group continually refuses to allow someone to join them, the teacher must investigate the reason why. If there is some non-religious issue that cannot be resolved, then a second group may need to be established so that the new convert gets fellowship. The issue will eventually have to be resolved, but the formation of a second group will allow further time to work out the problem.

What format should your meetings take? This is a question that no one can answer. Martin Luther had no idea what the average evangelical service today would look like when he started his work of reformation in the Roman Catholic church. The important issue was not the form, but the content of the meetings. Is God being glorified and are the needs of the believers being met? The form you use should be the choice of the converts and not something that you, the teacher, imposes upon them.

Linking new converts with those from a traditional Christian background

Some Muslim countries have a minority population of people from a Christian background. Countries like Egypt, Lebanon, Syria, Iraq, Chad and Jordan all have Catholic and/or Orthodox churches. During the last century, evangelical churches have been planted by reaching out to people from these backgrounds. If you work in a country with an evangelical church of this nature, then I believe you should consider yourself blessed indeed. While there are some who ignore these believers, I have personally seen these churches open their doors to embrace believers from Muslim backgrounds. This hasn't happened instantly. In fact many years of labor were invested, but the resulting body of Christ was much stronger than when it was comprised of two or three isolated communities.

While it is true that there are major difficulties between those from Muslim and Christian background communities, the largest area of concern when trying to form community, is usually that of trust and mistrust. This mistrust between Christian and Muslim background believers (MBB) is usually no larger than the lack of trust that exists between any two Muslim converts, before the discipler worked hard to bring them together. During the last decade evangelical churches in many Muslim countries have started to open their doors to MBB believers. While there have been struggles, overall the results have been very encouraging, and today many evangelical churches in Muslim countries have at least a couple of MBBs attending their services. In some situations churches have attempted to have special meetings for new believers from a Muslim heritage. A growing number of pastors readily baptize those who have come to Christ.

While there is still a long way to go to remove all mistrust, I have been greatly encouraged by what I have seen happening. In one instance, an evangelical church invited a convert to be on their board of elders. He was open to the idea, but challenged the church to think further. He said that once he was an elder, there would be other suitable converts who were fit and able, and wanting to serve. Was the church ready to open the door of leadership to what might someday become a MBB majority?

Cell Churches, House Churches & Networks of House Churches

Among those who are forming new churches around the world, great numbers are in favor of using either house churches or cell churches as their structural basis. While some readers may be familiar with the concept of cell churches there is still enough confusion in the minds of some to warrant some explanation of the topic. Hence, we will look at a few basic principles in starting a cell church, developing new cells, and training new leadership. There are a number of good books available on this subject, some of which are listed in the church planting handbook and on the website (http://rmuller.com). However, please be creative. When working in a new situation, you should not carefully follow some formula found in books, but rather follow the leading of God so that the emerging community of believers reflects what God would have for them in their situation.

What Cell Churches are not!

Cell churches are not churches that meet in small groups. Most of us are so familiar with what we call a church in the West that we struggle to understand what and how cell churches operate.

Most churches in the West are program-oriented. The church bulletin on Sunday morning outlines the programs for the coming week. Various groups meet during the week, each one a part of the program of the church. Some small groups may meet for Bible study and prayer on Wednesday. Another group may meet during the week to support working mothers, another for unwed mothers, and of course a group for the youth of the church. There are usually small groups called Sunday school classes and sometimes even a group for seniors. Some churches have women's missionary groups, and others have special prayer groups.

The focus of such groups is often an activity or program. When the groups meet together on Sunday, they have a large group activity, and announce all the programs that are available for people to join. This is a very organized Western approach, but it is not a cell church.

What is a Cell Church?

Cell churches are made up of cells, not congregational meetings. Each cell is a living thing, which is capable of growth, living on its own, and multiplying into more cells. Each cell consists of a small group of people who may meet together several times a week. The aim of the cell is not an activity, but ministry to the people that make up the living cell. Some cells meet for prayer and singing one night, Bible studies another night and for coffee and prayer in the morning. Cells can meet together as often as they want, and for as many purposes as they want. In practice, cell groups have often found it helpful to meet in different places for different purposes. Some locations give themselves to praise, singing and worship, while others are better for study or relationship building.

When all of the cells in a church meet together in a large meeting it is an occasion for praise and worship. Remember, cells in this case are not a division of the Sunday morning church, but rather they are the main focus of the church. Some cell churches may gather the cells together every month, and others only several times a year. The object of the larger meeting is not to minister to the individual needs of the cell members, but to praise God for what He has done, to share testimonies from the various cells, and to give the individual cells a wider look at what God is doing. In some cases these larger gatherings were called "Spiritual Days" pr "Celebrations" to help identify them from cell meetings.

How do cell churches operate?

A cell can be any size, but in ministry among Muslim background believers it is often better to keep them small, at least initially. As with any healthy cell, it should have a living nucleus. Whether this is three, four or ten people is up to the church planter. There are usually one or two people who are known as the cell leaders or elders. The cell church pastor usually doesn't lead any of the cells but rather visits and pastors all of the cell leaders.

Our practice in the West is to try to include everything in one church service. We have singing, worship, praise, Bible reading, a sermon, something for the children, announcements, and often, squeezed in at the end, the breaking of bread. Many cell groups have a special gathering for each of the above events. Sometimes a special meeting is called to support and pray for an individual member, and sometimes they may just gather to have a social event together. Even then you may find members slipping off to a quiet corner or bedroom to pray together over some issue, rejoining the group a few minutes later.

There are many advantages to using the cell-church structure. First, cells can meet often and in different places, helping new converts to relate to following Christ in a variety of settings. It also provides new believers with a wealth of occasions, as well as plenty of time, to interact with other Christians in an informal setting. New believers don't need to relate to a large group, but can learn to trust and relate to a small group of like-minded believers. As cell meetings don't look like regular church meetings, they don't usually attract attention to themselves, and may be a more secure form of meeting. Meetings can be called at any time, at anyone's house to meet emergency needs. Also, in cell churches leadership can be more easily developed, as cell leaders lead only a few and are not necessarily seen as "sheiks" or "big bosses."

As cells usually meet in homes, often the best place to start a cell is in the home of the teacher. Since this home is usually open for new converts to come and just spend time there quietly, they should already feel at home. Once two or three converts are brought together, they can begin to study, praise and relate together in this setting.

Allowing the converts to give direction

Remember that the cell church is not your church. This ministry is not your ministry, it is God's; the church belongs to him and to the believers in it. Someday the missionary will go away. In a cell church setting this may happen sooner rather han later, perhaps even after a couple of months. Make sure that others, not just you, establish the new church. It is vitally important that this is done from the very beginning.

If the believers want to have songs written out, let them write them out. If they would like more chairs, let them get them. Remember that as an individual member (and you are just that, one individual member) you should only pull the load of one member. If you begin the ministry doing everything for the new believers, they will never learn to stand on their own. Although you may start out leading a cell, as soon as possible you should pass the leadership of that cell onto a member who has the qualifications of an elder.

There is one practical problem with this: -the qualifications for an elder are clearly spelled out and are quite strict. It usually takes years for someone coming from a completely non-Christian background to fit the qualifications of an elder. Therefore church planters are left with the dilemma of either leading the churches for years until people meet the qualifications of an elder, or they find the person who is closest to fitting the qualifications and make him an elder, even though he falls short of fulfilling all the qualifications.

For this reason many emerging cell-churches in non-Christian areas do not label the leader as an elder, but rather a "leader of the group." Then those who eventually meet the qualifications of an elder and rise up to be the overseers of the cells or house churches, are given the title of elders.

As the cell grows it will need to be split into two cells under the leadership of two leaders. In time, the teacher may become the elder or pastor of the cell leaders. Eventually even this position should be given over to a capable national leader.

In one situation in which I was involved in getting believers together, I decided that I would not preach, teach or lead without their permission. We had only one meeting before I asked the Lord to show me who should be the leader. I approached the man the Lord showed me and asked him to be the leader. He said he couldn't, because he wasn't able. I didn't take "no" for an answer, and made an agreement with him. I would meet with him on Tuesday nights to help him prepare a short message. On Friday he would give that message to the group. After a couple of weeks of this arrangement, this man began to take the leadership and work on his own. The venue of the meetings soon changed from my home to his, and the more mature believers began to take on the pastoral care for the others.

A couple of years later, when we left that country, most of the people in the group thought we were just the foreigners that attended; very few realized that we had started the group in our own home. Leaving was not traumatic, because we had started leaving at the very first meeting. Getting on the plane was simply the last step in establishing the church.

Splitting the cell into two

Cells cannot be split into two unless there are two leaders. The object of a cell church is to multiply the number of cells, and thus there is a need to multiply the number of leaders. Usually cells need to be small so that the leaders can focus personal attention and pastoral care on the members of the cell.

In establishing your first cell, you need to be aware that most of the members of that cell will someday be leaders of other cell groups. These may be the first elders that God is giving you, and you need to work carefully with them. As someone shows leadership potential you can start to disciple him and eventually build a new cell around him. Several experienced church planters strongly recommend choosing two new leaders for initial training. Watch out for jealousy from others in the group. Never place one of these leaders above the other. Once they have the respect of the group, you can start to build a new cell around them. When you start a new cell, make sure that there are two in place to lead it. Then one by one, new cells will start to form on their own. Your job as a teacher then becomes making sure that the leaders are fed spiritually and that their needs are being met.

Characteristics of Someone Who May Make a Good Leader

First of all, don't put all your eggs in one basket! There is a very real possibility that the first few leaders you train will not end up being satisfactory. The list I give here may seem odd at first, but after you work among people who struggle with honor and pride, the list may make more sense. This list is born out of experience, not theory. Along with this list, check out the biblical lists in I Timothy 3 and in Titus I.

Look for a person who has an "I don't know" attitude, rather than someone who is eager to teach everyone.

Don't be dazzled by a good evangelist. Many who are good evangelists are not necessarily good teachers or good leaders.

Watch for these undesirable attitudes: pride, self-ambition, jealousy, hatred, gossiping, big dreams, big talkers, worshipers of self, projectors of a very good image.

If the person is not a natural leader now, have him work with someone until you can see his leadership potential developing. Most leaders are made, not born.

Look for humility, willingness to learn, and love for God, others and the community.

Characteristics of a Leader Trainer (That's you)

The list below was compiled by two Arab leaders who had been trained by a teacher and were later asked to analyze the traits and characteristics of why they thought their trainer did an excellent job. Do you have these characteristics? (1) He identified with the people. (2) He was honest and sincere. (3) He was compassionate and real. (4) He was readily available. (5) He was willing to confront and to say specifically where and when things were wrong. (6) He demonstrated leadership both in the ministry and in his family life. (7) He inspired people to make decisions by themselves, rather than telling them what to do. (8) He had stickability and stayed at it when things got rough.

Points for Training New Cell Leaders

First and foremost, the trainer needs to demonstrate that leaders must have a shepherd's heart. Along with this, the new leaders must learn to draw their identity and security from God. If they are easily hurt, angered, or rejected, then they will hurt, anger and reject others. Jesus' identity and worth came from the Father when the Father declared, "This is my beloved Son, and I am fully pleased with him" (Matthew 3:17). Jesus' ministry had not yet begun, yet the Father was pleased with him and loved him. Leaders need to know God's pleasure and love without the need of being great or doing anything for God. The foundation of all ministry comes from our identity in Christ. This may be a big battle for your emerging leaders. Ministry flows out of relationship with God, not serving the cell. Remember Satan's challenge, "If you are the Son of God..." in the temptations of Christ. The whole basis of Satan's temptations and denials is to alienate us from God and from hearing his "My beloved son," and feeling his love.

The trainer must demonstrate that authority and power come through servanthood. Jesus told his followers that whoever wanted to become great must serve. If we want to be first, we must go to the end of the line. Jesus Christ, the creator of all, became a servant to show us his way. However, many people serve only until they become leaders. Then they stop serving. If we don't serve one another, we lose the anointing, the power and the blessing. Leaders need to show and lead the way. Once this happens, the group will learn to serve each other, carrying one another's burdens.

Along with servanthood, the trainer must be willing to confront those in the community of new believers who hurt, anger and reject others. This is not an easy task and great wisdom, both of the culture and regarding personal issues, needs to be sought from the Lord.

Remember that believers from a Christian background need assurance of faith. But those from a Muslim background need assurance of belonging. Muslim converts believe in God, but they may not understand the God of the Bible. Time needs to be spent looking at who and what God really is.

It is also important for the trainer to demonstrate that leaders should have a spirit of abundance rather than a spirit of poverty. A spirit of poverty says, "I only have a little, I can't give it away." A spirit of abundance gives things away, is open-handed, doesn't cling and doesn't protect. It says, "These things are not mine, nor ours, they're all his!" If you and your leaders learn to release things with open hands, then God will put more into those hands.

You will also need to train your cell group leaders to be models to the new believers of how to pay the price, to die to self and to count the cost. While Judas betrayed Jesus, he may not have hurt Jesus as much as Peter did. Peter claimed to love him yet denied him. Every church plant has its Peters. There will be those who are close to us in the ministry, and suddenly we feel betrayed by them. Leaders must be willing to give up reputation, family, friends, and face loneliness, if needed.

In the end, remember that leaders need to be broken in their strengths and taught to walk in brokenness before God. Someone once commented "Never trust a leader who walks without a limp." You can never be too small for God to use; you can only be too big.

Questions for Reflection or Discussion

1. What are the differences between cell churches, house churches and networks of house Churches? Check the Internet for discussion on this subject.

2. Are your church planting efforts patterned only after something you as a foreigner have studied or experienced, or do they also include some things that reflect the local culture and worldview? What could be changed or included to make it more familiar to the general population?

3. What church-building model are you using? (cell church, house church, traditional church, or something else) Why?

4. Are you providing opportunity for new (local) leadership to develop? How soon have you encouraged people to participate or do they sit and watch you do church for them? How can you improve what you are doing?

5. How do you call people to come to church? Do members of your church have to own a watch and be able to read numbers or how can they know when it is time to come to pray? If you live in a modern city this may not be an issue, but in much of the world, especially among illiterates it can be a problem.

6. Is the church planting model you are using easily reproducible by the local people? Could they plant a new church and carry on if your church planting team had to evacuate?

7. Read I Timothy 3 and in Titus 1. What leadership qualifications come first? Where does Paul put teaching and doctrinal issues in the list? Why did Paul not put doctrine, preaching and teaching at the head of the list?

Chapter Thirty One
Creating Community

Several years ago I heard a story of a church in a large city that demonstrated Christian community. A lady whose husband was a Muslim attended the church. He worked as a taxi-driver and allowed his wife to attend the church, but he himself showed no interest. Then one day he had a car accident. That evening several of the church leaders visited his home to express their concern for the family. They asked the man what his financial commitments were, and promised to help him with his mortgage, car payments, and daily expenses until his taxi was repaired. They offered the services of one of the members of their community to help him repair his car. When he asked why they would do this, they replied that his wife was a part of their Christian community. Needless to say, the husband began to warm to the community, and a short time later be started to attend some meetings, and soon after that found Christ as his Savior.

What was it that drew this man to Christ? Was it theology or the love that was expressed to him through Christian community? So often we fail to appreciate the power that Christian community can have. It is essential that we work from the very beginning to create the kind of atmosphere that this kind of community can thrive in. If we as church planters do not appreciate or know how to foster this kind of community, we will plant churches that struggle on this level.

Building Christian Community

We must begin with ourselves. A church planter that cannot build community is like a carpenter that cannot start a home. He can build buildings but cannot create the home that should be inside them.

At the beginning of this book we started by looking at some of the tools that the church planter should have in his toolbox. However, none of the evangelistic ools that are common today can build Christian community. Christian community must be built by those who are living it. They then allow others to enter into the community they have built for themselves.

In the first chapters of this book we learned that the secret to being a messenger that God can use is "brokenness." In much the same way, the secret to forming true Christian community is transparency and brokenness as a community. There is a cost to this.

The Cost of Community

Years ago in the country of Spain, two missionaries stood on the street corner preaching to people who passed by. They faithfully pursued their preaching until one night a young man responded to their teaching. That young man was a drug addict. After they prayed with him, the missionaries realized they had a problem. What should they do with this man? Should they send him back to the needle strewn alley? How could they take him home with them? The cost seemed too great.

However, as they prayed and quickly thought about it there on the street, they decided to take him home. That young man, a drug addict, slept on their living room sofa. He started withdrawal symptoms in their living room. They ministered to him as he shivered and shook. They cleaned up his vomit and made chicken noodle soup for him. They prayed and massaged him as the chemicals left his system.

A few days later his friends came looking for him. When they discovered that their friend was quitting drugs they too wanted to quit. Soon that living room was the center of a new Christian community in Spain. From one living room emerged first one group, then two, and then it quickly spread to other places. Within a year or two ex-drug addicts were leading new groups. Within fifteen years they had gown and divided into fifty groups. Today, that community has grown into a worldwide network of Christian communities known as Betel. Thousands of people struggling with addictions have found Christ through the outreach of these Christian communities. I have heard that today the largest church in Madrid, Spain, is now a Betel community, and that Betel communities have since sprung up all over Europe and are now in North America, Africa, and Asia.

One of the reasons Betel grew was that they had discovered three keys to successful Christian ministry. They had viable messengers, and a dynamic message expressed in the language and worldview of drug-addicts, and they had Christian communities that drug addicts could not just join but thrive in. Betel is made up of communities of ex-drug and alcohol addicts and is not simply a program that addicts move through and graduate from. In essence, Betel illustrates the powerful impact that can happen when all three issues of the messenger, the message and the community are addressed.

One of the common occurrences that cross-cultural church planters face is that of the cost of community. Christian ministry is often handed to us on a platter, but there is a cost attached to it. We may not realize it at the time, but we are being offered an opportunity to be involved in starting a Christian community. If we feel the cost is too high and decline, the ministry will be offered to others. But whoever takes up the call must pay the price. However, when the price is paid and community is started, God's blessing usually follows in wonderful ways.

Building Community-Minded Leaders

If you are the church planter, then you are the leader of the new community that will soon come into being. Are you a community-minded leader? Can you impart this vision into the new leaders you leave behind? If you cannot practice and offer real Christian community on a small scale, how do you expect the new followers of Jesus to practice it on a larger scale? Consider some of the leadership principles that the Scriptures teach us.

"But Jesus called them unto him, and said, 'You know that the princes of the Gentiles exercise dominion over them, and they that are great exercise authority upon them. But it shall not be so among you: but whosoever will be great among you, let him be your minister; And whosoever will be chief among you, let him be your servant: Even as the Son of man came not to be ministered unto, but to minister, and to give his life a ransom for many.'" (Matthew 20:25-28)

If we are to be servants and ministers to others, then we must be willing to share our time, our finances, and all our resources with others in order to form real Christian community. If we as missionaries hold back, then we have set the precedence for those who come to faith or join our new community. One of the drawbacks that Western missionaries usually face is that "they have so much, and others have so little." Sharing resources seems so hard, and so one-sided, but if we help it may create paternalism and dependency. The questions are not easy to answer and as a result few missionaries end up building real Christian community.

Church Discipline

Church discipline is an act of the community, and it expresses community values. If discipline is lacking, this will have an immediate impact on the Christian community, and eventually on the surrounding community. Discipline is the flip side of stewardship. We are willing to help others, but we will not tolerate abuse within the community. Our Christian community is too valuable to have it or its members abused by others. If the community stands together on issues, then the community will grow in strength.

Notice that the Bible verses about discipline and shunning are nestled in between verses about church and community in Matthew 18:15-22. These verses are also filled with opportunities to restore and rebuild relationships and community.

"If your brother sins against you, go and tell him his fault, between you and him alone. If he listens to you, you have gained your brother. But if he does not listen, take one or two others along with you, that every charge may be established by the evidence of two or three witnesses. If he refuses to listen to them, tell it to the church (*ekklesia*). And if he refuses to listen even to the church (*ekklesia*), let him be to you as a Gentile and a tax collector.

Truly, I say to you, whatever you bind on earth shall be bound in heaven and whatever you loose on earth shall be loosed in heaven... Then Peter came up and said to him "Lord, how often will my brother sin against me and I forgive him? As many as seven times? Jesus said to him "I do not say to you seven times but seventy-seven times." (Matthew 18:15-22, ESV)

Church discipline is all about forgiving and rebuilding relationships. However, if someone from within the church community abuses the community, he should know that he has been excluded from the community.

Western Individualism

One of the great struggles that the Western church planter faces is that he or she may have very little experience in building Christian community. So much of Western culture values individualism. As a result, many Westerners struggle in the area of community. I feel this is adequately described in the words of Neil Krahn below:

"Contrary to North American or Western thought, individualism is a huge deception. While many Westerners pride themselves in their individualism, it should be noted that the Biblical consideration of the body is a metaphor for community,

295

and that no one part of the body can live by itself. Not a one. Personal identity is not found in a self-actualization of some sort, except if that self-actualization is understood to be finding one's place in the body. On the other hand, a hand does not cease to be a hand when it finds itself part of the body, so that there is a personal identity of some sort in the body. This is also the argument which makes service the path to personal fulfillment (as opposed to ambition, the pursuit of personal goals). That is, our own personal survival depends on each of us doing our part to keep the body healthy – the body comes first (so that the arm protects the head...)." (Neil Krahn, Wisdom Institute)

What Westerners must discover is that individualism is not just a road-block to success as a Christian; it may be a form of sin that needs forgiveness. Don't pride yourself on being independent to the extreme that you are proud that you do not need anyone else to help you. Individualism flies in the face of Biblical teaching, and this attitude should be enough to disqualify some as leaders, elders and missionaries of the church.

Conclusion

Planting churches in other cultures is not only possible, it is the desire and plan of God. The Bible contains the Gospel message, clearly laid out for every cultural setting. You and I are being called to be messengers of this Gospel, and are commanded to take it to cultures other than our own. The Church in the first two millennia of its existence spread out across the world, ministering to others and establishing churches wherever she went. Today we are being called to finish the job. Most of the cultures of the world that are yet to be evangelized are labeled as resistant. But what are they resistant to? If we come with our cultural baggage and with a narrow understanding of what the Gospel message is, it will not be understood, and thus not easily accepted. But resistance, apparent or real should not hold us back. We have the tools to do the job. We have the resources to do the job. We have the knowledge to do the job. We have the command and provision of almighty God. The only thing we lack is the will to do it.

For most of us, tremendous courage and motivation are required to move us from our comfort zones into the unknown. Few of us want to leave our own culture and venture into an alien world where we never fully feel at home. Yet, that is what Christ did for us. He left the comforts of heaven and came to earth in order to bring us out of darkness into light. We are called to be imitators of him as we bear his message to others. Not only that, the fellowships of believers that we gather should be filled with the testimonies of men and women who have been set free from sin and are no longer held in the grips of guilt, shame and fear.

Leaving our comfortable culture may seem costly, but in the end we will have to agree with the words of Dr. Helen Roseveare, that well known missionary doctor to the Congo, who stated, "There really is no cost, only the privilege of serving the King of Kings."

I trust that God will use what is written here to help and encourage you in your efforts to plant viable Christian communities in other cultures.

Questions for Reflection or Discussion

1. What did the Lord impress on your heart as you read through some of the issues surrounding 'creating community?'

2. Have you found that there is a cost to creating community? How hard has this been? Is it harder for some than for others? Why is this? Does it depend on culture or upbringing?

3. Read Matthew 20:25-28. How is Jesus' teaching on servant leadership being taught and demonstrated to your new church plant? Is it interpreted as your culture, or are the local people starting to demonstrate this in their lives?

4. Have you had to deal with church discipline issues yet? Do you feel that the church community is strong enough to work together on these issues?

Now that you have finished reading the book, how would you answer the following questions:

1. What are the important elements that are needed to build a functioning biblical Christian community of believers?

2. How does one help an existing church become one of these functioning biblical Christian communities of believers?

3. How can we assist Muslims, Hindus, and Buddhists in their move from one community to another?

4. Summarize in a couple of sentences what you learned in the "Community" section of this book.

Bibliographies, Appendices and Other Resources

The bibliographies, appendices and other resources for this book have been published on the Internet and are also included at http://rmuller.com.